IRPP

INSTITUTE FOR RESEARCH ON PUBLIC POLICY

INSTITUT DE RECHERCHE EN POLITIQUES PUBLIQUES

FOUNDED IN 1972, THE INSTITUTE FOR RESEARCH ON Public Policy is an independent, national, nonprofit organization. Its mission is to improve public policy in Canada by promoting and contributing to a policy process that is more broadly based, informed and effective.

In pursuit of this mission, IRPP

- identifies significant public policy questions that will confront Canada in the longer term future, and undertakes independent research into these questions;
- promotes wide dissemination of key results from its own and other research activities;
- encourages non-partisan discussion and criticism of public policy issues by eliciting broad participation from all sectors and regions of Canadian society and linking research with processes of social learning and policy formation.

The IRPP's independence is assured by an endowment fund, to which federal and provincial governments and the private sector have contributed.

CRÉÉ EN 1972, L'INSTITUT DE RECHERCHE EN POLITIQUES publiques est un organisme national et indépendant à but non lucratif.

L'IRPP a pour mission de favoriser le développement de la pensée politique au Canada par son appui et son apport à un processus élargi, plus éclairé et plus efficace d'élaboration et d'expression des politiques publiques.

Dans le cadre de cette mission, l'IRPP a pour mandat :

- d'identifier les questions politiques auxquelles le Canada sera confronté dans l'avenir et d'entreprendre des recherches indépendantes à leur sujet;
- de favoriser une large diffusion des résultats les plus importants de ses propres recherches et de celles des autres sur ces questions;
- de promouvoir une analyse et une discussion objectives des questions politiques de manière à faire participer activement au débat public tous les secteurs de la société canadienne et toutes les régions du pays, et à rattacher la recherche à l'évolution sociale et à l'élaboration de politiques.

L'indépendance de l'IRPP est assurée par les revenus d'un fonds de dotation auquel ont souscrit les gouvernements fédéral et provinciaux, ainsi que le secteur privé.

IRPP

INSTITUTE FOR RESEARCH ON PUBLIC POLICY

INSTITUT DE RECHERCHE EN POLITIQUES PUBLIQUES

The Canadian social union without Quebec: 8 critical analyses

introduced by

Alain-G. Gagnon

and

Hugh Segal

Printed in Canada
Dépôt légal 2000

National Library of Canada
Bibliothèque nationale du Québec

CANADIAN CATALOGUING IN PUBLICATION DATA

Main entry under title:
The Canadian social union without Quebec:
Eight critical analyses
Also published in French under title: L'union sociale canadienne sans le Québec.
Includes bibliographical references.
ISBN 0-88645-184-1

1. Federal-provincial relations—Quebec (Province).
2. Framework Agreement on Canada's Social Union
3. Federal-provincial relations—Canada. 4. Canada—Social policy. 5. Constitutional law—Canada. 6. Federal government—Canada. I. Segal, Hugh II. Gagnon, Alain-G. (Alain-Gustave), 1954- III. Institute for Research on Public Policy.
JL19.C39 2000 320.971 C00-900291-X

Suzanne Ostiguy McIntyre
VICE-PRESIDENT, OPERATIONS

Sarah Fortin
PROJECT DIRECTOR

TRANSLATION
Scribe d'Aujourd'hui
Francesca Worrall
Peter Graefe

COPY EDITING
Francesca Worrall

PROOF READING
Marylin J. Banting

PRODUCTION
Chantal Létourneau

DESIGN AND PRODUCTION
Schumacher Design

COVER ILLUSTRATION
Marie Lafrance

PUBLISHED BY
Institute for Research on Public Policy (IRPP)
Institut de recherche en politiques publiques
1470 Peel Street, Suite 200
Montreal, Quebec H3A 1T1

DISTRIBUTED BY
Renouf Publishing Co. Ltd.
5369 Canotek Road
Ottawa, Ontario K1J 1J3
Tel.: 613-745-2665
Fax: 613-745-7660

SEVERAL PEOPLE HAVE GIVEN INCALCULABLE HELP IN PREPARING THIS COLLECTION. WE wish to thank Lise Trudeau of Scribe d'Aujourd'hui and Peter Graefe for translation; Francesca Worrall for revision and Marilyn Banting for proof-reading; Luc Turgeon and Murray Mincoff for their help with the manuscript; and all of the IRPP team, especially Chantal Létourneau for layout, Paul Howe for his editing skills, Suzanne Ostiguy McIntyre for her usual help in all aspects of production and Sarah Fortin who directed the project for IRPP.

We are most grateful to all the authors for their collaboration in preparing this book. Their promptness and eagerness were greatly appreciated.

Finally, we wish to thank Henry Milner, editor of *Inroads*, for permission to reproduce Claude Ryan's analysis, as well as the Secrétariat aux Affaires intergouvernementales canadiennes (SAIC), for permission to publish an English translation of the seven studies commissioned by the government of Quebec.

Alain-G. Gagnon
Director, Québec Studies Program, McGill University
Hugh Segal
President, Institute for Research on Public Policy

vii
Acknowledgements

viii
Table of contents

xi
Note to readers

1
Introduction
by Alain-G. Gagnon
and Hugh Segal

9
Alain Noël
General Study of the Framework Agreement

37
André Binette
Principles

71
Jacques Frémont
Mobility Within Canada

93
Ghislain Otis
Informing Canadians—Public Accountability and Transparency

129
Alain-G. Gagnon
Working in Partnership for Canadians

155
André Tremblay
Federal Spending Power

189
Guy Tremblay
Dispute Avoidance and Resolution

209
Claude Ryan
The Agreement on the Canadian Social Union as Seen by a Quebec Federalist

227
Appendix 1
Framework Agreement on Canada's Social Union (the Saskatoon consensus)

229
Appendix 2
Securing Canada's Social Union Into the 21ST Century (the Victoria proposal)

243
Appendix 3
A Framework to Improve the Social Union for Canadians (the Framework Agreement)

251
Selected Bibliography

253
Biographical Notes

256
List of Publications

Note to readers

IN THE PROCESS OF TRANSLATING THESE STUDIES, ALL EFFORTS HAVE BEEN MADE TO find an English version of the documents quoted or refered to by the authors. In cases when it was not possible, the references from the original French text are given and the mention [Translation], when applicable, is added at the end of the note.

For all quotes from the Framework Agreement, the Saskatoon consensus and the Victoria proposal please refer to the documents reproduced in the appendixes.

Since the beginning of the 1990s, federal-provincial relations have been marked by several fundamental changes.[1] These changes have had an impact on many policy areas, including health programs, labour mobility, post-secondary education and general training, as well as fiscal transfers, child benefits, tuition fees and financial aid to students. Frequently taking place in an atmosphere of confrontation, and often as a result of decreases in financial support from Ottawa, these developments have given rise to a desire among the provinces to develop new ground rules to govern federal-provincial negotiations in the social policy arena.

The culmination of several years work, the Social Union Framework Agreement, signed in February 1999 by nine provinces, the territories and the federal government, is undoubtedly one of the most important initiatives by Canadian governments to facilitate intergovernmental relations. On the first anniversary of its signing, it is still difficult to assess its likely political ramifications, but one can reasonably say that it represents the beginning of a new era that will have significant repercussions on federal-provincial relations and social policies in the years to come.

At present, the Framework Agreement is raising more questions and generating more hopes and concerns than it is providing answers.[2] One thing is certain, however: its promises of collaboration, transparency and efficiency will only be fulfilled if the heads of government have the express will to do so, and if the Quebec government joins its counterparts in signing the agreement. One cannot speak of a Canadian social union without the participation of such an important partner.

The absence of Quebec's signature on the Framework Agreement constitutes, without any doubt, the agreement's most serious weakness. Unfortunately, this situation has not attracted the attention it deserves. All too often the blame is laid on the current Quebec government's sovereigntist stance. But it is important to recall that the agreement was also rejected by Quebec's federalist Official Opposition. In fact, the sovereigntists, the provincial Liberals under Jean Charest and the Action Démocratique under Mario Dumont all saw it as an affront to the exclusive jurisdiction of the National Assembly.

Since the Framework Agreement includes a clause stipulating that by the end of the third year, "...governments will jointly undertake a full review of the agreement and its implementation and make appropriate adjustments to the Framework as required" there is a possibility that new negotiations will take place in the near future. It is important, therefore, to examine more closely and to understand the motivations behind the Quebec government's refusal to sign the Framework Agreement.

To this end, the translation and publication of the studies commissioned by the Quebec government in the winter of 1999 to assess the Framework Agreement and its implications for Quebec seemed to be a good starting point and an appropriate way to encourage further discussion.[3]

These studies contain a wealth of information and present an acute analysis of the evolution of the provincial consensus from August 1998 (the Saskatoon consensus) to January 1999 (the Victoria proposal). They provide us with a better understanding of Quebec's position, as well as a critical evaluation of the Framework Agreement itself. In addition to these seven studies, there is also an analysis of the Framework Agreement by Claude Ryan, which originally appeared in the journal *Inroads*.

Let us recall the broad outlines of the events that led to the signing of the Framework Agreement. The social union initiative had its origins in the early 1990s, a period dominated by the battle against the deficit which translated into substantial reductions in transfer payments to the provinces. With the introduction of the Canada Health and Social Transfer (CHST) in its 1995 budget, Ottawa cut funding for post-secondary education, health care and social services by more than one-third, that is, six billion dollars over a two-year period,[4] and provoked an outcry in several provincial capitals. As a result of this federal decision, provincial governments had to assume a much greater share of the cost of social programs.

Not surprisingly, this situation was the main item on the agenda of the Annual Premiers' Conference in August 1995. The Ministerial Council on Social Policy Reform and Renewal was struck at that meeting and continued to operate until the adoption of the Framework Agreement on February 4, 1999. In December 1995, the Ministerial Council presented a progress report that recommended constraining the federal spending power, clarifying the jurisdictions of each order of government, and minimizing program overlap with a view to more efficient and more responsible management.[5] In June 1996, the first ministers endorsed the report and the federal government joined the Council, which was asked to "design options for mechanisms and processes to develop and promote adherence to national principles and standards." From a limited social agenda, the governments' orientation expanded to a broad framework agreement on a social union.

The provinces became even more determined in their efforts as the federal deficit came under control and as Ottawa slowly regained its ability to use its spending power to influence social policy. In its February 1997 budget, the federal government announced the creation of the Canadian Foundation for Innovation, the Health Transition Fund, the Canada Millennium Scholarship Fund, and the National Child Benefit. Rather than restoring social transfers to the provinces or reducing the tax room it occupied to reflect its diminished role in social policy, Ottawa chose to invest in highly visible and direct programs in support of family, education and health care, all under provincial jurisdiction.

In 1997, the premiers (except Quebec) endorsed the Ministerial Council's report on "New Approaches to Canada's Social Union," which provided for a range of options for decision-making and dispute resolutions, and produced the Calgary Declaration, which dealt with provincial equality, diversity, Quebec's unique character and the workings of federalism. At their December 1997 meeting, federal and provincial first ministers officially agreed to negotiate a framework agreement on the social union.

In 1998, after a marked absence, Quebec finally agreed to participate fully in the provincial effort to negotiate a social union agreement with Ottawa.[5] Prior to participating in these negotiations, Quebec demanded the unconditional right to opt out with full compensation for provinces that wanted to fully assume their responsibilities in areas of exclusive provincial jurisdiction. These conditions had been agreed to by the other provinces in August 1998.

A broad consensus was thus achieved between the provinces and territories of the Canadian federation — a consensus that united rich and poor provinces of different political stripes (Conservative, Liberal and New Democrat), as well as Quebec. This agreement is now known as the Saskatoon consensus. In January 1999, the provinces put together a new proposal *Securing Canada's Social Union into the 21th Century* (the Victoria proposal) reiterating the main elements of this consensus.

In the end, during negotiations with the federal government in Ottawa in February 1999, the provinces conceded a number of key elements, notably on the right to opt out. In Quebec's opinion, this was a complete reversal by the other provinces, and was unacceptable. It was thus without Quebec's support that the provinces, on February 4, 1999, finally signed the Social Union Framework Agreement.

Soon after, the Quebec government decided to call on seven specialists (constitutionalists, lawyers, and political scientists) to study the repercussions of the Framework Agreement.[6] Each expert was asked 1. to examine one chapter of the agreement and to compare the pertinent sections agreed to by the provinces, first in the Saskatoon consensus and then in the Victoria proposal, to determine the gap between the provinces' initial negotiating position and the final outcome; and 2. to compare the Framework Agreement and Quebec's traditional demands in relation to each theme.

In the first study, which deals with the Framework Agreement as a whole, political scientist Alain Noël argues that the agreement once again isolated Quebec. He emphasizes that, as on previous occasions, the other partners of the federation had shown indifference to the aspirations of the Quebec government and the Official Opposition in the National Assembly. Noël also discusses the unfavourable repercussions for Quebec of the new method of calculating the distribution of the Canadian Health and Social Transfer. This formula was adopted with no prior notice by the federal government only a few weeks after the signing of the Social Union Framework Agreement.

In the second study, law professor André Binette examines chapter 1 of the Framework Agreement, which deals with principles, and maintains that it allows the federal government to take on new responsibilities in the sensitive areas of post-secondary education and social services, irrespective of constitutional jurisdictions. Binette argues that the Framework Agreement does nothing to clarify the allocation of powers, promoting instead further overlap. In addition, provinces are thereupon subject to a federal accountability framework should they elect to use their right to opt out. The author argues that two avenues remain for Quebec, given Ottawa's position: public consultation asking Quebeckers to express their opinion on patriation of full fiscal powers to the National Assembly, or Quebec's attainment of sovereignty.

Law professor Jacques Frémont examines chapter 2 of the agreement, which deals with the issue of mobility or freedom of movement within Canadian territory. Frémont notes that the Framework Agreement imposes considerable restrictions on the provincial governments that were signatory to the agreement because they, for the most part, have jurisdiction in the fields involving the issue of mobility. The author argues that the Framework Agreement has substituted a "social logic" for a "free trade logic" to regulate the movement of the population of Canada and that the signatory governments have limited their sovereignty well beyond the requirements of the Canadian Constitution and existing standards in this matter. According to Frémont, this could lead to the disappearance of residence criteria in the exercise of provincial jurisdictions.

Constitutional expert Ghislain Otis discusses the repercussions for Quebec of the third chapter, which deals with public accountability and transparency. The author stresses the major changes in these spheres and concludes that the federal government is asserting its domination in provincial fields. He further concludes that the Canadian provinces agreed to grant Ottawa a primary role in their exclusive jurisdictions. Otis notes a major reversal with respect to accountability, since a province that wishes to opt out of a new federal Canada-wide initiative must commit to respecting "the accountability framework" laid down by the federal government together with the provincial majority. Ottawa will also be able to impose changes to existing programs, simply by giving notice and without public consultation, which gives it greatly increased room to manœuvre.

In the fifth study, political scientist Alain-G. Gagnon demonstrates how Quebec finds itself more constrained than ever within the Canadian federation following the present federal offensive relating to the allocation of powers. The author also contends that the Social Union Framework Agreement goes squarely against several years of efforts by both orders of government to promote the principle of accountability. Gagnon concludes that principal foundations of the Quebec position in constitutional matters are called into question: dualism and provincial autonomy are rejected; the exercise of provincial jurisdictions must increasingly take into account the federal spending power; and the binding ties of social cohesion built up over the years could henceforth be presented as being contrary to the vision held by the federal government.

In the sixth study, constitutionalist André Tremblay concentrates on chapter 5 of the Framework Agreement, which deals with the federal spending power. The author argues that Canadian federalism is being replaced by a more unitary system. According to A.Tremblay, the imposition of standardizing Canada-wide norms reduces the system's flexibility and adaptability and challenges Quebec's distinct character. The author concludes that the provinces have just "imprisoned themselves inside the shackles of Canada-wide standards, priorities, conditions and objectives, to which will be added a framework of accountability and account rendering." He maintains that it is important for the

Quebec government to explore in more depth potential legal and political courses of action with the aim of achieving greater vertical fiscal balance with the jurisdictions of each order of government.

Law professor Guy Tremblay looks at chapter 6 of the Framework Agreement, which covers dispute avoidance and resolution. He concurs that the Social Union Framework Agreement promotes greater centralization of powers, and reminds us that it only identifies fields of collaboration that come under exclusive provincial jurisdiction. The Framework Agreement does not lay down any mechanism that forces Ottawa to respect its own commitments. Furthermore, G.Tremblay notes that the agreement legitimizes federal intrusions into provincial fields, without any real constraints.

Claude Ryan, former head of the Liberal Party of Quebec, dissects the Framework Agreement from several angles and deplores the fact that Quebec, for the third time, has been abandoned by its provincial counterparts in the negotiating process: in 1981, during the patriation of the Constitution; in 1990, at the time of the failure of Meech Lake Accord; and in 1999, with the Social Union Framework Agreement. Ryan, who describes himself as a moderate federalist, shows to what extent the initiative undermines several federal principles. In addition, he deplores the fact that Quebec's unique character was not recognized as a distinguishing element of the Canadian federation, and stresses the importance of giving expression to this fundamental character in policies on education, health and social services. Finally, Ryan questions clearly and directly federal minister Stéphane Dion's view that the Framework Agreement has a wider scope than the Meech Lake Accord.

All these experts conclude that major transformations are underway and are concerned about the centralization of power in Ottawa, which continues unabated. The questions these scholars raise will encourage reflection on the relations between Quebec and the rest of Canada and also federal-provincial relations in general. Their conclusions represent a profound questioning of the present approach to federalism and cast doubt upon its operation in Canada. They are worthy of the close attention of all concerned with the future of Canadian federalism.

Alain-G. Gagnon
Hugh Segal

1 See Alain-G. Gagnon, "Québec's Constitutional Odyssey," in James Bickerton and Alain-G. Gagnon (eds.), *Canadian Politics*, 3rd ed. (Peterborough: Broadview Press, 1999), pp. 270-99.

2 See the proceedings of the conference "Perspectives and Directions: The Social Union Framework Agreement," Regina, February 3-4, 2000 (forthcoming).

3 The document will be published simultaneously in French by the Quebec Studies Program at McGill University under the title *L'union sociale canadienne sans le Québec* (Montreal: Éditions Saint-Martin/Programme d'études sur le Québec, 2000).

4 Ian Robinson and Richard Simeon, "The Dynamics of Canadian Federalism," in Bickerton and Gagnon (eds.), *Canadian Politics*, p. 257.

5 Ministerial Council on Social Policy Reform and Renewal, *Report to Premiers* (December 1995).

6 To better understand the context in which this decision was taken, see Christian Dufour, *Rapport sur le projet d'union sociale en regard de la vision québécoise du fédéralisme canadien*, Secrétariat aux Affaires intergouvernementales canadiennes (July 1998) and Joseph Facal, "Pourquoi le Québec a adhéré au consensus des provinces sur l'union sociale," *Policy Options*, Vol. 19, no. 9 (November 1998), pp. 12-13.

General Study of the Framework Agreement

On February 4, 1999, the federal government and the governments of all the provinces and territories of Canada except Quebec agreed to a "Framework to Improve the Social Union for Canadians" (the Framework Agreement). This agreement broke the interprovincial consensus that had lasted until a few days before and put an end to a process that began without Quebec in late 1995. It also marked a crucial stage in the historical conflict between the provinces and the federal government by legitimizing the federal government's view on the spending power, in return for only minor concessions. The Framework Agreement makes the spending power "essential" for "[pursuing] Canada-wide objectives" and only restricts it minimally, while asking the provinces and territories to "meet or commit to meet the agreed Canada-wide objectives and agree to respect the accountability framework." More importantly, the Framework Agreement once again isolates Quebec, confirming the ability and willingness of the other governments to define and redefine the country without seeking the approval of the Quebec government (or even the official opposition) and without recognizing the distinctiveness of Quebec society. The Framework Agreement was also reached a few days ahead of a major change in the Canadian Health and Social Transfer's distribution formula, which also disfavoured Quebec.

Overall, the Framework Agreement represents a significant setback for Quebec. At the same time, in clarifying the situation and further institutionalizing the divergence between Quebec and the rest of Canada, the "social union" creates a novel and uncertain situation that provides the Quebec government with an opportunity to affirm its own priorities and to highlight the concrete implications of the Canadian political impasse. The Framework Agreement thus constitutes a real setback, but it also opens new opportunities and could even allow for the modification of the political situation in the coming years.

This study considers the Framework Agreement as a whole, and has two main objectives. It first seeks to evaluate its content both in relation to the provincial consensus that still existed four days earlier and with respect to Quebec's traditional demands. It then proposes to reflect more speculatively on the strategies adopted in this case by the Quebec government, on the lessons that can be drawn from this experience, and on the prospects for Quebec within the Canadian federal framework. It must be noted that the analysis presented here is an overall viewpoint on the broad question, proposed by an attentive observer who remained outside the process. The purpose is less to provide a precise account of what occurred than to promote reflection by situating the agreement in a larger historical and theoretical framework.

The first part of the text compares the Framework Agreement with the positions jointly defined by the provinces during the negotiation process. From this viewpoint, the situation is relatively clear: the provinces basically got nothing that had not already been unilaterally offered by the federal government, and they made important concessions. Of particular importance, they explicitly recognized the legitimacy of the federal spending power without succeeding in genuinely limiting its use. The second part repeats the exercise, but this time from Quebec's viewpoint. It concludes that the Framework Agreement is a clear setback that isolates Quebec, and makes progress on the Quebec government's traditional demands even more improbable.

The next section deals with the issue of objectives and strategies. It poses the simple but unavoidable question of whether the Quebec government should have got involved in a process that risked leaving it as the loser. And if so, was it well advised to go so far down the path of renewing the social union and of approving a pan-Canadian logic that is contrary to its own vision of Canadian federalism? In retrospect, the common front strategy may look like a mistake. Many arguments nevertheless justify its use. For one thing, the result would not have been much different had Quebec abstained. By getting involved in the process, Quebec at least helped define and legitimize an alternative approach that will remain a reference point in future debates on the social union.

The final part discusses the options open to Quebec within the new framework. Three aspects seem particularly promising for the future. First, by being implemented without Quebec's support, the Social Union Framework Agreement creates a *de facto* asymmetry, and this could come back to haunt the federal government. Second, the Framework Agreement only creates a very general framework for managing the social union, allowing Quebec some opportunities to impose its own vision in the sectoral negotiations that must complement the framework. Third, the new framework will reinforce the federal government's tendency to create social programs through the tax system, a tendency that Quebec can counter by taking the lead in social policy.

The Provinces' Rapid Surrender

> We all know what we want. We want more money. We want a restoration of our health-care money from Ottawa... I think everyone agrees essentially, and if we can keep the constitutional lawyers away from Ottawa on Thursday, we'll have a deal.
>
> Mike Harris, Premier of Ontario[1]

> I'm taking a different approach than on some issues and trying to be as constructive as I can. Substantially, I'll be supporting the federal government. I'm not going there with a big shopping list of demands.
>
> Glen Clark, Premier of British Columbia[2]

THE SOCIAL UNION FRAMEWORK AGREEMENT IS NOT A CONSTITUTIONAL ACCORD. It is a non-legally-binding administrative agreement that is in principle valid only for three years. Politically, however, it is a major breakthrough for the federal government, since it recognizes many of the principles it advanced in the negotiations. It is therefore highly probable that these principles will be further established and institutionalized. By joint agreement, the provinces and territories of the rest of Canada, along with the federal government, created a framework for managing the country's social policies. This new framework will delimit the ongoing negotiation process that characterizes federal-provincial relations on these questions. The Framework Agreement should therefore quickly come to play a major role by defining the framework for these negotiations in a clear and novel manner.

The keystone of the Framework Agreement is the provinces' and territories' explicit and almost unrestricted recognition of the legitimacy of the federal spending power in fields of provincial jurisdiction. This recognition takes several forms. First, the agreement suggests that the federal government uses its spending power, "under the constitution," which is eminently contestable from a legal point of view, since the judicial status of the spending power remains uncertain.[3] As well, the agreement calls on the governments to act "within their respective constitutional jurisdiction," without explicitly recognizing that social policies are in most cases an exclusive provincial responsibility. Finally, the document describes the use of the federal spending power as "essential to the development of Canada's social union" and credits it for the "new and innovative social programs" that the provinces have implemented over the years. All in all, to cite editorialist Michel Venne, the Framework Agreement's text is "an ode to the federal spending power. It almost invites Ottawa to use it more and more."[4]

In the past, the provinces were prepared to recognize the spending power, but only in exchange for measures circumscribing and governing its use. In particular, two conditions were proposed over time, either individually or together. These were (1) the necessity of creating a large intergovernmental consensus before introducing a new program, and (2) the recognition of a provincial right to opt-out with full compensation. The Social Union Framework Agreement echoes these demands, but in a minimalist fashion. On the one hand, the federal government vows not to create new transfers to provinces without first gaining the consent of a majority of governments. On the other hand, it accepts that a provincial government that already meets the "agreed Canada-wide objectives" and respects the "accountability framework" can "reinvest any funds not required for the objectives in the same or a related priority area." The majority rule remains well below the constitutional 7/50 rule (seven provinces representing 50 percent of the population), since the support of six provinces containing as little as 15 percent of the population would be sufficient to impose new Canada-wide objectives. As for the opt-out right, it is simply non-existent, since dissident provinces, including Quebec, which has not signed, are held to attaining the "agreed Canada-wide objectives." It is only the "non-required funds" that can be reinvested in a related domain. To require the opposite, namely reinvesting non-required funds in the same domain, would obviously be absurd.

As limited as they are, these constraints on the spending power only affect new transfers to provinces for health, post-secondary education, social assistance and social services. For direct transfers to organizations and individuals, the federal government commits only to "give at least three months notice and [to] offer to consult." Yet, for several years now, these direct transfers to individuals and organizations have been the federal government's preferred instrument. Transfers to the provinces are not anymore a source of innovation, if one ignores broad budgetary modifications and changes to the distribution formula among the provinces. The federal government itself, in the 1996 Throne Speech, proposed to circumscribe its capacity to create new co-financed programs.

Finally, the Framework Agreement enunciates a number of principles that all seek to define a pan-Canadian perspective, with little concern for provincial autonomy and respect for diversity. In particular, the equality of all Canadians, mobility everywhere in Canada and the rejection of "residency-based policies or priorities" are affirmed. Transparency and information sharing are also emphasized. The agreement also foresees flexible dispute-resolution mechanisms.

Even ignoring Quebec's concerns, the terms of the Social Union Framework Agreement seem quite distant from the provinces' initial demands. Before Quebec joined the provincial common front, the premiers had already advanced articulate and relatively ambitious demands for rebalancing the federation. In a substantial discussion paper presented by the provincial and territorial ministers responsible for social services (except for Quebec's) in December 1995, the provinces started to define a new vision of the Canadian social union. Observing the federal government's financial withdrawal — both from programs like unemployment insurance and pensions and in transfers to provinces — and noting the unilateral, unpredictable and incoherent manner in which this withdrawal was accomplished, the provincial ministers proposed a top-to-bottom revision of social programs in order to better respect the division of powers and to improve equity, accountability and efficacy.[5] According to Thomas Courchene, whose work contributed to the credibility of the provincial strategy, the approach departed from traditional provincial positions because it gave an expanded, institutionalized role to the Annual Premiers' Conference and even more, because it led the provinces to define their own pan-Canadian vision.[6] Denouncing Ottawa's unilateralism, the provinces proposed a better foundation for Canadian social policies that would respect the division of powers and rely on a host of joint decision-making and dispute-resolution mechanisms.

In August 1998, the Saskatoon agreement enlarged this approach by adding a consensus concerning the "ability to opt-out of any new or modified

Canada-wide social program in areas of provincial/territorial jurisdiction, with full compensation, provided that the province/territory carries on a program or initiative that addresses the priority areas of the Canada-wide program." A common front of all provinces and territories thus came into existence, and this front held together up to the eve of the signing of the Framework Agreement.

The provinces took up the objective of defining a reference framework in conjunction with the federal government that would be faithful to a certain number of values, would respect the division of powers, and would ensure the stability, predictability and flexibility of Canadian social programs. The Victoria proposal, that established what was still a common position on January 29, 1999, proposed, in particular:

- to favour the equality of all Canadians as well as access to adequate services, promote "individual and collective responsibility" and ensure the viability and maintenance of "affordable, efficient and accountable programs";
- to recognize that, by virtue of the constitution, the provinces and territories have primary responsibility for social programs;
- to commit to "avoiding overlap and duplication" and to clarify the "roles and responsibilities" of each order of government;
- to respect "freedom of movement" and to eliminate "unreasonable barriers to mobility while maintaining governments' ability to pursue legitimate public policy objectives";
- to ensure adequate, predictable and stable federal/provincial/territorial financial arrangements by restoring transfer levels to their levels before the cuts of recent years, by giving a five-year duration to the different arrangements, and by giving provinces three years' notice in writing for all downward adjustments in major transfers;
- to facilitate collaboration between governments, especially by developing outcome measures for Canada-wide programs;
- to submit all new or modified Canada-wide programs to the consent of a majority of the provinces, and to allow the right to opt out with full compensation for these programs;
- to establish a dispute-resolution mechanism that could involve the recourse to a third party where necessary.

Some of these objectives are found, in more or less modified forms, in the Social Union Framework Agreement. This is notably the case with the most general pan-Canadian principles such as equality, access to services, respect for the principles of medicare, and the idea of sufficient, affordable and durable financing. The most important objectives from the provincial viewpoint, however, are cast aside.

The first important difference between the provincial objectives and the Framework Agreement concerns the status of the different governments. Rather than recognizing the provinces' primary responsibility for social policy, the Social Union Framework Agreement simply evokes the respect of each government's "respective constitutional jurisdictions and powers." It is no longer a question of clarifying roles and avoiding duplication and overlap. Rather, the purpose is to "publicly recognize and explain the respective roles and contributions of governments." Far from recognizing provincial primacy, the Framework Agreement in fact affirms and highlights the federal government's role. Indeed, numerous statements present the provinces as subordinate governments frequently tempted by dubious practices and requiring supervision through precise rules. The provinces must "recognize and explain" the federal government's role, "use funds transferred from another order of government for the purposes agreed and pass on increases to [their] residents," "make eligibility criteria and service commitments for social programs publicly available," "monitor and measure outcomes of [their] social programs and report regularly to [their] constituents on the performance of these programs," "share information and best practices," "have appropriate mechanisms for citizens to appeal unfair administrative practices," "report publicly on citizen's appeals and complaints, ensuring that confidentiality requirements are met," and, it goes without saying, "meet the agreed Canada-wide objectives and...respect the accountability framework."

The case of mobility provides a good illustration of this change in perspective. While the provincial project sought to eliminate unreasonable barriers to mobility while allowing governments to pursue legitimate objectives, the Framework Agreement presents all barriers as nefarious, calls on the provinces to eliminate them completely within three years and inverts the burden of proof. It is no longer necessary to show that the use of a residence criterion is unacceptable. Rather, provinces must demonstrate that any such policy is "reasonable and consistent with the principles of the Social Union Framework." The very idea of residence criteria, used almost universally for post-secondary education in the United States, appears here as unacceptable.

Eager to submit the provinces to various criteria of transparency and accountability, the federal government itself does not provide more than a general commitment to ensuring sufficient, predictable and stable funding. It was probably not realistic for the provinces to expect a return to the pre-1995 financial situation.[7] But different measures might have provided protection against sudden and unilateral changes to the rules of the game. The only obligation imposed on the federal government by the Social Union Framework Agreement is to consult at least a year in advance in the case of existing social transfers, and to provide at least three months notice for direct federal spending. These very light constraints were immediately revised downwards a few days after the signing of the agreement when the February 16, 1999 federal budget introduced a major change in the distribution formula of the Canadian Health and Social Transfer without any advance notice or formal consultation process.[8] Canadian Intergovernmental Affairs Minister Stéphane Dion explained that the idea of moving in this direction had been debated for several years, and that in his view this was enough to comply with the terms of the Framework Agreement. On February 23, he wrote that the new distribution formula was announced "after a lengthy debate which fully meets the requirements for consultation set out in the social union agreement."[9] The agreement accepted by the provinces thus offers no guarantee of stability or predictability in federal spending. An issue only has to be debated publicly in order to meet the obligation to consult.

A similar logic prevails concerning the dispute-resolution mechanisms. While the provinces proposed the constitution of joint committees capable of producing public recommendations to which the governments involved would have to respond, the Social Union Framework Agreement only speaks of asking the advice of third parties without creating a clear or demanding conflict-resolution mechanism. The vocabulary of the provincial proposition is maintained, but most of the content is gone.

Finally, as we have already seen, the central goal of circumscribing the federal spending power was largely vitiated. It was the provinces themselves that advanced the majority rule, which was probably not very prudent. This permissive rule, however, was inscribed in a framework covering all federal transfers and spending in areas of provincial jurisdiction, and allowing opting out with full compensation. The majority rule remains, but only applies to social transfers.

Subordinate role for the provinces; strict mobility rules; lack of commitment regarding the sufficiency, stability and predictability of program financing; weak dispute-resolution mechanisms; nearly virtual controls on the federal spending power: in all respects, the Social Union Framework Agreement falls far short of the proposals jointly elaborated by the provinces since the publication of the December 1995 report. As two researchers from the C.D. Howe Institute concluded, the Framework Agreement retains next to nothing of a decade's worth of efforts to find an accommodation concerning the federal spending power, and still permits ill-advised initiatives like the Canadian Millennium Scholarship Foundation.[10]

How can one explain that the provinces signed an agreement so far from their collective position so quickly and so easily? Bill Robson and Daniel Schwanen from the C.D. Howe Institute attribute this result to the lure of increased federal health funding. They note that "it is clear that the lure of money swayed the nine provinces that signed the deal away from their previous unanimous stance in favor of restraining the spending power."[11] Mike Harris' comments cited at the top of this section, as well as the less direct but equally clear remarks made by other ministers and premiers, seem to support this view.[12] Money, however, cannot explain everything. The provinces could have counted on federal reinvestment in health transfers anyway, given federal budget surpluses, the priority of health care in public opinion at the time of the negotiations, and commitments already made by the Liberal government.[13]

To understand the outcome of the negotiations from the provincial point of view and to recognize its future implications, one needs to consider the likely role of three factors other than budgetary considerations. First, the provincial alliance was a marriage of convenience. The smallest and poorest provinces generally support centralization since it tends to benefit them. It is therefore not surprising that they defected to the federal position. Second, the vision advanced by the provinces was a pan-Canadian one, as was the federal vision. The proposed mechanisms were different, but their objectives were not really so far apart. Premier Glen Clark, cited above, was not mistaken in saying that he supported the federal government in substance. The provinces' ambivalence in part explains the final result. Finally, English-Canadian public opinion on these questions is either indifferent or favours the federal government. This stance reduces provincial bargaining leverage in negotiations with a determined and rich federal government. Alberta Premier Ralph Klein summarized the situation on the eve of agreement by noting that "the social union to the severely normal Canadian out there doesn't mean a tinker's dam."[14] Divided amongst themselves, close to the federal position on the basic issues and with little support from their constituents, the provincial governments were thus weakly disposed to resist the federal government once the funding question was resolved.

Many observers have recently spoken of a fundamentally new dynamic in federal-provincial relations. This is the case, of course, for the leader of the Quebec Liberal Party, who counts on this dynamic to renew federalism.[15] But this view is also widely shared both in Quebec and the rest of Canada.[16] It is true, as we have seen, that the provinces did take the initiative of defining common positions and institutionalizing their annual meetings. The Social Union Framework Agreement, however, drafted by Ottawa and only amended by the provinces,[17] retains nothing of this process and reflects the status quo far more than it does a wind of change.

In this respect, it is instructive to return to Richard Simeon's detailed 1972 analysis of federal-provincial relations in the 1960s. Other than Quebec, noted Simeon, the provinces never questioned the federal government's role. They were more interested in transfers of money than responsibilities, although they wished to be involved in major decisions. He concluded that "for the provinces cooperative federalism implies they should be involved in policy formation at an early stage; for Ottawa it is less a question of joint decisions than a willingness to listen to provincial views after a policy has been developed."[18] The provinces, however, had difficulty fulfilling their objectives concerning cooperative federalism because the smallest and poorest provinces wanted a strong central government, because English-Canadian politicians were more ambivalent than those from Quebec and wished to preserve a pan-Canadian vision, and because their constituents did not favour decentralization. Only Quebec proposed more fundamental changes with conviction.[19] The Social Union Framework Agreement, which leaves Quebec alone in its positions and which places after-the-fact consultation ahead of joint decision-making mechanisms, seems to owe more to this well-worn dynamic than to a genuinely new approach.

A Setback for Quebec

We are awash in hollow symbolism.

Alain Dubuc, *La Presse*[20]

IN THE DAYS AFTER THE SIGNING OF THE FRAMEWORK AGREEMENT MANY COMMENTATORS suggested that it represented a gain for Quebec, despite the limits discussed above. For the first time ever, they argued, the federal government had agreed to limit its spending power. While these limitations were perhaps weaker than what Quebec and the other provinces wanted, they nevertheless represented a step forward, and further progress could be made in three years time. After all, the federal spending power had known no limits before the agreement.[21] Alain Dubuc wrote in *La Presse* that, at worst, "the direct interventions that Ottawa has always made can continue despite Quebec's opposition… The fact that Quebec did not sign the agreement changes nothing." Dubuc concluded that in this context, denunciations of the agreement as a significant setback had to do with "hollow symbolism."[22]

It must be reaffirmed, however, that some significant and concrete setbacks are embedded in the document. The Framework Agreement places provinces in a subordinate role and submits them to new obligations, including the near interdiction of residence criteria. (This obligation does not directly apply to Quebec as a non-signatory, but it will nevertheless constitute a new norm that the federal government has the capability to enforce.) The much-vaunted new interprovincial dynamic barely registers in the agreement's text. One must also stress the significance of the direct and positive recognition of the federal spending power. It is true that this power has been used frequently over many years, despite its uncertain juridical and constitutional status. One must also admit that the Social Union Framework Agreement is not a constitutional document and that this recognition has no immediate legal implications. Nevertheless, the recognition of the federal spending power changes the balance of power between the federal and provincial orders. It is precisely for this reason that the provinces had always refused to commit themselves on this question.

To understand the significance of recognizing the federal spending power, even administratively, one has to consider the very logic of this instrument. Indeed, the issues surrounding it are not primarily constitutional or legal. In the past, both Ottawa and the provinces avoided directly subjecting the federal spending power to judicial review. They preferred to resolve their differences through negotiations rather than risking defeat in an uncertain judicial context. Neither party really wished to see the Supreme Court make a decision about the spending power.[23] In most cases, the use of this power forces the federal government to negotiate with the provinces anyway.[24] The need to negotiate and collaborate is obvious in all fields where the federal government makes transfers, since it is the provinces that define the programs and offer the services.[25] But negotiations are also necessary in cases of direct federal spending in areas of provincial jurisdiction, whether these take the form of transfers to organizations and individuals or of tax expenditures. The Millennium Scholarship Foundation and the National Child Benefit are good examples of this dynamic. In all sectors where the federal government has shown an interest and where direct or tax expenditures are plausible, some level of federal-provincial collaboration is inevitable. This holds as much for child poverty as it does for youth employment, home care, services for people with disabilities or homelessness.[26] In such a context, marked by negotiation more than by explicit reference to constitutional rules, the provincial recognition of the spending power can weigh heavily.

Keith Banting, a political scientist who largely favours centralization, argued in 1988 that the Meech Lake Accord's recognition of the federal spending power would have greater political impact than judicial significance. For Banting, the provinces' unanimous agreement to recognize the federal spending power and specify the conditions for its use "would strengthen the spending power far more than a favourable ruling of the Supreme Court ever could." The federal government would not necessarily use this instrument more often, but it would have at its disposal an extra bargaining chip in negotiating the conditions associated with any new initiative.[27] The provinces, having renounced the right to opt out with compensation, would have no alternative but to have their citizens pay taxes for services they could not receive.[28] To take an example, child care services already place Quebec citizens in this situation, since the federal government does not compensate Quebec for the tax credits its citizens can only partially use given the establishment of $5-per-day child care spaces.

Since the Quebec government has not signed the Social Union Framework Agreement, theoretically the impact of recognizing the spending power should be reduced. It is, however, not clear that the federal government sees this refusal as a significant limit to its actions. Unlike what has traditionally occurred, Ottawa made little effort to get Quebec to sign the agreement, and quickly insisted that it applied to all the provinces anyway.[29] Quebec's position is further weakened by the lukewarm reaction shown by the official opposition and numerous commentators, and by the relative indifference of public opinion. The legitimacy of Quebec's very conventional position is further undermined by the position taken by observers like Claude Castonguay who, as a minister, played a key role in defining an autonomist vision for Quebec social policy, but who is now pleased with an agreement that "will apply to Quebec even without its signature."[30] Even if it abstains, Quebec moves backwards. The federal government's spending power in provincial jurisdictions and its capacity to impose its priorities have never been more firmly established.

More generally, Quebec has never been so marginalized in the Canadian federation.[31] It was only with great hesitation and a certain malaise that the provinces, specialists and Canadian public opinion approved the federal constitutional approach in 1981-82. This time, everything happened very quickly, over a few days, with little afterthought. The uneasiness of those who demanded an open and public process in the days of Meech and Charlottetown simply evaporated. For Robson and Schwanen, Ottawa and the provinces "have forced Quebec to stand alone in defense of its constitutional rights."[32]

Although isolated and confronted with a rich central government capable of imposing its prerogative, Quebec still holds some cards. Since the use of the spending power always necessitates at least minimal collaboration and negotiation between the federal government and the provinces, the game is not over. Indeed, Quebec's abstention creates a dilemma for the federal government. Either it must agree to give Quebec its part of new-program funding even if it does not respect all the conditions, or it must support the odious practice of denying Quebec citizens the resources to which they have a right.[33] This problem is not entirely new, but it could become more significant if the collaboration between the federal and provincial governments increases.

The consolidation of the federal spending power and the isolation of a Quebec government basically defending traditional positions represent significant setbacks for Quebec that go much beyond "hollow symbolism." The federal government is henceforth better positioned to define the priorities and the rules of the game in many domains of exclusive provincial jurisdiction.

A Detour Via Saskatoon

> This is a re-balancing exercise in name only when one considers that the existing constitutional arrangements do not recognize the identity, aspirations, priorities or needs of the Quebec people...this exercise will in fact be another pan-Canadian exercise that the provinces welcome with open arms.
>
> Lucien Bouchard, Premier of Quebec[34]

Only a few months before the August 1998 Saskatoon consensus the Quebec government refused to join the other provinces in the social union process. As Premier Bouchard explained in August 1996, the provinces were engaged in "another pan-Canadian exercise" that would lead "to the abandonment of Quebec's fundamental demands and to their gradual erosion via intergovernmental and administrative means." The Quebec government thus could not "engage itself in intergovernmental decision-making processes that would result in subjecting Quebec to norms to which it had not consented, even in areas under its jurisdiction."[35] Beyond "directly attacking Quebec's current prerogatives and responsibilities with respect to the definition and management of its social policies," the provinces' proposed intergovernmental mechanism would "have the consequence of recognizing a federal responsibility in the definition of social policies" and of "legitimizing the historic federal pretensions in this field."[36]

The announcement of the National Child Benefit, which imposed upon Quebec norms and mechanisms defined by the provinces and the federal government even while the social union talks were progressing, as well as the probability that this scenario would repeat itself in other sectors, forced a change in strategy. In December 1997, Premier Bouchard enunciated the specific conditions under which Quebec would agree to participate in the social union discussions. These conditions included openness to an unconditional right to opt out with full compensation, a moratorium on all new federal measures and initiatives and the refusal to recognize the federal spending power or "any role for the federal government in the field of social policy."[37] At first, the provinces rejected any discussion of a right to opt out but gradually came to consider it before finally arriving at a unanimous agreement, which was signed in Saskatoon in August 1998.

The Saskatoon agreement established a consensus on the right to opt out with full compensation, provided that a "program or initiative that addresses the priority areas of the Canada-wide program" is offered. For Quebec, this was a significant, almost unprecedented advance. The 1981 "Gang of Eight" constitutional agreement only offered a right to opt out with "reasonable compensation" in cases of constitutional modifications that reduced provincial powers.[38] The Meech Lake and Charlottetown Accords in turn only dealt with new, shared-cost national programs and only allowed for opting out with compensation in cases where a province adopted a program or initiative compatible with the national objectives.[39] The Saskatoon agreement extended the opt-out right to new and modified programs of all types (shared-cost or not) and no longer required compatibility with national objectives.

This clause of the Saskatoon consensus clearly constitutes a concession to Quebec, since the provinces had not endorsed the right to opt out with compensation before that point. This concession was not extended, however, without a safeguard, as the text of the agreement clearly specifies that the opt-out provisions represent a "provincial/territorial consensus negotiating position." As stated, the Saskatoon agreement appeared eminently negotiable.

In return for this concession, the Quebec government took the important step of joining the discussions on the social union, of accepting, in part, the vocabulary of the social union and of Canada-wide programs, and of recognizing a federal role in social policy. The Saskatoon consensus represents a compromise on the three conditions laid out in December 1997. The right to opt out is no longer unconditional, there is no moratorium on new initiatives, and a federal role in social policy is recognized, albeit only implicitly. More fundamentally, the Quebec government joined a process whose major premises it had previously criticized, even while knowing that the consensus it backed was precarious and no more than a negotiating position for many provincial partners.

The Quebec government's choice was not without risk, as subsequent events have made clear. But it is fairly understandable, given that abstention would not have produced better results. At a minimum, the government cannot be accused of not making concessions or sincerely participating in the process.

The Saskatoon consensus was nevertheless paradoxical. The Quebec government joined a common front with partners who were weakly committed to its central objective concerning the opt-out provision. In doing so, it signed onto a pan-Canadian process that was itself in contradiction with another of its major political objectives, namely, the recognition of Quebec as a people. Indeed, the partners in Saskatoon were also the authors of the Calgary Declaration, which only incidentally recognized Quebec's "unique character." This declaration, which Premier Bouchard argued placed Quebec in "the reductive formula of the equality of provinces," was not put under question in Saskatoon.[40] On the contrary, its logic informs the decision to extend the opting out formula to all. The Quebec government left a fundamental or even existential question on the sidelines to make a common front with the provinces.

In intergovernmental relations, the Quebec government has always sought to achieve two major objectives. These are respect of its jurisdiction and autonomy and recognition of Quebec as a people or as a distinct society. When it stresses the respect of its jurisdiction, the Quebec government speaks as a province, even while refusing the pan-Canadian discourse of many provinces in favour of the classical conception of federalism where each government is sovereign in its constitutional sphere. When it insists on recognition, the government reasons more like a national state, or as the state of a nation.

This dual approach goes back to the origins of Canadian federalism. It is anchored in a vision of Canada as a double pact, between the old colonies of British North America agreeing to create a federation on the one hand, and between two nations that recognize the dualist nature of this federation on the other. In entering Confederation, the French Canadians of Lower Canada were seeking both autonomy and recognition. As historian Arthur Silver writes,

> By 1864 French Canadians had long accustomed to thinking of themselves as a nation and of Lower Canada as their country. Consequently, what they sought in Confederation was to strengthen the French-Canadian nation by strengthening Lower Canada. They wanted to be separated as much as possible from the other provinces, to have an autonomous French-Canadian country under the control of French Canadians. The greatest possible amount of provincial sovereignty was to be combined with a modicum of federal association. This meant that Confederation would be an "alliance" or "association" of autonomous provinces, with a central government dealing only with certain limited matters of common interest while the provinces took care of their respective nationalities. In this federal alliance Quebec would be the French-Canadian country, working together with the others on common projects, but always autonomous in the promotion and embodiment of the French-Canadian nationality.[41]

Henri Bourassa would later summarize this situation by speaking of a double pact between what would become the Canadian provinces, and between two founding peoples. Bourassa affirmed the dualist dimension of the federation in a context where the notion of provincial autonomy, left to itself, risked legitimizing the oppression of francophones outside Quebec. But the thesis had a more general relevance in that it portrayed Canada as a pact with two complementary dimensions, one federal and the other binational. This double pact is not found either in historical documents or in law, and one can even say that it is not what the English-Canadian elites had in mind when they adopted a constitution that very imperfectly reflected this idea.[42] It was nevertheless the dominant conception in Quebec from the very beginning, with Confederation seen as a means of founding a "partnership between peoples" and of establishing Quebec as an autonomous political framework for a nation, within a decentralized federation.[43]

Thus, in the Canadian context, the Quebec government acts sometimes as an autonomous province able to make common cause with other provinces, and sometimes as a national state standing alone against the multiple representatives of another nation. At times, the two viewpoints co-exist and enrich each other. In the early 1960s, for instance, the Quebec government obtained a *de facto* special status in social policy by linking its demands for provincial autonomy to the affirmation of its prerogatives as a national government.[44] In a similar manner, despite all its limits, the Meech Lake Accord had the great merit of explicitly recognizing this double logic by providing both the recognition of a distinct society and greater autonomy for those provinces that wanted it. It was this double dimension that made Meech such an important accord. As it has frequently been said, the Quebec government has never put forward such modest demands in constitutional negotiations. This is entirely true, but one must also add that it has never obtained so much either. For the first time since 1867, Quebec obtained both autonomy and recognition. The autonomy was highly circumscribed and the recognition very limited, but the two dimensions were nevertheless both present and explicit. By contrast, in the 1960s, Quebec made much more substantial gains in obtaining *de facto* special status in the management of many social policies. But in not explicitly recognizing the political and social foundations of these concessions, the governments of the time left the door open to the banalization of this special status, which occurred a few years later when the federal government deliberately proceeded to erase any institutional recognition of Quebec's difference.[45]

On other occasions, the Quebec government has dissociated autonomy and recognition to concentrate on autonomy, which appears easier to obtain. This is the case with numerous sectoral negotiations where the provinces can present a common position based on specific interests, often limited to public finance issues. Such common fronts are frequently fragile, however, as Claude Morin underlined as early as 1973 when he observed that the other provinces were largely preoccupied with funding issues, that they accepted the federal government's pre-eminent role and, above all, that they did not support Quebec's autonomist demands. Morin noted that when the provinces broke a common front they did not feel that they had betrayed a commitment because, in their view, Quebec was never truly part of the "group."[46]

In 1981, the Quebec government played the provincial card in a negotiating process with much more fundamental stakes. It ended up on the sidelines, unable to block an evolution that obliterated its veto, transformed the Canadian constitutional order, and reduced the powers of the National Assembly. In 1998, in the course of the social union discussions, Quebec again decided to make common cause with the provinces, leaving aside any question of recognition. We know what the results were.

As Premier Bouchard said in a press conference after the Calgary Declaration, the majority of Quebecers share certain common political goals. They desire "greater control over their affairs, and thus more powers for Quebec, and they desire that their existence as a people be recognized."[47] It is from this baseline of autonomy and recognition, which as we have seen is deeply rooted in Quebec's history, that Lucien Bouchard arrived at his negative assessment of the Calgary Declaration drafted by the other provincial premiers. In Saskatoon, one of these objectives was put aside in order to establish a common front, which was already difficult to achieve in terms of autonomy alone. This common front, which made the right to opt out with compensation simply a "negotiating position" and engaged Quebec in a pan-Canadian exercise, eventually broke apart, leaving Quebec with neither recognition nor autonomy.

Should all interprovincial strategies that do not integrate Quebec's historic objectives be rejected from the start? Past experience is not very encouraging in this respect. At the same time, can one really expect to negotiate everything at once? There are no conclusive examples here either. Furthermore, if common fronts have their limits, abstention is scarcely more promising.

The Quebec government has historically oscillated between strategies of withdrawal and of interprovincial alliance, with the choice depending on the circumstances. The withdrawal strategies have taken diverse forms, ranging from the use of the veto (in Victoria in 1971) to a refusal to participate in multilateral discussions (after the failure of Meech Lake), to outright abstention (from 1995 to August 1998 for the social union discussions). The alliance strategy has given rise to common fronts of various sizes (in 1981 and 1998, for example), as well as to formal accords ending in failure (Meech and Charlottetown Accords).

It is difficult to avoid the conclusion that common fronts have been precarious and, in the end, ineffective. The problem does not result from the partners' bad faith. As mentioned above, the other provinces are mainly preoccupied with financial issues, and they neither genuinely question the federal government's preponderant role, nor support Quebec's fundamental demands except where these buttress their negotiating position. For Quebec, the provinces are friends of convenience, on which few expectations can be placed.

This being said, there are good arguments for an alliance strategy.[48] Such an approach allows Quebec to avoid being isolated from other governments, to make its positions known and, most importantly, to contribute to defining an alternative to federal positions. Even if this alternative ends up being defeated, it nevertheless legitimizes Quebec's positions by showing the possibility of another approach. More generally, alliances allow the Quebec government to play a positive and constructive role and to show that Quebec is more than just a roadblock to change.

The fact that alliances are broken, yielding results far below the initial goals, is hardly surprising. Abstention likely would have the same results. The National Child Benefit, for instance, was negotiated without Quebec's input, with consequences similar to those of the social union talks. From this vantage point, the failure of an alliance appears without consequences. If, by contrast, the Quebec government makes compromises in order to maintain an alliance and these compromises are incorporated in a final agreement without their *quid pro quo*, the common front is more costly than abstention. The 1981 Gang of Eight alliance is a prime example.

In the case of the Social Union Framework Agreement, the Quebec government was perhaps too quick to accept the pan-Canadian perspective, obtaining no concessions on the question of recognition and no assurances about the strength of its partners' convictions with respect to the opting out proposal. Still, even here abstention would have produced similar results, without putting forward a credible alternative to the federal project.

This question will inevitably have to be reconsidered, since the Social Union Framework Agreement will require a series of sectoral negotiations. The Quebec government has every interest in enunciating clearly its fundamental positions concerning recognition and autonomy. At the same time, and despite the inherent difficulties of this approach, it will have to rebuild links with the other provinces in order to preserve its interests in the various sectors. Studies in negotiation suggest that parties can always make alliances around specific issues, even when they diverge over fundamental questions.[49]

Quebec's Options

> If we are faced with difficulties of a constitutional variety, it is because the legislature has not used the powers made available by its sovereignty and autonomy in order to enact its own family allowance policy.
>
> André Laurendeau, *Le Devoir*[50]

> The most important determinants of wealth and job creation in the next century will be education and training, quality of life, health, and our ability to attract public and private investment. We will not look to Ottawa for solutions in these areas.
>
> Bob Rae, Premier of Ontario from 1990 to 1995[51]

The foregoing analysis clearly highlights the limits of interprovincial alliances. Such alliances have their use in publicizing Quebec's viewpoint and contributing to the development of alternatives to federal policy. They offer little protection for Quebec, however, since the other provinces are often closer to the federal government's viewpoint than to Quebec's. Similarly, the constitutional debate has few chances to favour Quebec in the short term. The possibility of a winning referendum on sovereignty remains distant and, unlike in the 1960s, it no longer pushes the provincial governments to act prudently in the face of Quebec's demands.

In these circumstances, social policy will be the principal arena of conflict. If the Quebec government wishes to counter the federal government's will to redefine the Canadian welfare state from the centre, its best bet is to define a comprehensive and ambitious set of social policies encompassing all of its spheres of jurisdiction. From the end of the Second World War to the beginning of the 1960s the federal government was the social policy leader, in large part due to the provinces' conservative and passive policies. The Quebec government's opposition to the federal initiatives centered mainly on respect for provincial jurisdiction and on a defense of the status quo.[52] With the Quiet Revolution, Quebec moved to take the lead, to clearly impose its prerogatives, against a less progressive federal government.[53] More recently, the Quebec government has taken the lead in family and child care policy, making unilateral federal interventions more difficult. Generally, the government that is the first to occupy a field of jurisdiction and to define the parameters of government intervention has a good chance of prevailing.[54]

Contrary to the federal argument, there are no "pressures for a 'race to the bottom' in social programs and services" in Canada.[55] Some governments may have adopted more conservative and less generous policies, but these do not arise from an unavoidable competition that, in the absence of federal intervention, would force all provincial governments to adjust downwards. No one has managed to prove the existence of such a mechanism, either in Canada or the United States, and this is not for lack of trying.[56] Indeed, if Canadian social policies are more generous than American ones, it is precisely because the Canadian federation is more decentralized.[57] Moreover, it would be difficult to find a single program at the provincial level that has endured such severe restructuring and with such extensive consequences as is the case with employment insurance, an entirely federal program that now only protects a minority of the unemployed.

The real issue in social policy is not a hypothetical "race to the bottom." Rather, it is the autonomous capacity of each society to define and maintain progressive models in a context defined by globalization and rapid economic and social change. In Europe, for instance, there is less concern about a competition that would lead different societies to reduce their social protection than about the loss of autonomy that economic and political integration might entail. Europeans worry that their union might undermine the capacity of states to maintain and improve distinctive national models of social protection.[58] Similarly, in Canada, the possibility of developing consensus, meaningful social contracts, and a real sense of solidarity seems far greater at the provincial than at the federal level.[59] In social policy, the federal government can mainly act indirectly, through transfers or the tax system. Comparative analyses of Canada and the United States show that the federal government's redistributive impact is significant,[60] but the possibilities remain limited. The federal government quite simply lacks the tools needed to renew the welfare state by means such as integrating transfers to individuals, developing active labour market policies, linking health services to the more general context of social services, and promoting local and community development.[61] By contrast, Quebec is particularly well placed to evolve in this direction, provided it is given the necessary autonomy.[62]

Even in a difficult political context, the Quebec government still can pursue three strategies: it can continue to affirm its autonomy and its national character while continuously underlining that this orientation is not only that of the present government; it can remain open, without being naïve, to punctual alliances with other provinces in order to take advantage of possible convergences of interests and contribute to defining the issues in federal-provincial relations; and it can occupy the social policy terrain by developing an ambitious, progressive, and comprehensive social policy approach.

When all is said and done, social policy remains primarily a field of provincial jurisdiction. Quebec's different social actors and citizens turn spontaneously to the Quebec government when they deal with these issues. It is the Quebec government that should have the first, and last, word on these questions.

Conclusion

> The problem with the spending power is that, by enabling the federal government to use fiscal means to influence decisions that fall within provincial jurisdiction, it allows national majorities to set priorities and to determine policies within spheres of influence allocated under the Constitution to regional majorities. Thus, both by design and effect, the spending power runs counter to the political purposes of a federal system.
>
> Andrew Petter, Faculty of Law, University of Victoria[63]

THE CONCEPT OF SOCIAL UNION IS A RECENT CREATION IN CANADA. INTRODUCED IN the Charlottetown Accord to affirm the unity that Canada realizes through its social programs, the concept served to counterbalance what were seen as decentralist tendencies. This was the Canadian nationalists' social union. Taken up again by the provinces in the mid-1990s, the concept took on a second meaning, this time to designate an intergovernmental process for managing less unified and probably less generous social policies. Finally, in August 1998 in Saskatoon, the social union took on a third meaning to represent a Quebec vision that privileges the autonomous development of distinct provincial social policy models.[64]

On February 4, 1999, the first vision triumphed, conceding next to nothing to four years of intergovernmental efforts to give shape to the other two perspectives. That the provinces lost their hand is beyond doubt. Almost none of their demands for greater federal-provincial collaboration were met. Where their vocabulary was retained, it was without substance. Quebec, which joined and redefined the provincial process, also suffered a setback, although by not signing it is less bound to a process that will institutionalize the federal spending power for far longer than three years. This is not to say that the common front strategy was poorly chosen. The Quebec government could have proceeded somewhat differently in explicitly affirming the question of recognition, but it really did not have a better option. In the coming months, Quebec should continue to advance its traditional objectives while remaining open to possible alliances. Most importantly, it should define a comprehensive and ambitious social policy agenda that allows it to occupy the social field. International links with comparable small countries could also be profitably developed.

Arthur Silver notes that at the time of Confederation, Quebec francophones saw Quebec as the autonomous political framework of a nation that was the partner of another nation in a flexible federation. This perception was not shared. In the anglophone provinces, there was a desire to build a Canadian nationality that would be more than a political partnership. Silver notes that "within months of Confederation, a 'Canada First group' appeared, to promote the idea. If Canada was to realize its destiny, they believed, it must develop a 'national spirit' — a moral nationhood with a common vision and sense of purpose."[65] Since the Second World War, this desire to create a unitary nation has been transposed onto the promotion of pan-Canadian social policies. The philosopher Will Kymlicka explains that,

> ...their conception of Canada as a single national community includes the idea of unrestrained mobility rights, common national standards in social services, portability in social entitlements, as well as the right to use the English language in courts, schools and government functions from sea to sea...

> These features of pan-Canadian nationalism not only increase the mobility of English-speaking Canadians, they also increase their political power. If language rights and standards in social programs should be national in scope, this means that decisions must now be made at the federal rather than the provincial level. And this, in turn, means that decisions will be made in a forum where English-speaking Canadians form an overwhelming majority.[66]

Similarly, Andrew Petter has noted that the spending power permits the majority of the country to override provincial majorities, even on questions where the federal regime specifies provincial sovereignty. It is this power of the majority that the new Social Union Framework Agreement reinforces. This is why, in this case as in 1981-82, no one in English Canada raised concerns about the power of a few politicians making decisions behind closed doors.

The problem is real, but it is hardly new. Since Confederation, one way or another, Quebecers have always maintained and preserved the federal principle. This idea, which made Canada possible, implies that Quebec is an autonomous nation, capable of defining its own political and social orientations. Even within the current constraints, the Quebec government can still summon this vision by fully exercising the powers that it holds.

1 Statement made on February 2, 1999, quoted in Edward Greenspon and Graham Fraser, "PM Finds More Cash to Woo Provinces: On Eve of Talks with Premiers, He Prepares to Sweeten Health Offer," *Globe and Mail*, February 3, 1999, p. A1.

2 Statement made on February 2, 1999, quoted in Greenspon and Fraser, "PM Finds More Cash to Woo Provinces," p. A1.

3 Andrée Lajoie, "The Federal Spending Power and Meech lake," in Katherine E. Swinton and Carol J. Rogerson (eds.), *Competing Constitutional Visions: The Meech Lake Accord* (Toronto: Carswell, 1988), pp. 175-78.

4 Michel Venne, "L'accord du 24 Sussex," *Le Devoir*, February 6, 1999, p. A10. [Translation]

5 "Redefining the Social Services Roles and Responsibilities of Federal and Provincial/Territorial Governments," A Discussion Paper Submitted by the Provincial/Territorial Ministers Responsible for Social Services to the Ministerial Council on Social Policy Reform and Renewal, Victoria, December 12, 1995.

6 Thomas J. Courchene, "In Praise of Provincial Ascendancy," *Policy Options*, Vol. 19, no. 9 (November 1998), pp. 30-31.

7 John Richards, "Reducing the Muddle in the Middle: Three Propositions for Running the Welfare State," in Harvey Lazar (ed.), *Canada: The State of the Federation 1997; Non-Constitutional Renewal* (Kingston: Institute of Intergovernmental Relations, 1998), p. 92.

8 "Notes pour un point de presse du Premier ministre du Québec, M. Lucien Bouchard; réaction au budget fédéral," Premier's Office, Quebec, February 17, 1999; "Le Québec n'a jamais reçu de préavis des modifications annoncées au transfert social canadien," press release, Cabinet du vice-premier ministre et ministre d'État de l'Économie et des Finances, Quebec, February 19, 1998.

9 Stéphane Dion, "Letter to Premier Lucien Bouchard Regarding Federal Transfers to Provinces," Ottawa, Ministry of Intergovernmental Affairs, February 23, 1999.

10 William B.P. Robson and Daniel Schwanen, *The Social Union Agreement: Too Flawed to Last*, C.D. Howe Institute Backgrounder (Toronto: C.D. Howe Institute, February 8, 1999), p. 3.

11 Robson and Schwanen, *The Social Union Agreement*, p. 3. See also Jeffrey Simpson, "A Fistful of 'Social Union' Dollars," *Globe and Mail*, February 4, 1999, p. A14.

12 Greenspon and Fraser, "PM Finds More Cash to Woo Provinces"; Edward Greenspon, "PM and Premiers Gather, with Little to Lose: There Are Differences but Nobody Seems Too Worried About Them," *Globe and Mail*, February 4, 1999, p. A1.

13 See Daniel Leblanc, "Canadians Rank Health Care as Top Priority for Liberals' Attention; Poll Finds 43% of Respondents Put Issue First on List of Concerns," and Shawn McCarthy, "Martin Rejects Manning's Calls to Cut Spending: Finance Minister Says Now is the Time to Invest in the 'New Economy' Rather than Sacrifice Key Programs," *Globe and Mail*, February 2, 1999, p. A4.

14 Greenspon, "PM and Premiers Gather, with Little to Lose."

15 Jean J. Charest, "L'union sociale canadienne: la chance de progresser tous ensemble," *La Presse*, February 16, 1999, p. B3.

16 See, for example, Alain Dubuc, "L'union sociale n'est pas une croisade," *La Presse*, December 9, 1998, p. B2; Courchene, "In Praise of Provincial Ascendancy."

17 Norman Spector, "Same Place, Same Wallflower," *Globe and Mail*, February 9, 1999.

18 Richard Simeon, *Federal-Provincial Diplomacy: The Making of Recent Policy in Canada* (Toronto: University of Toronto Press, 1972), p. 182.

19 Simeon, *Federal-Provincial Diplomacy*, pp. 89, 164, 175, 181-82, 207-08, 213 and 232-34.

20 Alain Dubuc, "Signer ou ne pas signer?" *La Presse*, February 5, 1999, p. B2. [Translation]

21 Claude Castonguay, "Québec a raté une belle occasion," *Le Droit*, February 11, 1999.

22 Dubuc, "Signer ou ne pas signer?" [Translation]

23 J. Stefan Dupré, "Section 106A and Federal-Provincial Fiscal Relations," in Swinton and Rogerson (eds.), *Competing Constitutional Visions*, p. 209; Keith G. Banting, "Federalism, Social Reform and the Spending Power," *Canadian Public Policy*, Vol. 14, supplement (September 1988), p. S84.

24 Peter Hogg, "Analysis of the New Spending Power Provision (Section 106A)," in Swinton and Rogerson (eds.), *Competing Constitutional Visions*, pp. 157-58.

25 Thomas J. Courchene, "ACCESS: A Convention on the Canadian Economic and Social Systems," reproduced in *Assessing ACCESS: Towards a New Social Union* (Kingston: Queen's University Institute of Intergovernmental Relations, 1997), p. 81.

26 Harvey Lazar, "Non-Constitutional Renewal: Toward a New Equilibrium in the Federation," in Lazar (ed.), *Canada: The State of the Federation 1997*, p. 33.

27 Banting, "Federalism, Social Reform and the Spending Power," p. S84-S85.

28 Andrew Petter, "Meech Ado About Nothing? Federalism, Democracy and the Spending Power," in Swinton and Rogerson (eds.), *Competing Constitutional Visions*, p. 190.

29 Manon Cornellier, "Union sociale: Dion adopte un ton cassant vis-à-vis de Bouchard," *Le Devoir*, February 6, 1999, p. A6.

30 Castonguay, "Québec a raté une belle occasion." [Translation]

31 Rhéal Séguin, "Behind the Fateful Decision to Leave Quebec Out," *Globe and Mail*, February 3, 1999, p. A1; Michel Venne, "Le Québec face à lui-même," *Le Devoir*, February 21, 1999, p. A10.

32 Robson and Schwanen, *The Social Union Agreement*, p. 4.

33 Robson and Schwanen, *The Social Union Agreement*, p. 5.

34 "Le rééquilibrage des rôles et des responsabilité d'Ottawa et des provinces: une autre avenue de centralisation," Press Release, Premier's Office, Quebec, August 23, 1996. [Translation]

35 "Le rééquilibrage des rôles et des responsabilités d'Ottawa et des provinces: une autre avenue de centralisation." [Translation]; "Programmes sociaux: le Québec refuse la proposition des provinces de centraliser à Ottawa les pouvoirs du Québec en matière sociale," Press Release, Premier's Office, Quebec, August 23, 1996.

36 "Union sociale canadienne: la position du Québec," Document Submitted by the Premier of Quebec to the Annual Premiers' Conference, St. Andrews, August 6-8, 1997.

37 "Rejetant deux propositions québécoises, la conférence des premiers ministres expose les Québécois et les Canadiens au gaspillage du fédéral," Press Release, Premier's Office, Quebec, December 12 1997. [Translation]

38 "Constitutional Agreement," Canadian proposal for the patriation of the Constitution, April 16, 1981.

39 "Constitution Amendment, 1987, Constitution Act, 1867," art. 106A; "Consensus Report on the Constitution," Charlottetown, August 28, 1992, art. 25.

40 "Notes pour un point de presse du premier ministre du Québec Monsieur Lucien Bouchard, à la suite de la rencontre des premiers ministres à Calgary," Premier's Office, September 16, 1997. [Translation]

41 A.I. Silver, *The French-Canadian Idea of Confederation*, 2nd ed. (Toronto: University of Toronto Press, 1997), pp. 218-19.

42 Kenneth McRoberts, *Misconceiving Canada: The Struggle for National Unity* (Toronto: Oxford University Press, 1997), pp. 19-23.

43 Silver, *The French-Canadian Idea of Confederation*, p. 250.

44 Simeon, *Federal-Provincial Diplomacy*, pp. 59 and 174-75; Yves Vaillancourt, "Le régime d'assistance publique du Canada: perspective québécoise," Ph.D. dissertation, Department of Political Science, University of Montreal, Montreal, February 1992, pp. 11-12; Claude Morin, *Les choses comme elles étaient: une autobiographie politique* (Montreal: Boréal, 1994), pp. 169-70.

45 Simeon, *Federal-Provincial Diplomacy*, pp. 171-72; Vaillancourt, "Le régime d'assistance publique du Canada," pp. 340-44; McRoberts, *Misconceiving Canada*, pp. 141-42.

46 Claude Morin, *Le combat québécois* (Montreal: Boréal, 1973), pp. 83-90.

47 "Notes pour un point de presse du premier ministre du Québec Monsieur Lucien Bouchard...," [Translation].

48 Yves Vaillancourt (with Luc Thériault), "Transfert canadien en matière de santé et de programmes sociaux: enjeux pour le Québec," *Cahiers de LAREPPS*, no. 97-02, Laboratoire de recherche sur les pratiques et les politiques sociales, Université du Québec à Montréal, Montreal, October 1997, p. 91-92.

49 Simeon, *Federal-Provincial Diplomacy*, p. 155.

50 André Laurendeau on February 17, 1945 cited in Keith G. Banting, *The Welfare State and Canadian Federalism*, 2nd ed. (Montreal: McGill-Queen's University Press, 1987), p. 141.

51 Bob Rae, *From Protest to Power: Personal Reflections on a Life in Politics* (Toronto: Penguin Books, 1997), p. 337.

52 Yves Vaillancourt, *L'évolution des politiques sociales au Québec, 1940-1960* (Montreal: Presses de l'Université de Montréal, 1988), p. 119.

53 Simeon, *Federal-Provincial Diplomacy*, p. 55.

54 Keith G. Banting, "The Welfare State as Statecraft: Territorial Politics and Canadian Social Policy Reform," in Stephan Leibfried and Paul Pierson (eds.), *European Social Policy: Between Fragmentation and Integration* (Washington: The Brookings Institution, 1995), pp. 269-300.

55 "Collaborative Use of the Spending Power for Intergovernmental Transfers: The Race to the Top model," Ministry of Intergovernmental Affairs, Ottawa, February 5, 1999, p. 2.

56 On this, see Alain Noël, "Is Decentralization Conservative? Federalism and the Contemporary Debate on the Canadian Welfare State," in Robert A. Young (ed.), *Stretching the Federation: The Art of the State in Canada* (Kingston: Institute of Intergovernmental Relations, 1999), pp. 195-219.

57 See Noël, "Is Decentralization Conservative?"

58 Alain Noël, "The Federal Principle, Solidarity and Partnership," in Roger Gibbins and Guy Laforest (eds.), *Beyond the Impasse: Toward Reconciliation* (Montreal: Institute for Research on Public Policy, 1998), pp. 284-85.

59 Richard Simeon, "In Search of a Social Contract: Can We Make Hard Decisions as if Democracy Matters?" Benefactors Lecture, Toronto, C.D. Howe Institute, September 1994, p. 43.

60 Keith Banting, "The Social Policy Divide: The Welfare State in Canada and the United States," in Keith Banting, George Hoberg and Richard Simeon (eds.), *Degrees of Freedom: Canada and the United States in a Changing World* (Montreal: McGill-Queen's University Press, 1997), p. 301.

61 On this, see Alain Noël, "Vers un nouvel État-providence? Enjeux démocratiques," *Politique et sociétés*, no. 30 (Fall 1996), pp. 18-24.

62 Alain Noël, "La contrepartie dans l'aide sociale au Québec," *Revue française des affaires sociales*, Vol. 50, no. 4 (October-December 1996), pp. 99-122; Vaillancourt, "Transfert canadien en matière de santé et de programmes sociaux."

63 Petter, "Meech Ado About Nothing? Federalism, Democracy and the Spending Power," p. 189. Andrew Petter is now Minister of Intergovernmental Relations in British Columbia.

64 Alain Noël, "Les trois unions sociales," *Policy Options*, Vol. 19, no. 9 (November 1998), pp. 26-29.

65 Silver, *The French Canadian Idea of Confederation*, p. 250.

66 Will Kymlicka, "Multinational Federalism in Canada: Rethinking the Partnership," in Gibbins and Laforest (eds.), *Beyond the Impasse*, p. 30.

Principles

Introduction

We were asked to carry out a study of chapter 1 of the February 4, 1999 agreement between the Government of Canada and the provincial and territorial governments, with the exception of Quebec. This agreement is better known as the Social Union Framework Agreement.

The study will be approached from the standpoint of constitutional law and intergovernmental relations. There are other factors involved in the analysis of the agreement, particularly the socio-economic and financial dimension (the effects of the agreement on Quebec's economic equilibrium), modifications in the nature of the various categories of federal transfer payments, etc. These other aspects will be raised only to emphasize certain elements and will not be dealt with in depth.

General Perspective

The Social Union Framework Agreement is a major turning point in the history of Canadian federalism, one that introduces an unprecedented degree of rigidity, uniformity and centralization into the exercise of the Canadian provinces' socio-economic powers in the health, education and social services sectors. The agreement introduces a new dynamic into federal-provincial relations. In the long run this new dynamic will alter the very nature of Canadian federalism by substantially reducing the autonomy of the provinces and consecrating the primacy of the federal government in the majority of Canada's key governmental intervention areas. This is the general perspective that will guide this study.

The Social Union Framework Agreement cannot help but recall the Constitutional Agreement of November 1981, reached after the "the night of the long knives." The exclusion of Quebec on that occasion was the cause of a constitutional deadlock that has still not been resolved. This exclusion also assumed a great symbolic value that crystallized the redefinition of Canada. The Social Union Framework Agreement appears to be an extension of the November 1981 agreement. That agreement has in fact until now been partially compensated for by a relative degree of flexibility at the federal administrative level (agreements on training and labour, immigration and the GST) that to a certain extent took into account the specificity of Quebec or the scope of the provinces' jurisdictions (for example, the Agreement on Internal Trade). By the same token, between 1986 and 1992 major efforts were devoted to resolving the constitutional deadlock.

The current federal government has now given up on such efforts. It has opted for the Social Union Framework Agreement, a major administrative agreement that has a structuring effect on the conduct of the federation's affairs, an agreement that is therefore, at the political level, of a quasi-constitutional nature (even though the legal formulation fails to reflect the political reality here). The Framework Agreement will not be quasi-constitutional for the jurist, but will be for the manager of the state. The jurist will nonetheless recognize that the constitutional effects of the Framework Agreement may be considerable and threaten to increase over time.

The Social Union Framework Agreement thus appears to be the complement and corollary of the 1981 Constitutional Agreement. Both texts led to the political and symbolic exclusion of Quebec from the definition of Canada. The exclusion of Quebec was on each occasion the result of the refusal to recognize the unique status of Quebec, particularly by means of the right to opt out with compensation. The Social Union Framework Agreement exacerbates the effects of the 1981 agreement. It constitutes an intensification of the constitutional deadlock at the administrative level, a greater degree of rigidity of the federation in the name of a principle of equality that does not acknowledge a right to difference. It is a recognition by the other provinces of the legitimacy of Ottawa's attempts at standardization and of the primary status of the federal government.

With the benefit of hindsight, we will no doubt be able to state that in 1999 the English-speaking provinces agreed to put into writing the concept of federalism that had no doubt already reigned among most of them for a long time: the recognition of a vertical federalism in which they play a subordinate role, framed by the spending power and the "national" norms of the federal government. (We have already seen in the federal budget of 1999 the weakness of the provinces' political power, and how little impact the Social Union Framework Agreement has had on Ottawa's unilateral initiatives.)

The November 1981 Constitutional Agreement and the Social Union Framework Agreement are versions of one and the same theme played in major and minor keys: Canada's identity can no longer co-exist with that of Quebec. Canada is increasingly incapable of arriving at a definition of itself that takes into account Quebec's aspirations and desire for autonomy. The two societies are in fact separating, and the Social Union Framework Agreement is just the latest milestone along the way towards an irrevocable break. It is no longer even enough for Canada that Quebec accept Canada as such, without any constitutional reform. Canada is now asking Quebec for more. It is asking it to accept Canada in its new centralizing form, that is, in accordance with a dynamic that runs counter to the one that almost every Quebec government has wanted to introduce, one that respects the development of Quebec.

The 1999 administrative *coup de force* by Ottawa and the provinces complements the constitutional *coup de force* of 1981. It is its logical consequence and end. Although it came about in less dramatic circumstances, making it less visible in the eyes of public opinion, its effects on Quebec's aspirations are actually more concrete and more damaging.

General Comments on Chapter 1

The first point to be made here is that the governments assert that they are acting in accordance with their respective constitutional responsibilities and powers. This classic, apparently inoffensive clause actually masks a profound disagreement over the scope of the powers and responsibilities of the two levels of government, particularly between Ottawa and Quebec. If the federal government were to publish an exhaustive list of its powers and responsibilities and its definition of the powers and responsibilities of Quebec in up-to-date, accessible language, and if the government of Quebec did the same, ordinary citizens would no doubt be astonished at the enormous divergence of opinion in a great many sectors. Furthermore, a clause of this kind masks the fact that the balance of powers and responsibilities is subject to perpetual change, most often to Ottawa's advantage. Two of the most decisive factors in such change are constitutional jurisprudence and the administrative agreements themselves. To cite just one example, the jurisprudence of the 1970s, under which the Supreme Court of Canada assigned jurisdiction over communications to Ottawa, today deprives Quebec of a large share of control in the high technology, computer and multimedia sectors. Furthermore, the courts will hesitate to put intergovernmental agreements in question, seeing them as an important reference point with respect to the allocation of powers.

The second remark concerns the clause for the protection of Aboriginal peoples at the end of chapter 1. No such similar clause appears for the Quebec people in spite of the fact that the House of Commons and the Senate in December 1995 adopted a resolution recognizing a distinct society in Quebec that called on "the legislative and executive branches of [the federal] government to take note of this recognition and be guided in their conduct accordingly."[1] This resolution remained a dead letter; it never had any real effect. Whenever a decisive moment arrives, there is no longer a distinct society of Quebec in Ottawa's eyes, even less a Quebec people. Once more, Canada is incapable of arriving at a definition of itself that respects the identity of Quebec.

The Evolution of the Position of the Provinces

The Saskatoon Consensus

IN THE SASKATOON CONSENSUS, THERE IS A REFERENCE TO ANOTHER DOCUMENT EXPRESSing the provincial/territorial consensus on the negotiating position that had been developed at the ministerial level and to which the premiers unanimously subscribed. In the Saskatoon consensus, the provincial premiers stressed the importance of "a stronger partnership between the two orders of government," in order to protect Canadian social programs in the future. They also declared that it was not a matter of giving more powers to one or another of the two levels of government. They expressed a wish for the governments to work together within their constitutional jurisdictions.

Emphasis was laid on cooperative federalism, that is, on mutual respect between the two levels of government, and on the maintenance or strengthening of a certain balance between their respective powers. The relationship with the federal government that was envisaged was more horizontal than vertical in nature.

It is striking to remark that this approach is no longer to be found in chapter 1 of the Social Union Framework Agreement, which contains the principles that are supposed to guide the interpretation of the agreement. The only reference to federalism in this chapter is the government's undertaking to adopt these principles "within their respective constitutional jurisdictions and powers." We should note that the Saskatoon text only mentions respect of constitutional responsibilities. The reference to constitutional powers was no doubt added at the request of the federal government and opens the way for an unprecedented recognition of the federal spending power in chapter 5. The first sentence of chapter 5 states that "The use of the federal spending power under the Constitution has been essential to the development of Canada's social union." This sentence alone would have justified Quebec's not signing the Framework Agreement. We should also note that before Quebec participated in negotiations leading to the Social Union Framework Agreement, the Quebec premier declared that he refused to recognize the federal spending power either directly or indirectly: "Moreover, Quebec reaffirms its historic position concerning respect for its fields of jurisdiction."[2]

Although the courts agreed to consider the spending power legal under the 1867 Constitution Act, its exercise by the federal government seriously weakens the autonomy which, according to the interpretation that has been current in Quebec for a very long time, the Constitution Act is supposed to guarantee to the provinces. The spending power is not defined by the Constitution. Its exercise is a result of the imbalance between the constitutional responsibilities of the provinces and their financial and fiscal resources in the modern age, and of Ottawa's desire to establish a direct relationship with citizens in order to extend its visibility and to avail itself of a stronger state. It does not correspond — particularly in the case of unilateral federal initiatives in fields of jurisdiction clearly assigned in the Constitution to the provinces — to the concept of federalism that has traditionally been current in Quebec. We shall return to this aspect of the question at a later point.

In the Saskatoon consensus, the provincial premiers emphasized the need for "collaborative arrangements on federal spending in areas of provincial/territorial jurisdiction." The spending power, which was not recognized but simply remarked upon, appeared there as a troubling element that needed to be corrected.

In chapter 5 of the Social Union Framework Agreement, as we have seen, the legitimacy of the federal spending power is proclaimed loud and clear. More than a change of tone, this amounts to a completely different perspective that imposes the federal vision. This constitutes a major discrepancy between the two approaches.

With magnanimity, once it had obtained the major victory of official recognition of its spending power, the federal government consented in chapter 5 to "proceed in a cooperative manner that is respectful of the provincial and territorial governments and their priorities." It will be remarked that in the rest of the chapter the clauses preserve the federal government's freedom of manœuvre and initiative, and that the constraints that it will have to bear are very minor. It undertakes to consult the provinces and to notify them before modifying funding for social transfers. It undertakes to cooperate with the provinces to determine Canada-wide priorities and objectives. It will not create any new Canada-wide initiatives without the consent of the majority of the provinces, which is frankly a ridiculous clause when one considers the demographic weight of the four largest provinces. Furthermore, it imposes a framework of accountability on the provinces even in cases when their programs would allow them to take advantage of the possibility of transfer payments in the same, or a related, priority domain.

In chapter 5, the federal government succeeds in investing itself with the right to manage certain of the provinces' key socio-economic responsibilities, without ever considering power-sharing. Moreover, nowhere in the Social Union Framework Agreement, and more particularly, nowhere in chapter 5, is it stated that health care, post-secondary education, social assistance and social services fall under the jurisdiction of the provinces. The Framework Agreement is presented as a matter of vast shared responsibilities with primacy going to the federal party. Although Ottawa says it wishes to respect the provinces and their priorities, it is not committed to respecting the exclusivity of their constitutional jurisdictions because it does not recognize it.

From this point on, the reader will better grasp the meaning and the scope of chapter 1 of the Framework Agreement. Behind the stated principles lies the federal desire to gain greater legitimacy and visibility by establishing direct links with citizens and by confining provinces to a secondary role. Who could better express the fundamental values of Canadians and their aspirations to equality? Who could better fulfill their needs once it has defined them? Basically, chapter 1 is a program and a mandate whose primary political beneficiary is the federal government itself. It, after all, is the only government that claims to act on behalf of the entire Canadian population, and it is the common needs of every individual member of this population that are emphasized in chapter 1 and the rest of the Framework Agreement. Chapter 1 increases the visibility and legitimacy of Ottawa in domains where its presence has long been contested, even outside Quebec. The English provinces caved in and consented to a major shift in position that will ensure that a certain vision of decentralized, cooperative federalism will never again be credibly proposed outside Quebec, even though it continues, intermittently, to be invoked in official pronouncements.

Another major discrepancy between the Saskatoon consensus and the text of the Social Union Framework Agreement is to be found in the question of the opting-out formula. The provincial premiers insisted, in August 1998 in Saskatoon, on the fundamental importance of reaching a consensus on this question. Their position at that time was that in sectors of provincial jurisdiction each province should be able to opt out of any new social program or modified Canada-wide program with full compensation, on the understanding that the province would offer a program or an initiative in the same fields of priority activity as the Canada-wide programs. This position already represented a significant compromise for Quebec.

We have seen that the Social Union Framework Agreement recognizes no provincial field of jurisdiction. Here are the relevant clauses from chapter 5:

> A provincial/territorial government which, because of its existing programming, does not require the total transfer to fulfill the agreed objectives would be able to reinvest any funds not required for those objectives in the same or a related priority area.
>
> The [g]overnment of Canada and the provincial/territorial governments will agree on an accountability framework for such new social initiatives and investments.
>
> All provincial and territorial governments that meet or commit to meet the agreed Canada-wide objectives and agree to respect the accountability framework will receive their share of available funding.

These clauses apply to the new Canada-wide initiatives for health care, post-secondary education, social assistance and social services, which are financed by means of federal transfers to the provinces. They are not intended for direct federal transfers to individuals and to organizations, like the Millennium Scholarship Fund. In these cases, federal action is limited only by the obligation of providing three months' prior warning and consultation. The distinction between federal transfers to provincial governments and federal transfers to individuals or organizations did not appear in the Saskatoon consensus.

It appears, upon reading the first of the three paragraphs cited above, that a province that is already offering a program in the domain targeted by the federal initiative and did not need to use all of the transfer to attain the agreed objectives could, in order to round-off its program, reinvest the nonrequired funds in the same, or in a related field. The provinces' room for manœuvre in the Social Union Framework Agreement is actually far narrower than indicated in the Saskatoon consensus. The objectives of the Canada-wide program and those of the existing provincial program will have to be agreed upon between Ottawa and the province, thereby limiting the latter's discretion in the exercise of its own jurisdiction.

Furthermore, it needs to be understood that the new accountability framework that will be put in place is as much aimed at the governments benefiting from the watered-down opting-out formula as at the others. In fact, according to the last paragraph quoted, only the provinces that attain or undertake to attain the Canada-wide objectives agreed with Ottawa and the other provinces, and agree to respect the accountability framework, may receive federal funding. This could have markedly limited Quebec's freedom to manœuvre within its own constitutional jurisdictions, which are supposedly exclusive.

Finally, provinces that already have a program in the domain of the federal initiative can use the transferred funds in the same or a related field. The definition of what is related must presumably be approved by Ottawa. We once more find ourselves in an exclusively provincial jurisdiction whose scope Ottawa will now have the right to define. There was no limit of this type in the Saskatoon consensus, which allowed any province offering a program in the same domain as a Canada-wide program to opt out of the latter with full compensation. It was clear that the province could then use these funds at its discretion in the field of its choice, without being monitored by the federal government.

The Victoria Proposal

There are some major discrepancies between the last interprovincial position of January 29, 1999, known as the "Victoria proposal," and the Social Union Framework Agreement. In general terms, the Victoria proposal emphasizes the status, constitutional responsibilities and legitimacy of the provinces relative to the public services provided to citizens in the fields of education, health and social services. These considerations are conspicuous by their absence in the Framework Agreement reached between the English-speaking provinces and Ottawa on February 4. It would be accurate to talk of a complete about-face in this instance, since we move from one text focused on horizontal or cooperative federalism in which all the governments are co-holders of legitimacy, to another focused on vertical federalism in which the provinces appear as links in an administrative chain.

There are several examples to illustrate this about-face. Section 1 of the Framework Agreement, entitled, "Principles" corresponds with chapters 1 and 2 of the Victoria proposal entitled, "Respecting Canadian Values" and "Guiding Principles." Chapter 1 of the Victoria proposal stresses the importance of improving relationships between governments by clarifying the sharing of responsibilities and by eliminating duplication:

> Canadians want and deserve governments working better together by clarifying responsibilities, eliminating overlap and duplication, and enhancing accountability.
>
> This Agreement offers Canadians financially sustainable health care and social programs, more accountable government, flexibility to meet different needs in different provinces and territories, and greater harmony among governments. Working together more effectively will strengthen the social union and benefit all Canadians.

Section 2 of the Victoria proposal goes further (see subsection entitled "Managing Canada's Social Union"), since it unabashedly asserts the primacy of the constitutional functions of the provinces in the field of social policy:

> Under the Constitution, provinces and territories are primarily responsible for social policy and the delivery of social programs.
>
> Governments believe strongly in increasing accountability to the public and improving the effectiveness and efficiency of the social union. To this end, governments are committed to:
>
> - reducing and avoiding overlap and duplication;
> - clarifying roles and responsibilities by assigning, where appropriate, responsibility for areas of the Social Union to one order of government or the other; and,
> - minimizing areas of joint responsibility where this would improve the effectiveness and efficiency of the social union.
>
> Governments are committed to working together in partnership where this would result in improved services to Canadians and explaining to Canadians their respective contributions to social programs.

There is a deep gulf between these provisions and those in chapter 1 of the Social Union Framework Agreement. In the latter, the proper functioning of the federation, the reduction of overlap and the clarification of power-sharing are no longer part of the priorities, principles or values of Canadians. In a text so clearly dedicated to establishing a preponderant role in the social domain for itself and the legitimacy of its spending power, Ottawa could not subscribe to an affirmation of the primary responsibility of the provinces under the Constitution. In a text aimed precisely at setting aside the traditional interpretation of the Constitution, an interpretation that was built on a scrupulous respect for shared jurisdictions and the substantial autonomy of the provinces, there could be no question of Ottawa clarifying the roles and responsibilities of the two levels of government by clearly assigning the responsibility for certain domains of the social union to one of them. Nor could there be any question of reducing areas of joint intervention, since — given the wording of the Constitution — it risked losing in the exercise. It is more in Ottawa's interest to maximize such areas.

In the vision of the federation held by the federal government, the power-sharing formula of 1867 does not work. The provinces are spoilsports, who ideally ought to be no more than administrative branches of a unitary, concentrated state. From that moment on, all provisions reinforcing the status and emphasizing the primary jurisdictions of the provinces in the domains targeted by the Framework Agreement became unacceptable. The federal government's response to the clauses just cited is typified in the formal recognition of its spending power in chapter 5 of the agreement.

This change of perspective can be seen in other examples. Chapter 4 of the Victoria proposal entitled, "Programs Canadians can count on" sets forth the interprovincial vision that was announced in the preceding chapters. This vision can be described as "provincialist" in that it proposes a role of heightened visibility for the provinces. Contrary to the Social Union Framework Agreement, chapter 4 of the Victoria proposal applies to fiscal transfers and federal payments, to existing programs and new programs, to transfers to individuals and organizations as well as provincial governments, and federal programs aimed at only one or a few provinces or at Canada-wide programs.

The most significant clauses in chapter 4 are the following:

> The federal government will work with provinces and territories to ensure that all major federal/provincial/territorial funding arrangements provide provinces and territories with adequate resources to meet their responsibilities to Canadians, including those described in this agreement. To ensure that Canadians are treated equitably, the federal government will work with

provinces and territories to ensure that they have the financial resources to allow them to provide reasonably comparable levels of public services at reasonably comparable levels of taxation.

Adequacy and long-term balance will be addressed through:

- The federal government working with the provinces and territories to ensure that major federal/provincial/territorial funding arrangements adequately reflect provincial/territorial spending responsibilities...
- The federal government working with the provinces to ensure that equalization payments adequately address the fiscal imbalances that exist between the provinces' revenue-raising capacities...
- The federal government working with the provinces and territories to ensure sufficient federal resources through existing financial arrangements to address current and growing cost pressures in the areas of health, education and social services...
- Under this Agreement, if the federal government withdraws from the funding of social programs, or if there is a realignment of responsibilities within the federation, commensurate federal resources must accompany these changes to provide provinces and territories with adequate funds to carry out their new or enhanced responsibilities.

These clauses give substance to the statement of principle of the primary constitutional responsibility of the provinces in the fields of social policy and the provision of social services (chapter 2). The role of the federal government, in the view of the provinces, consists in supporting them in order to allow them to fully acquit themselves of their constitutional responsibilities. The federal government must thus ensure that the provinces have sufficient resources to provide comparable services at a comparable rate of taxation to all Canadians. In this view, the provinces require Ottawa to give them fiscal and financial support that does not threaten their own primacy in the social domain.

The provinces also identify one of the major structural imbalances in the Canadian Constitution: that between the fiscal and financial resources of the provinces and their constitutional responsibilities or jurisdictions. We know how costly provincial responsibilities in the sectors of health, education and social services are. The provinces, however, do not have fiscal powers as wide as those of Ottawa, which has used its fiscal powers and its borrowing power to enter into provincial fields of jurisdiction, rather than correct imbalances by respecting provincial autonomy.

In Victoria, the provinces attempted to deal with more fundamental issues by including the problem of equalization payments in the Social Union Framework Agreement in an attempt to correct fiscal disparities. The clauses quoted from chapter 4 of the Victoria proposal are nowhere to be found in the federal-provincial Framework Agreement. For Ottawa, it was unacceptable for the provinces to attempt to take part in its decisions about budgetary procedures and the distribution of fiscal and financial resources between levels of government. For the federal government, this distribution must remain unilateral, since it constitutes a vital element in the relationship of power in which it enjoys the advantage. Its fiscal, borrowing and spending powers form a huge trilogy by means of which it dominates the provinces in the domains formally assigned to them by the Constitution. This fiscal and financial trilogy is one of the primary sources of the power of the federal state. It is out of the question to let the provinces get too close to it.

In chapter 5 of the Victoria proposal, the provinces reiterate their basic viewpoint:

"Provincial and territorial governments have primary responsibility for core social programs. The federal government also has an important role in the Social Union."

According to this text, the provinces are not simply providers of federal services, they have a primary responsibility. The federal government has a back-up role that permits the provinces to fulfill the responsibilities — including the design of social policies — that fall to them under the Constitution. Subsequent events showed the lack of firmness of the English-speaking provinces on these questions. This does not alter the fact that the clause quoted above was compatible with the traditional position of Quebec on this issue, as will be seen later.

Still in chapter 5 of the Victoria proposal, the provinces once more pose the question of social union through reference to constitutional jurisdictions:

"The ability of a province/territory to address priority areas of Canada-wide programs within its jurisdiction is essential to an effectively functioning Social Union."

On the subsequent page, with regard to federal programs in one or several provinces, the reference to provincial jurisdiction leads to the requirement of obtaining the consent of the province before a federal program can be applied on its territory:

"Federal spending in an area of provincial jurisdiction which occurs in a province or territory must have the consent of the province or territory involved."

This approach is entirely absent from the Social Union Framework

Agreement, which contains no mention of the responsibilities and jurisdictions of the provinces. Nor does it contain any mention of the Constitution, aside from one single reference in chapter 1, which is contradicted by the power relationship so disadvantageous to the provinces that is expressed in each of the subsequent chapters.

As for the right to opt out, chapter 5 of the Victoria proposal repeats in more formal terms the position stated in the Saskatoon consensus:

> The federal government will provide full financial compensation to any provincial or territorial government that chooses not to participate in any new or modified Canada-wide program, providing it carries on a program or initiative that addresses the priority areas of the new or modified Canada-wide program.[3]

Another profound difference in approach between the Victoria proposal and the Social Union Framework Agreement is contained in chapters 6 and 7 of the proposal, entitled "Clear roles for governments" and "Accountability for Canadians."

Chapter 6 states:

> Canadians need to know which order of government to hold responsible for specific decisions in areas of social policy. Clarifying roles and responsibilities in the management and delivery of social programs will enable Canadians to hold their governments accountable for decisions they make.

The opening words of chapter 7 are as follows: "Clarify the roles of [g]overnments and inform Canadians of the responsibilities of each government."

The importance attached here to the clarification of the roles and responsibilities of governments and to the transparency of these roles and responsibilities in the eyes of citizens has no equivalent in the Social Union Framework Agreement, which was drafted in order to give the federal government maximum visibility and unprecedented legitimacy in the targeted sectors. This was achieved at the cost of clarification of the roles of government which, once more, might have benefited the provinces and prevented Ottawa from obtaining its political objectives. Utilizing the advantages conferred by its large financial and fiscal resources to the fullest, Ottawa embarked on a kind of short-sighted nation-building campaign that may turn out to be one more factor of disunion and instability for the Canadian federation.

To conclude this first part, although no great discrepancy emerges from the Saskatoon consensus and the Victoria proposal (since the latter constitutes a formal elaboration of the former) there is a profound divergence between the Victoria proposal and the Social Union Framework Agreement. It is astonishing to remark that in a single week, the positions of the provinces, with the exception of Quebec, could have swung around so completely. It has to be concluded from this that they only associated with Quebec for bargaining purposes, that negotiations with Ottawa were taking place concurrently, unknown to Quebec, and that the firmness of their constitutional convictions gave way at the decisive moment, when they were faced with the necessity of choosing loyalty to Canada over solidarity with a province that was seeking secession. These elements were all present in the Constitutional Agreement of November 1981 that isolated Quebec.

The English-speaking provinces endeavoured to make the federation work even at the cost of centralization. Quebec could not accept to pay this price because this would threaten its national identity. It was this simple equation, so fraught with consequences, that caused the Social Union Framework Agreement to falter over the relationship between Quebec and Canada.

The English-speaking provinces do not see the Framework Agreement as a threat to their aspirations, since they have a shared national identity that can be expressed by a strong central government whose legitimacy they contest far less. The principal source of unease for the future does not come in their eyes from the federal government, but from the possible withdrawal of Quebec from the Canadian federation. They played a double game and left Quebec on its own as soon as their autonomist position threatened to compromise the chances of a financially advantageous agreement, and risked attracting the accusation from their own public opinion of having played the game of the Quebec separatists. In so doing, they lost a large amount of their political and constitutional credibility.

Comparison Between the Social Union Framework Agreement and Quebec's Traditional Positions

When one compares the Social Union Framework Agreement and the various relevant positions defended by Quebec governments for over half a century, it is clear that the agreement does not fit with Quebec's traditional positions and no Quebec government that hoped to uphold these positions could ever sign it.[4] In this analysis of Quebec's traditional positions we look at three periods: before 1960; from the government of Jean Lesage to René Lévesque (1960 to 1976); and from 1976 to today.

Before 1960

Before 1960, the government of Maurice Duplessis had defended classical positions on the autonomy of the Canadian provinces and the necessity of preserving the financial independence of the provinces to assure their autonomy. The Duplessis government formulated many of its positions on the occasion of various intergovernmental conferences held after the Second World War. Following the Rowell-Sirois Report of 1939, the federal government attempted to consolidate control over the fiscal powers of the provinces that had been temporarily assigned to it during the war. It wanted greater freedom of initiative and action to finance and erect the welfare state. It was within the context of Maurice Duplessis' resistance to these federal aims that his conception of the status of provinces and intergovernmental relations was advanced:

- ...the very essence of Confederation is made of provincial authorities, within the scope of their jurisdiction and a sovereign central authority, within the scope of its jurisdiction. When Confederation was discussed and decided upon, it was based on the principle of complete provincial autonomy.[5]
- The provincial autonomy cannot be safeguarded by substituting a federal grant for the financial independence of the [p]rovinces.[6]
- The federative system which necessitates, fundamentally, an attribution of public tasks, must also provide a correlative division of revenue sources... A central government which would appropriate to itself the sources of taxation would, by this very fact, reduce the provinces to legislative impotence. Effectively, a province with no other revenues than federal subsidies would become a kind of inferior organism, under control of the authority which could measure out its means of subsistence.[7]
- The exclusive rights of the Provinces in matters of social legislation, education, civil rights, etc. must be safeguarded in their entirety if Confederation is to endure.[8]
- Of what use would it be for the provinces to have the right to build schools and hospitals if they are dependent on another authority in order to obtain the necessary funds? Their sovereignty with respect to education and hospitalization would then be meaningless.[9]

We know that the Duplessis government objected strenuously and long to federal grants to universities. In 1955, it prohibited Quebec universities from accepting these grants. In a letter to the federal justice minister in 1954, Duplessis objected to the federal policy of intervening directly in institutions under provincial jurisdiction, rather than providing the provinces with sufficient financial resources to permit them to fulfill their constitutional obligations.[10]

Mr. Duplessis' successor, Mr. Paul Sauvé, took the same position:

- Quebec considers that federal grants to universities encroach on an area reserved exclusively for the provinces.[11]
- In my opinion...it is very clear that the central administration should not tax for provincial purposes, and if, at a given time, in the near or distant future, Ottawa agrees on this, there will be no more conflict in the area of taxation.[12]

From Jean Lesage to René Lévesque (1960-1976)

After 1960, the Quebec government modernized its approach. It was no longer just a question of valuing autonomy for itself, but of seeing it as a means of allowing a people to develop and flourish as it wished:

> In short, we are not defending the autonomy of the provinces simply because it is a question of a principle, but rather because autonomy is to us the basic condition, not of our survival which is assured from now on, but of our assertion as a people.[13]

In 1964, Lesage presented his concept of cooperative federalism, which in his view ought to respect the autonomy and responsibilities of the provinces:

> Cooperative federalism does not mean simply obtaining the consent of the provinces to centralizing policies. Rather, for Quebec, it means beginning of a new era in federal-provincial relations and the dynamic adaptation of Canadian federalism. Federalism should express itself in three ways: 1) regular cooperation when decisions are made concerning new policies; 2) constant consultation on the application of policies; 3) sufficient financial resources granted to the provinces to enable them to carry out their greater responsibilities.[14]

Jean Lesage frequently denounced the federal government's use of the spending power, and vigorously claimed an opting-out right that gave preference to the fiscal transfer formula. Here are a few examples:

- Conditional grants made by the [f]ederal government to provinces in connection with joint programs administered by the provincial governments create all sorts of difficulties. We understand why, when the [f]ederal government decides to participate in such programs, it requires that certain conditions be fulfilled by the provinces, but these conditions themselves cause frequent complications.
  Experience shows that often these joint programs do not permit the provinces to use their own revenues as they wish nor to take local conditions sufficiently into account. Moreover, they raise administrative difficulties that are the cause of a loss of efficiency or duplication of effort and increased costs. The provinces must have in their service persons specially charged with making reports to Ottawa concerning the execution of these programs and the [f]ederal government must, in its turn, hire employees to see that the conditions laid down by Ottawa are fulfilled by the provinces.[15]
- But these programs are now sufficiently well established on the provincial scale to enable the [f]ederal government to cease taking part in them and to vacate these fields. The [f]ederal government should be prepared to accept this request. Obviously, in such a case, it would be necessary to compensate the provinces fully for the additional financial responsibilities assumed by them. This financial compensation should take the form of additional taxation rights specifically reserved for the provincial governments and of corresponding equalization payments. If this were done, each province would be free to use its revenues as it sees fit in the fields of jurisdiction that belong to it.[16]
- These grants thus become a compulsion which, for all practical purposes, places the provinces in a state of subordination vis-à-vis the central government. As a matter of fact, if some of the provinces, because of their constitutional position, do not want to submit to the conditions established by the central government, they are seriously penalized because they are deprived of sums to which their citizens have nonetheless contributed. Above all, it is this situation which, since 1960, has forced Quebec to participate in several joint programs. However, this participation has always been for us but a makeshift solution while waiting for a satisfactory solution to this problem. We believe that the time has now come to solve this question once and for all...
  In the case of future shared-cost programs, and of those already existing but in which Quebec is not participating at present, we would like to be granted financial equivalence which would then be transposed into an additional freeing of taxation fields taking as a basis for calculation the relative proportion of Quebec's population in relation to the whole of the Canadian population.[17]
- Quebec is resolved to end the system of shared-cost programs and, consequently, has withdrawn from such programs instituted by the federal government and demands either fiscal compensation or the tax point equivalent. These shared-cost programs cause costly duplication, reduce provincial initiative in areas recognized by the

Constitution to be within provincial jurisdiction and distort the order of priorities established by the provinces.[18]

- Quebec demands that the federal government transfer to Quebec, in the form of tax equivalents, the amounts the federal government wanted to allocate to programs that encroach on provincial jurisdiction: i.e., student loans, education allowances.[19]

Under Daniel Johnson, the situation was practically the same. The continuity of the Quebec state's basic positions was remarkable. The following quotations sum up the positions of the government formed by the Union Nationale from 1966 to 1970:

- Quebec does not foresee renewing the joint programs from which it has already withdrawn, or committing itself to join any new programs of this kind.
  In return, Quebec demands unconditional compensation to enable it to ensure services for its population which are consistent with its own needs...
  Quebec hopes that once and for all it will be understood that for socio-cultural reasons, Quebec unreservedly insists that its constitutional jurisdiction be respected, and that it will brook no federal interference with this jurisdiction, whether that interference be direct or indirect.[20]
- The federal spending power should be limited to federal matters alone. However, unconditional grants could be paid to provinces either according to a general equalization formula or to stabilize their revenue.[21]
- Joint programs impede the free growth of our people by imposing on them priorities likely to upset those they would otherwise adopt, in addition to reducing their effective budget autonomy... For a nation like ours, their effect is to freeze its sources of taxation and take away full control over areas of activity which are rightfully its own. Joint programs therefore are generally incompatible with the basic aims pursued by the French-Canadian nation.[22]
- Governments that are ultimately responsible for given fields of activity must have access to resources that they can handle as they see fit and allocate in the way they want to carry out their responsibilities... Conditional grants, subsidies or transfers are wholly unacceptable.[23]

During his first term in office, Robert Bourassa did not deviate from the positions held by his predecessors. He expressed himself in precise terms that still reflect the current reality:

- ...each level of government must have access to sufficient revenue to meet the cost of programs falling under its jurisdiction.[24]

- No one would dare deny that the policies in matters of health services and social services come primarily under the jurisdiction of the provinces. Nevertheless, in actual fact, the federal government has always set priorities and fixed available resources through the means of rigid financial programs.
  Though ideally the federal power to spend in areas of provincial jurisdiction should not exist, Quebec is prepared to agree to it provided any province that does not participate in a joint program be entitled to financial compensation that would guarantee its freedom to abstain.[25]
- ...I wish to emphasize that the Government of Quebec wishes to terminate the provisional arrangements concerning programs of hospitalization and health insurance in order to replace them with a definitive withdrawal formula. This formula should meet two preliminary conditions:
  1) It should result in unconditional payments, that is to say, they should no longer be submitted to administrative control;
  ...
  I believe that these conditions could be met effectively by granting to the provinces an abatement of tax points on revenue sufficient to cover the real costs of programs. This method of financial compensation is unconditional and increases annually at a rate sufficient to compensate for the rise in costs...
- Quebec considers [the] question [of compensation for the withdrawal from certain cost-sharing programs] extremely important because it prefers to continue collecting its own taxes rather than having to receive financial compensations.[26]

During the inaugural speech of 1973, the Bourassa government made reform of the federation's tax system its first priority:

> The Government's major priorities in federal-provincial relations are as follows: the question of the financing of the federation in order to achieve a distribution of fiscal resources more in accordance with the constitutional responsibilities of the federal and provincial governments;...[27]

From René Lévesque to Today (1976 to present)

In Quebec, the idea of sovereignty was propelled to the foreground after November 1976 with the formation of the first sovereigntist government under René Lévesque. This government did not put into question the fundamental positions of its predecessors on the spending power and the division of powers, but employed them to demonstrate the structural deficiencies in Canadian federalism that ran counter to Quebec's aspirations. This criticism of federalism was one of the justifications put forward for the accession to sovereignty. At the same time, René Lévesque criticized the centralizing tendencies of the federal regime, which increasingly ignored the letter of the Constitution and the spirit of federalism, making the defense of Quebec's autonomy increasingly difficult. The constitutional status quo cannot exist in such conditions; either Quebec acquires the powers necessary to allow it to flourish freely or its status and its constitutional jurisdiction will be diminished and constantly eroded. The Social Union Framework Agreement is the most recent manifestation of these centralizing tendencies.

The Lévesque government's resumption of the historical positions of its predecessors is illustrated in the following extracts:

- Quebec believes that the federal spending power should be limited solely to the matters listed as under exclusive or concurrent federal jurisdiction. However, it will be necessary to rule on the mode of compensation applicable to provinces that may eventually abstain.[28]
- [Quebec objects to the numerous federal cuts which] gradually push the Quebec [g]overnment into an increasingly tight financial position in the hope of bringing it to reorganize as its own, the federal priorities, federal programs and federal distributions to citizens.[29]
- Quebec denounces the encroachment on provincial jurisdiction caused by the imposition of federal national standards that, through the federal spending power, erode the distribution of powers between the two orders of government. It is unacceptable to Quebec that the federal government implement an inspection and monitoring system in a sector of provincial jurisdiction such as health, that it pay grants to municipalities directly and make payment of its contributions subject to compliance with the criteria of national objectives, in particular in education. If provincial jurisdiction is to be defended, the provinces must effectively exercise their powers, fully occupy their areas of jurisdiction and the federal spending power must be limited, with the latter a priority.[30]

An examination of René Lévesque's record of intergovernmental relations in 1984 reveals that he not only continued his predecessors' denunciation of federal spending power, but he went further than they ever did. He declared that the generalized and unilateral use of this federal power was a distortion of Canadian federalism that was profoundly transforming its nature:

- We see a will to centralize powers in Ottawa, without precedent in modern Canada...It must be foreseen that a large part of this movement will continue.

On this question, Quebec's interest overlaps with that of the other provinces, for the sovereign exercise by all provinces of the areas of jurisdiction they have traditionally exercised under the BNA Act of 1867 and the decisions of the courts, is clearly being challenged. Ottawa, particularly using its unlimited spending power, has not only undertaken to alter to its advantage the distribution of powers within Canadian federalism, but is attacking the very nature of this system. The federal offensive is particularly obvious when it affects the powers exclusively reserved to the provinces in three sectors at the heart of their jurisdiction: health, municipal affairs and education.[31]

- We are seeing a mutation, in the deep sense of the term, of what the essence of Canadian federalism has been these past few decades: the provinces' areas of jurisdiction are no longer ever considered exclusive by Ottawa, which arrogates the right to intervene for every purpose to impose ITS "national" standards in this field, supposedly for the greater good of all Canadians...[32]

Unfortunately, following the Social Union Framework Agreement, it is no longer possible to assert that the English-speaking provinces share Quebec's concern for the respect of their autonomy and their constitutional powers. The transformation in the basic nature of Canadian federalism that René Lévesque perceived has progressed even further today. It has advanced to such a degree that the other provinces have now consented irremediably to weaken their own status. From now on, Quebec will find itself alone in defending a vision of federalism upon which the provinces turned their backs when they followed the direction imposed by Ottawa. In 1999, the deterioration of Canadian federalism progressed to a degree unwitnessed by any previous Quebec government.

On his return to power, Robert Bourassa attempted to reform the Canadian Constitution to respond to what he perceived as one of Quebec's central grievances with respect to the Canadian federation. Among the five conditions that he set for Quebec's ratification of the Constitution Act of 1982 was the limiting of the federal spending power. These conditions were expressed in 1986 by the minister responsible for Canadian intergovernmental affairs. Here is a passage from that speech on the subject of the spending power:

> Cultural security also signifies Quebec's ability to act alone in its fields of jurisdiction without interference from the federal government through its spending power. You are no doubt aware that this power allows Ottawa to

> spend sums of money in any area it wishes whether it falls under federal jurisdiction or not. At present, there is no exclusively provincial area of jurisdiction that is not susceptible in either a direct or indirect way to being affected by the federal spending power. The spending power has become a "sword of Damocles" hanging menacingly over any province wanting to plan its social, cultural or economic development...
>
> Placing boundaries on the application of the spending power could be a major contribution to the amelioration of the Canadian federation.[33]

Quebec's demand was reflected in the proposed 1987 constitutional amendment, better known as the Meech Lake Agreement. This agreement would have inserted a new clause into section 106A of the Constitution Act 1867, which would have set a certain limit on federal funding power. This clause read as follows:

> 106A. (1) The Government of Canada shall provide reasonable compensation to the government of a province that chooses not to participate in a national shared-cost program that is established by the Government of Canada after the coming into force of this section in an area of exclusive provincial jurisdiction, if the province carries on a program or initiative that is compatible with the national objectives.
>
> (2) Nothing in this section extends the legislative powers of the Parliament of Canada or of the legislatures of the provinces.[34]

Paradoxically, section 106A provided for an opting-out right only in the event of a Canada-wide program that was co-financed in an exclusively provincial jurisdiction. The unilateral exercise of federal spending power in such a sector was not forbidden, so section 106A only partially satisfied Quebec's traditional positions.

Since the 1987 constitutional amendment proposal was never adopted, the problem has remained in its entirety. Daniel Johnson Jr., who succeeded Robert Bourassa in 1994, reiterated the position of his predecessors:

> But above all, the reduction of overlaps must be consistent with a framework for the exercise of the federal spending power, if we wish to allow the two governments to exercise their responsibilities as efficiently as possible. This objective should also contribute to each government acting clearly within the areas of jurisdiction assigned to it by the Constitution.[35]

After the Parti Québécois was returned to power in September 1994, the government, led first by Jacques Parizeau and then by Lucien Bouchard, once more demanded respect for Quebec's constitutional powers and the right to opt out of federal programs, accompanied by fiscal compensation:

> ... Quebec will insist on respect for its constitutional jurisdictions and will demand their full exercise; it will continue to denounce the federal government's interference and will insist on full financial compensation in the form of tax points, particularly in the case of any new agreement or federal initiative in a sector within Quebec's jurisdiction.[36]

When the other provinces undertook negotiations with the federal government in 1996 on the topic of social union, Premier Bouchard issued a statement, invoking the historical positions of the various governments of Quebec:

> The government has neither the intention nor the mandate to abandon any dimension of Quebec constitutional jurisdiction, whether the operation involved is of a constitutional or administrative nature...Quebec governments have tried for a long time and independently of their option regarding the status of Quebec to steady its jurisdictions in order to foster the mastery by the Quebec people of its social, economic and cultural development, as well as its political institutions. What the provinces are offering us is centralization, a step backward, and a denial of the historical path of Quebeckers ...
>
> Quebec cannot embark on the road to a new equilibrium whose general direction and special measures lead to the abandonment of Quebec's fundamental claims and the gradual erosion of these claims through intergovernmental and administrative means. What is now proposed to Quebec is the construction of a Canadian government that is more powerful, a Canada that is more centralized and less respectful of the will of Quebeckers.[37]

It is not surprising that the present government of Quebec, aware that its positions are only the latest in a long, historical continuum, cannot subscribe to the Social Union Framework Agreement.

Comparison Between Quebec's Traditional Positions and the Social Union Framework Agreement

No long analysis is necessary to demonstrate that the Framework Agreement is incompatible with the interests and aspirations of Quebec as understood and defined by the successive governments that have come to power in Quebec in the last half-century. One has only to read the Framework Agreement and then read the positions taken by the various premiers of Quebec or other official spokespersons on matters dealt with in the agreement to arrive at this conclusion. It is manifest that the current Quebec government's refusal to sign the Framework Agreement is a direct continuation of previous positions whose constancy and firmness, transcending partisan differences, cannot fail to inspire respect. While the remedies prescribed for the ills afflicting Canadian federalism are different, namely accession to sovereignty or the reform of federalism, the diagnosis offered does not vary. This federalism, in its present state, is unacceptable to Quebec. Only a marked strengthening of the status of Quebec and a considerable increase in its powers and jurisdictions could maintain and foster the development of Quebec.

The spending power is a unilateral federal power whose generalized use diverts and undermines power-sharing to the point of actually putting into question the very notion of exclusive provincial jurisdiction. By transforming Canada, at the very best, into a quasi-federation, it has posed major difficulties for every Quebec government since the end of World War Two and has been deemed unjustifiable by every one of them. The spending power crystallizes the imbalance in the balance of power between Ottawa and the provinces, and is one of the most powerful elements of the centralizing dynamic that runs through the federation. The various Quebec governments have valiantly and continuously striven to contain its effects. On occasion, they have been able to count on a certain resistance to federal interference by the other provinces. This possibility, which has always been uncertain, will from now on be seriously compromised. Present and future Quebec governments will only be able to count on themselves and the Quebec people to defend and strengthen the status of Quebec.

For Maurice Duplessis, the Canadian federation was founded on the principle of the complete autonomy of the provinces, and this autonomy could not be safeguarded by substituting federal transfers for the financial independence of Quebec. He attempted to ensure this independence by creating a Quebec income tax and the Quebec Ministry of Revenue. For Jean Lesage, the principle of autonomy was the specific condition for the affirmation of the Quebec people. He reinforced the financial independence of the Quebec state by a series of withdrawals from federal programs accompanied by fiscal transfers, and by the creation of the Caisse de dépôt et placement. For Robert Bourassa, every order of government had to have access to sufficient revenues to cover the cost of the programs under its jurisdiction. He attempted to consolidate Quebec's fiscal autonomy by reaching an agreement with Ottawa on the payment and management of the Goods and Service Tax in Quebec.

One cannot imagine that any of these premiers would have agreed to recognize, as the Social Union Framework Agreement does, the legitimacy of the federal spending power and its quasi-discretionary use in areas of provincial jurisdiction, or the limiting of the provinces' discretion in the exercise of their own powers. Nor would they have accepted the obligation contained within the Framework Agreement to justify to Ottawa, like a subordinate government, the use of funds that are provided for the sole purpose of correcting a defect inherent in the Canadian Constitution: the profound discrepancy between Quebec's constitutional responsibilities, particularly in the areas of health, education, social services (as well as other sectors such as the protection of the environment), and the fiscal and financial resources that are made available to it by the Constitution. When, in addition, this relates to the development of a unique, distinct people on whose behalf these responsibilities are exercised, only a government that had repudiated the identity of this people and its own *raison d'être* could acquiesce to the federal desire to standardize it.

The Social Union Framework Agreement and the Status of Quebec

In this section we shall briefly examine the future effect of the Social Union Framework Agreement on the development of Canadian federalism in English Canada, on the identity of Quebec and on the status of Quebec.

Canadian Federalism in English Canada

A good point of departure for this discussion is a 1996 study conducted by Thomas Courchene for the Ontario government and distributed to the governments participating in the negotiations on social union.[38] In it Courchene emphasizes the need to strengthen the Canadian economic and social union. In the context of globalization and ongoing changes in relations with the United States, it is crucial to make the Canadian federation function better, particularly to preserve Canadian social programs. He considers the Canadian federation to be very decentralized, which is detrimental to internal integration of provincial markets. He also believes that the Canadian government intends to hand over major power to the provinces, and that the resulting massive reduction in federal transfers will weaken the federal government in its dealings with them:

> What is increasingly required is "positive integration" — a pro-active meshing of provincial systems (skill transferability) and federal-provincial systems (consumption tax harmonization). This cannot be done without the full participation of the provinces. Hence, delivering a full blown socio-economic union requires both top-down (vertical) and bottom-up (horizontal) integration. That this is the case is becoming progressively more evident.
>
> As more powers are passed down (back?) to the provinces, as indicated in the 1996 Speech from the Throne, provincial involvement becomes ever more essential. Moreover, as Ottawa pares cash transfers to the provinces under the Canadian Health and Social Transfer (CHST), from roughly $ 18 billion this year to the announced floor of $ 11 billion at the turn of the century, it is losing both its moral authority and its financial capability for enforcing unilateral top-down standards.[39]

In the author's provincialist vision, the political and constitutional weight of the provinces will be such that Ottawa will no longer be able to impose its views upon them. Only joint action between partners on a collegial basis will permit the effective management of the federation.

He argues that the respective roles of the two levels of government in the social domain have to be clarified. Furthermore, the order of government that controls public monies must be the same as the one that receives them. Intergovernmental transfers must be designed so as to permit the order of government responsible to be easily identified and held accountable.[40]

He asserts that the federal government should be able to exercise its spending power in areas of provincial jurisdiction if the provinces obtain an opting-out right with financial compensation. He is not opposed to asymmetry among provinces. Quebec may be accorded more power on condition that all Canadian citizens hold uniform rights. In his opinion, the convention that he proposes on this basis would symbolize the nature and identity of the Canadian federation.[41]

In the convention on social union Courchene proposes, federal financial transfers would be replaced by tax point transfers, except for equalization adjustments. He recognizes that Ottawa is opposed to fiscal transfers, but believes that it is possible to convince it, as well as Canadian public opinion, that they are well-founded:

> Given that the federal government is on record as being against further PIT tax-point transfers, the only possible way that this can become a reality in ACCESS is for the provinces to demonstrate to themselves, to the federal government and, most of all, to Canadians that they indeed have the will and the ability to design and deliver an effective internal social union convention...
>
> This exercise will hardly be easy, particularly since both health and welfare policy areas are in full evolutionary flight, but the goal is achievable. Indeed, it must be achievable since a pan-Canadian social safety net is a core Canadian value. And, increasingly, it is only with support of the provinces that Canada can fully deliver on this goal. That this basic message has not been filtered down to citizens constitutes a major stumbling block. With its call for mutual-consent principles in the 1995 budget (and reiterated in the 1996 budget and the Throne Speech), Ottawa has reconciled itself to this reality. It now needs to communicate this to Canadians.[42]

Further on, the author quotes another study with approval, which affords him an opportunity to reformulate his premises and his concept of intergovernmental relations:

> In a recent article, Richard Zucker (1995) focusses on this very issue. He argues that because of the demise of the federal spending power and because of the on-going decentralization, new arrangements are required to minimize the potential negative spillovers arising from vertical policy interdependencies. Zucker refers to these potential arrangements as "reciprocal federalism." The name is particularly apt since the concept recognizes, at base, that the provinces need Ottawa to act in certain ways in order that provincial policies become more effective. Similarly, Ottawa needs some help from the provinces in order that federal policies become more effective.[43]

Courchene's view, which is held by numerous intellectuals in English Canada, and has occasionally been taken up by several provincial governments, has been contradicted by the facts. First of all, it was based on an optimistic view of the federal government's intentions in the post-referendum climate of 1996. At that time, Ottawa was making many plans to decentralize the federation by pulling out of certain fields of jurisdiction (which incidentally were reserved for the provinces by the Constitution [see the Throne Speech of 1996]). We now know that this withdrawal was superficial and did not significantly change the balance of power between the orders of government. Furthermore, as soon as the state of public finances permitted (and even when it didn't), the federal government resumed its conditional intervention in health and education, as was demonstrated in the federal budget of 1999, the Millennium Scholarship Fund, child benefits and several other programs. The federal government has never seriously attempted to limit its intervention in provincial jurisdictions.

At the ideological level, Ottawa could not go along with the provincialist vision of Courchene and others in English Canada who share it in good faith. Ottawa could not renounce its own fundamental vision, that of strengthening its own power in order to maintain the existence of Canada. For the federal government, the existence of Canada is endangered by two major impulses: the possibility of Quebec secession and the constant, permanent attraction of relations with the United States. Ottawa has historically conceived the strengthening of its own powers as a necessary condition for the maintenance of Canada. To subscribe to the provincialist vision put forward by a certain current of thought in English Canada, which partially mirrors the autonomist standpoint of Quebec within the federation, would in Ottawa's eyes eventually increase the risk of dismantling the federation.

The provincialist vision in English Canada emerges seriously weakened from the Social Union Framework Agreement of February 4, 1999. At the ideological and political levels, the concept of Canadian federalism in English Canada now seems to have undergone a major about-face. The English-speaking provinces have completely given up on one of their major historical grievances: limiting the federal spending power. The limits supposedly exercised on this power in the Framework Agreement are insignificant compared with the historical recognition of its legitimacy and its validity. In fact, the Framework Agreement sanctions the entry of the federal government into exclusively provincial jurisdictions, and the provinces have committed themselves not to exercise their exclusive powers without Ottawa's authorization. The collegial vision of Canadian federalism expressed by Courchene and others, which recognizes the interdependence of the orders of government and the decentralization of public intervention, could only be viable if it were based on an effective limitation of Ottawa's appetite for power and its desire to dominate the provinces. This plan to contain the federal government appeared in the Saskatoon consensus and Victoria proposal. It was rapidly dropped by the premiers of the English-speaking provinces, who never seriously sought to see it adopted.

Canadian Federalism from Quebec's Standpoint

For Quebec there are lessons to be drawn from the Social Union Framework Agreement. One of the conditions laid down by the Bourassa government for Quebec's adherence to the 1982 Constitution Act was the limitation of the federal spending power. Since this historic demand has been flouted, the signing of the Social Union Framework Agreement makes Canadian federalism increasingly unacceptable to Quebec.

Furthermore, the government of Quebec can no longer seriously count on the support of the other provinces in order to remedy any structural weaknesses in the Constitution. The method of nominating Supreme Court judges and senators, for example, has always been contrary to the elementary principles of federalism and has often been denounced by other provinces as well as Quebec. With respect to the spending power, the Framework Agreement constitutes the abandonment by the other provinces of any attempt at reforming federal institutions and the formal recognition of the virtues of the status quo. The English-speaking provinces have adopted a reactionary stance in the constitutional field, leaving all initiatives to Ottawa and public opinion. From now on, moreover, Ottawa will never be persuaded to modify a status quo whose dynamic is to its advantage, except through public opinion expressed in a referendum. Henceforth, the nature of Canadian federalism has changed, as the provinces have agreed to a substantial weakening of their constitutional status.

We have seen that a common front of the 10 provinces could not make Ottawa budge. It is too attached to its historical and ideological pursuits, aware of the fragility of interprovincial consensus and assured of the support of the English-speaking provinces in the struggle against the assertion of the national character of Quebec. Realism demands that Quebec no longer support this type of exercise. The concept of federalism that will from now on be current in English Canada is incompatible with the traditional positions of Quebec, which manifestly enjoy the constant support of the Quebec population, as demonstrated in every general election and survey for several decades.

Canadian federalism outside Quebec will in the future follow its own course, a course in which Quebec will no longer be able to recognize itself. Canada has already separated from Quebec in this sense. The political and constitutional Canada that is being constructed outside Quebec is not large enough for Quebec. It is gradually smothering Quebec's aspirations, which are founded on the constant, historic desire to strengthen its autonomy and master its own development. The defense of the autonomy of the government and of the National Assembly of Quebec is a vital element in the identity and the development of the Quebec people.

The Status of Quebec After the Social Union Framework Agreement

After succeeding in trivializing the wishes of the other provinces, Ottawa will now be able to devote itself more to the standardization of Quebec. As soon as a conflict breaks out with the provinces over a major issue of provincial jurisdiction, the recipe will be perfectly predictable. Ottawa will be able to invite the provinces to a joint structure of some kind, in which collegiality will serve as a screen for its domination. The direction and management of the whole of the federation's affairs will be increasingly incumbent on the federal government, which in time will be able to solicit the blessing of the courts for an extension of its powers.

Quebec will be able to continue to put forward another conception of collegiality which does not seek to exchange federal transfers of money for a federal decision-making presence in its own spheres of competence. A joint management of the Canadian federation that respected the autonomy of Quebec would recognize substantial opting-out rights with full compensation and federal transfers in the form of tax points. Quebec must never renounce these two fundamental demands. On the contrary, it must reiterate them and continue to explain the need for them to the Quebec people.

It is to be expected that Quebec will, through its refusal to enter into the centralizing current, be more and more considered an anomaly. The Canadian federation risks becoming increasingly asymmetrical, not because Quebec has obtained new powers, but because it will hold on to those that it enjoys under the Constitution. Quebec's desire for autonomy risks, in the future, being subjected to systematic attacks by the federal government in every area of provincial jurisdiction. These attacks will take several forms — budgetary, media, legal and diplomatic — all aimed at convincing public opinion in Quebec and elsewhere in the world that Quebec society has to get into line, and that it is reasonable to attempt to suppress its aspirations and dissolve them within the Canadian whole. The status of Quebec will no doubt be subject to bitter pressure in the years to come or at least as long as the current federal government is in power, for it seems to have exhausted the appearance of flexibility it demonstrated following the last referendum. A change of government in Ottawa could bring momentary respite, which would only be of short duration, however, since the centralizing logic owes more to the structure of the system than to temporary circumstances.

The Social Union Framework Agreement is a symbol of the state of the Canadian federation in 1999 and an indication of the future of intergovernmental relations between Ottawa and the other provinces. From Ottawa's standpoint, it represents a historic victory that consolidates the central government's position within the federation. For the English-speaking provinces, it constitutes an abandonment of their status as autonomous governments, in the sense that autonomy is understood in Quebec, in exchange for the hope of more constant financial support. The crisis in federal public finances will have allowed Ottawa to demonstrate to the provinces the extent of their dependence, their interest in setting aside their claims centered on power sharing and their vision of federalism. For Quebec, it will from now on be clear that the Canadian state is attempting to construct itself at the expense of the state that the Quebec people for several decades have strived to develop. The legitimacy of the Quebec state in the eyes of the Quebec people is incontestable, but the tools of intervention and the margin of autonomy that the Quebec state has acquired for itself, particularly since the Quiet Revolution, are more threatened than ever.

Conclusion: Toward the Fiscal and Financial Autonomy of Quebec

The defense and promotion of a substantial level of autonomy for Quebec have been a constant in its history. For over a half century, the various Quebec governments, transcending any partisan leanings, have emphasized that this general autonomy should particularly be ensured in fiscal and financial terms. These are ultimately the foundation of the Quebec state's ability to act in the jurisdictions that have been entrusted to it by the Canadian Constitution. This quest for wider autonomy is founded on the will of the Quebec people, in its attempt to express its identity.

In the face of renewed attempts by the Canadian government to deny the identity of the Quebec people and to make the government of Quebec a subordinate, dependent government, Quebec has an obligation to react. Resistance that is passive or diluted by exhausting sectorial conflicts will not permit citizens to gain an overall view or to deepen their understanding of events. With the signing of the Social Union Framework Agreement, a historic milestone has been passed. Ottawa will no longer even pretend to respect Quebec's autonomy or its traditional reading of the Constitution.

Two avenues are open to the Quebec people. One of these, Quebec accession to sovereignty, is the path chosen by many, but they do not yet form a majority. Another is to ask the Quebec people to grant, through a referendum, full fiscal powers to the Quebec National Assembly. This option could unite a large majority of sovereigntists and non-sovereigntists, who would incontestably demonstrate the legitimacy of Quebec's traditional positions. The results of such a popular consultation could serve as a brake — at least temporarily — on Canada's centralizing spiral, and force the federal government to tolerate effective, more substantial autonomy for Quebec.

1 House of Commons, *Journals*, 1st session, 35th Parliament, no. 273, December 11, 1995, 2232.

2 Declaration by the Premier of Quebec, *First Ministers' Conference*, Ottawa, December 12, 1997 in Secrétariat aux affaires intergouvernementales canadiennes (SAIC), *Québec's Historical Position on the Federal Spending Power, 1944-1998* (Quebec: ministère du Conseil exécutif, 1998).

3 In this connection, we refer the reader to our comments above on the comparison between the Saskatoon consensus and the relevant clauses of the Social Union Framework Agreement.

4 The documents consulted here come from the Secrétariat aux affaires intergouvernementales canadiennes (SAIC), *Québec's Traditional Constitutional Positions 1936-1990* (Quebec: ministère du Conseil exécutif, 1991); SAIC, *Québec's Historical Position on the Federal Spending Power.*

5 Opening speech by Maurice Duplessis, *Dominion-Provincial Constitutional Conference*, Ottawa, January 10-12, 1950, p. 16 in SAIC, *Québec's Historical Position on the Federal Spending Power, 1944-1998*, p. 7.

6 Memorandum by the government of Quebec at the Dominion Provincial Conference on Reestablishment, *Dominion and Provincial Submissions and Plenary Conference Discussions*, Ottawa, 1946, p. 396 in SAIC, *Québec's Traditional Constitutional Positions 1936-1990*, p. 7.

7 Memorandum submitted by Maurice Duplessis, *Canadian Intergovernmental Conference*, Ottawa, October 1955, pp. 6-7 in SAIC, *Québec's Historical Position on the Federal Spending Power, 1944-1998*, pp. 7-8.

8 Memorandum submitted by the government of Quebec to the *Dominion-Provincial Conference on Reestablishment*, Ottawa, April 25, 1946, p. 365 in SAIC, *Québec's Historical Position on the Federal Spending Power, 1944-1998*, p. 8.

9 Memorandum submitted by Maurice Duplessis, *Canadian Intergovernmental Conference*, Ottawa, November 1955, p. 3 in SAIC, *Québec's Historical Position on the Federal Spending Power, 1944-1998*, p. 9.

10 SAIC, *Québec's Traditional Constitutional Positions 1936-1990*, p. 11.

11 Statement by Paul Sauvé, *La Presse*, September 18, 1959 in SAIC, *Québec's Traditional Constitutional Positions 1936-1990*, p. 12.

12 Statement by Paul Sauvé, *La Presse*, September 17, 1959 in SAIC, *Québec's Historical Position on the Federal Spending Power, 1944-1998*, p. 10.

13 Opening Statement by Jean Lesage, *Federal-Provincial Conference*, Ottawa, November 1963, p. 40.

14 Speech by Jean Lesage, honorary doctorate, Université de Moncton, May 17, 1964, p. 2 in SAIC, *Québec's Traditional Constitutional Positions 1936-1990*, pp. 18-19.

15 Opening speech by Jean Lesage, *Federal-Provincial Conference*, Ottawa, July 25-27, 1960, pp. 129-30 in SAIC, *Québec's Historical Position on the Federal Spending Power, 1944-1998*, p. 11.

16 Opening speech by Lesage, *Federal-Provincial Conference*, p. 130 in SAIC, *Québec's Historical Position on the Federal Spending Power, 1944-1998*, p. 14.

17 Statement by Jean Lesage, *Federal-Provincial Conference*, Quebec City, March 31-April 1, 1964, pp. 15-17 in SAIC, *Québec's Historical Position on the Federal Spending Power, 1944-1998*, pp. 15-16.

18 Opening statement by Jean Lesage, *Federal-Provincial Conference*, Ottawa, July 1960, p. 31 in SAIC, *Québec's Traditional Constitutional Positions 1936-1990*, p. 17.

19 Statement by Jean Lesage, *Federal-Provincial Conference*, Quebec City, 1964, pp. 21-23 in SAIC, *Québec's Traditional Constitutional Positions 1936-1990*, p. 18.

20 Quebec memorandum to the *Fourth Meeting of the Tax Structure Committee*, September 13, 1966, p. 2 in SAIC, *Québec's Historical Position on the Federal Spending Power, 1944-1998*, p. 19.

21 Brief submitted by Daniel Johnson, *Federal-Provincial Conference*, Ottawa, February 5-7, 1968 in SAIC, *Québec's Traditional Constitutional Positions 1936-1990*, p. 25.

22 Memorandum submitted by Quebec to the *Fourth Meeting of the Tax Structure Committee*, September 14, 1966, p. 50 in SAIC, *Québec's Historical Position on the Federal Spending Power, 1944-1998*, p. 19.

23 Declaration by Jean-Jacques Bertrand, *Federal-Provincial Finance Ministers' Conference*, Ottawa, November 4-5, 1968, pp. 10-11 in SAIC, *Québec's Historical Position on the Federal Spending Power, 1944-1998*, p. 20.

24 Statement by Robert Bourassa, *Federal-Provincial Finance Ministers' Conference*, Winnipeg, June 5-6, 1970, p. 22.

25 Statement by Robert Bourassa, *Constitutional Conference*, Ottawa, September 1970, p. 16 in SAIC, *Québec's Traditional Constitutional Positions 1936-1990*, p. 18.

26 Statement by Robert Bourassa, *First Ministers' Conference*, Ottawa, November 15-17, 1971, pp. 31-32, 40 in SAIC, *Québec's Historical Position on the Federal Spending Power, 1944-1998*, pp. 27-28.

27 Opening speech, *Journal des débats*, March 15, 1973, p. 1 in SAIC, *Québec's Historical Position on the Federal Spending Power, 1944-1998*, p. 25.

28 Government of Quebec, *Dossier sur les discussions constitutionnelles 1978-1979*, Ministry of Intergovernmental Affairs, p. 6.

29 Notes for an intervention by the Quebec Minister of Finance, *Federal-Provincial Conference of First Ministers on the Economy*, Ottawa, November 27-29, 1978. Secretariat of Canadian Intergovernmental Conferences, p. 12.

30 Statement by René Lévesque on the current situation and priorities for the future, *Annual Premiers' Conference*, Charlottetown, 1984, in SAIC, *Québec's Traditional Constitutional Positions 1936-1990*, p. 61.

31 Intervention by René Lévesque on the current situation and the priorities for the future, *Annual Premiers' Conference*, p. 2 in SAIC, *Québec's Historical Position on the Federal Spending Power, 1944-1998*, pp. 32-33.

32 Intervention by René Lévesque on the current situation and the priorities for the future, *Annual Premiers' Conference*, p. 4 in SAIC, *Québec's Historical Position on the Federal Spending Power, 1944-1998*, p. 30.

33 Speech by Gil Remillard, then Minister Responsible for Canadian Intergovernmental Affairs, to the conference "Rebuilding the Relationship: Quebec and its Confederation Partners," Mont Gabriel, May 9, 1986 in Peter Leslie (ed.), *Canada: The State of the Federation 1986* (Kingston: Institute of Intergovernmental Relations, Queen's University, 1986), Appendix, p. 101.

34 *Strengthening the Canadian Federation: The Constitutional Amendment, 1987* (Ottawa: Government of Canada, 1987).

35 Letter from Daniel Johnson to Marcel Masse, Federal Minister of Intergovernmental Affairs, February 15, 1994 in SAIC, *Québec's Historical Position on the Federal Spending Power, 1944-1998*, p. 37.

36 Statement by Jacques Brassard, Minister Responsible for Canadian Intergovernmental Affairs, *Journal des débats*, December 4, 1997, p. 9087 in SAIC, *Québec's Historical Position on the Federal Spending Power, 1944-1998*, p. 42.

37 Press Release, "Le rééquilibre des rôles et des responsabilités d'Ottawa et des provinces: une autre avenue de centralisation," August 23, 1996, p. 2. [Translation]

38 Thomas Courchene, "ACCESS: A Convention on the Canadian Economic and Social Systems," Study conducted for the Minister of Intergovernmental Affairs of Ontario (August 1996) in *Canadian Business Economics*, Vol.4, no. 4 (July-September, Summer 1996), pp. 3-26.

39 Courchene, "ACCESS," p. 5.

40 Courchene, "ACCESS," p. 6.

41 Courchene, "ACCESS," p. 8.

42 Courchene, "ACCESS," pp. 13, 14.

43 Courchene, "ACCESS," p.16.

Mobility Within Canada

Introduction

On February 4, 1999 representatives of the Canadian federal government and of nine of the ten Canadian provinces and territories signed the Social Union Framework Agreement. Quebec alone declined to participate. We were asked, in this short paper, to analyze in greater detail chapter 2 of the Framework Agreement entitled "Mobility within Canada," particularly the provision on mobility put forth by the provinces in the Victoria proposal of January 29, 1999. There are two objectives in this study. First, we track the evolution of the provincial position from that adopted in the summer of 1998 (the Saskatoon consensus) to the one prevailing in January 1999 (the Victoria proposal) to determine the gap between the initial position of the provinces and the final result of the negotiation. Second, we assess the gap between the final result of the negotiation and the position traditionally conveyed by Quebec with regard to freedom of movement.

To examine the whys and wherefores of this question, we will first analyze the origins of the concept of freedom of movement stated in the Social Union Framework Agreement. This analysis will concomitantly shed light on the main differences between the prior provincial proposal and the final agreement, and identifies the most significant points in this clause. We will then be able to examine more closely how chapter 2 of the Framework Agreement is formulated in light of provisions pertaining to this topic found in various instruments, including the Canadian Charter of Rights and Freedoms and the Agreement on Internal Trade (AIT). Then we will determine Quebec's traditional positions with regard to freedom of movement.

This analysis allows us to measure the gap between the traditional positions and the Framework Agreement proposal.

Origin of the Concept of Freedom of Movement Within the Framework Agreement

THE CONCEPT OF FREEDOM OF MOVEMENT, AS SEEN IN THE FRAMEWORK Agreement, was discussed among all Canadian governments, including Quebec. These discussions mainly took place in Saskatoon and Victoria, and two documents emerged from these discussions, the Saskatoon consensus and the Victoria proposal.

The Saskatoon Consensus and the Victoria Proposal

At the 39th Premiers' Conference held in Saskatoon on August 5-7, 1998, the premiers discussed the possibility of signing an agreement on the Canadian social union. Nonetheless, the final press release from the conference did not include anything specific regarding mobility. We thus conclude that discussions on this precise point were general, and the question of mobility was of greater interest to the federal government. The provincial premiers considered that the provisions of article 6 of the Canadian Charter of Rights and Freedoms and those of chapter VII of the AIT covered this domain sufficiently. It was only later, during a meeting in Victoria on January 29, 1999, that the provinces agreed on the wording of a proposal regarding freedom of movement. This text, clumsy as it was, nonetheless represented the initial formulation of a law governing freedom of movement, which, as we shall see, closely replicated the logic of the relevant provisions of the AIT.[1]

Social Union Framework Agreement

Chapter 2, the mobility provision of the Social Union Framework Agreement, is considerably different from the text proposed by the provinces in the Victoria proposal. These five paragraphs reiterate some of the points advanced by the provinces in the preceding month and add new ones. This text primarily sets forth the principle regarding freedom of movement and outlines the consequences relating to effects over time. In addition, the chapter proposes an application of the principle.

Gap Between the Framework Agreement and the Victoria Proposal Regarding the Mobility Rights of Canadians

There is a considerable gap between the proposal the provinces set forth in the Victoria document and the position that was ultimately adopted by the provinces (other than Quebec), territories and federal government in February 1999. The Victoria proposal made at least implicit reference to existing mechanisms (such as the Canadian Charter of Rights and Freedoms and the AIT) by confirming their value and logic. The clause ultimately adopted in the Framework Agreement, in contrast, extends, at least to a certain extent, the logic of the normative instruments already applicable in this area and imposes a series of new obligations on the signing governments. Before examining these obligations in detail, it is worth discussing the rationales in question, together with the reinforcement of the AIT, the follow-up mechanisms introduced by chapter 5 of the Social Union Framework Agreement and the terminological adjustments that were introduced between the two versions of the provision.

Free trade logic is replaced by a social logic It is clear that if the argued objectives of the mobility clauses of the Victoria proposal and the Framework Agreement are essentially the same (freedom of movement is an essential element of Canadian citizenship and citizens AIT are free to take advantage of favourable opportunities anywhere in Canada), the means of attaining these goals vary considerably from one provision to the other. The Victoria clause is mainly supported by existing provisions of the AIT and quotes that document explicitly in the third paragraph by referring to provisions that relate to mobility of labour. At least implicitly, it favours this approach in the preceding paragraph by referring to the notion of "legitimate public policy," taken from article 709 of the AIT. In other words, mobility is essentially defined according to the interprovincial circulation of labour.

Chapter 2 of the Framework Agreement seems to depart from this logic, at least to a certain extent, by emphasizing the role of social considerations. The second paragraph refers to new social initiatives and the third paragraph describes social policies and programs exclusively. It suggests that barriers to mobility therefore actually (or potentially) originate primarily from existing or future social programs. The question of whether residency-based requirements of social programs effectively restrict freedom of movement of Canadians is left manifestly unanswered. Note that the new logic expressed by the provision of the Framework Agreement is consistent with a text bearing on a Canadian social union. Moreover, it is clear that this subtle shift from free trade logic to social logic will have an impact on the interpretation of the provision, in a legal or other context.

The foundations of the clause on elimination of mobility barriers have been reviewed In the Victoria clause, the governments undertook to eliminate unreasonable barriers to mobility while allowing the same governments to pursue legitimate public objectives. On the one hand, the nature of the barriers was not specified, and nor was what would constitute a reasonable barrier. On the other hand, there was a deliberate attempt to stress, as the AIT did, that governments might circumvent the mobility right in some circumstances that are not defined. From the terminology used ("legitimate public policy objective"), one can assume that this is an implicit reference to article 709 of the AIT. The formulation of the clause in the Framework Agreement is different. Practices or policies founded on residency criteria are described restrictively. These criteria are defined based on a closed list of sectors: post-secondary education, training, health, social services and social assistance. Lastly, while the relevant clause in the Victoria proposal grants governments room to manœuvre ("unreasonable barriers," "legitimate public policy objectives"), in the Framework Agreement they have less leeway. Now the governments must prove that these policies and practices are "reasonable and consistent with the principles of the Social Union Framework." Once again, therefore, the clause as it appears in the Framework Agreement imposes a reinforced and more precise logic, articulated according to the ultimate objective of the Framework Agreement.

Mobility rights are extended to future and existing programs. Whereas the Victoria clause apparently applied only to existing programs, the clause in the Framework Agreement applies to both existing (paragraph 3) and future (paragraph 2) programs.

The requirements of the AIT are reinforced by a requirement of full compliance. Whereas the Victoria clause simply reiterated the support of federal and provincial governments for the provisions of the AIT pertaining to mobility of labour, the Ottawa clause, still with regard to AIT, goes much further by calling for full compliance with these provisions by July 1, 2001. To our knowledge, nothing in the AIT requires full compliance with the provisions, let alone by any deadline. These requirements are therefore new in every respect, even though they appear to ensue directly from the spirit and letter of the AIT.

A follow-up mechanism has been introduced The Victoria clause did not, strictly speaking, include a mechanism to follow up the progress achieved with respect to its implementation. This is undoubtedly explained by the fact that this clause is mainly based on AIT provisions concerning the mobility of labour, which are themselves subject to its own general provisions with regard to follow-up. Paragraph 4 of the clause of the Framework Agreement introduces a traditional mechanism of annual reports that will be examined by a Ministerial Council.

The clause relating to freedom of movement of Aboriginal peoples and the right to social and federal programs has been eliminated The Victoria proposal contains a paragraph that effectively guaranteed Aboriginal peoples full access and transferability of federal social programs both on and off reserves. This clause has simply disappeared from the Framework Agreement. We do not believe that the provision of the declaration in principle guaranteeing that the Framework Agreement would not affect ancestral rights or treaty issues will have an equivalent effect to the clause set aside.[2] One can assume that the federal government has chosen not to impose such obligations on the mobility of Aboriginal Canadians.

Terminological nuances have been introduced There are more or less significant terminological differences between the Victoria proposal and the Framework Agreement versions of the clause governing freedom of movement.

- When one compares the first paragraph of each version, the Victoria clause stipulates that governments "support and promote" the principle of mobility, whereas in the Framework Agreement version governments merely "believe" in the principle of mobility, which indicates a weaker insistence on the principle expressed;
- Whereas the Victoria clause refers to "social and economic opportunities," the Framework Agreement clause merely mentions "opportunities," without specifying their type or nature. There is thus an attempt to avoid limiting the type of opportunities to which Canadians can aspire under this provision.

Obligations and constraints are imposed on signing governments The analysis of the document signed in Ottawa in February 1999 demonstrates that, compared with the earlier Victoria agreement, signing governments have undertaken several obligations or constraints. These include:

- Governments are now prohibited from creating new obstacles to mobility during the launching of new social policy initiatives (paragraph 2). Note that this is a pure and simple prohibition, without any loopholes;
- Governments are obliged to eliminate any policy or practice based on residency criteria in several important social sectors, such as post-secondary education and social assistance (paragraph 3);
- Sector Ministers are obliged to submit annual reports that inventory the residency-based accessibility barriers (paragraph 4);
- Governments are constrained to fully comply with the provisions of the AIT regarding mobility of labour (paragraph 5); and
- A firm deadline is imposed, i.e., July 1, 2001, to do so (paragraph 5).

In light of the preceding analysis, it seems evident that the differences between the provision adopted in Victoria and that of the Framework Agreement are substantial. From a provision that essentially confirmed the applicable law, the parties chose to adopt a clause that imposes obligations and serious constraints on the signing governments. Note that these obligations affect provincial governments considerably more than they do the federal government, because ultimately the provinces have jurisdiction over these areas. Moreover, the only clause that directly refers to federal jurisdiction, that relating to the mobility rights of Aboriginal Canadians, has simply been set aside. In addition, as we have seen, the Framework Agreement intentionally changed the logic on which the standard is founded. In short, a provision that respected what the provinces had granted in the past has been transformed into a clause that imposes several changes on the new understanding of the concept of freedom of movement within Canada.

The Principle of Freedom of Movement in Relation to Existing Standards

The provision of the Social Union Framework Agreement pertaining to mobility does not exist in a vacuum. In effect, the legal system already includes several important provisions that address, to varying degrees, issues regarding the mobility of Canadians. In other words, the requirements of the provision regarding freedom of movement supplement the existing normative structure. We will briefly examine the probable impact of this provision of the Framework Agreement both with respect to article 6 of the Canadian Charter of Rights and Freedoms, the AIT and the existing bilateral agreements to which Quebec is a party. We will also discuss the delicate issue of the normative effect of the Framework Agreement.

From the outset, it should be remembered that these diverse instruments are not identical: one is constitutional, and the others are essentially contractual, while affecting third parties. The Framework Agreement is also contractual, but produces restrictive effects only on the co-signers. This discussion is therefore situated in a complex normative universe and shrouded in uncertainty with regard to the normative impact of the provision of the Framework Agreement relating to freedom of movement.

Normative Effect of the Social Union Framework Agreement

At first glance, it is not easy to identify with any precision the exact nature of the Framework Agreement. For one, it may be a "simple" intergovernmental policy agreement that would affect only the signers, similar to the Meech Lake Agreement in 1987 or the Charlottetown Agreement in 1992. If such is the case, the legal nature of such an agreement is at best contractual, and it cannot have legal effects on parties other than the signers. The sanction for violation of its terms would consequently be governed by strict provisions and would remain essentially a political issue. Examination of the text of the Framework Agreement, in particular chapter 6 entitled "Dispute Avoidance and Resolution," may lead one to believe that the Framework Agreement indeed constitutes a simple agreement. Its drafting style, in particular the frequent use of the conditional, clearly reveal its policy status. The parties undertook to adopt certain principles (chapter 1), the governments believe that freedom of movement is an essential element of Canadian citizenship (chapter 2, paragraph 1), the governments agree to cooperate and undertake concerted planning in specific sectors (chapter 2, paragraph 4) and so on. Therefore, the Framework Agreement, in order to produce concrete legal effects, will demand not only the introduction of institutional dispute avoidance and settlement mechanisms but also the adoption by each signer of laws and regulations that effectively entrench its standards into internal, provincial or federal law, as applicable.

In contrast, it is worth asking whether at least some of the provisions of the Framework Agreement can be interpreted as going beyond simple political statements, instead proposing commitments that will likely produce repercussions among the signing parties and perhaps on third parties, i.e., the general public. Accordingly, under the Framework Agreement, governments will ensure that new initiatives create no new obstacles to mobility (chapter 2, paragraph 2), and they will also eliminate, within the next three years, all policies and practices based on residency criteria (chapter 2, paragraph 3). Furthermore, they undertake to ensure full compliance with the provisions of the AIT (chapter 2, paragraph 5). These are certainly firm commitments that, subject to contractual scrutiny, may undoubtedly trigger effects in the case of violation, as each signing party is legally entitled to demand compliance. Perhaps the same applies to the other provisions of the Framework Agreement relating to federal spending power (chapter 5), for which Ottawa has defined very precise commitments.

If so, one must also ask whether third parties may seek to benefit from these commitments taken by the governments. This question is particularly appropriate with regard to the issue of freedom of movement, whereby some people may demand before the courts, as occurred a few years ago in a similar context of intergovernmental agreements,[3] that governments comply with the contractual agreements signed. For the purposes of the discussion below, however, we will assume that we are essentially dealing with a simple policy statement, which, until it is received by the legal systems of each province and the federal government, will not generate legal effects, so to speak.

Therefore, again for the purposes of the discussion below, we will consider that the Framework Agreement cannot effectively contradict, invalidate or question any existing normative system such as the AIT, bilateral agreements or, more importantly, the Canadian Charter of Rights and Freedoms. This observation raises two issues. First, one can presume that the Framework Agreement will eventually trigger legal effects when the provincial legislatures and the Canadian Parliament undertake a legal translation of the principles adopted in February 1999. It will subsequently be taken for granted that the principles stipulated in the Framework Agreement will not be constitutionalized in one way or another in the next few years.

Principle of Freedom of Movement and Mobility Rights Guaranteed by Article 6 of the Canadian Charter of Rights and Freedoms

Article 6 of the Canadian Charter of Rights and Freedoms gives force of law to the right of Canadian citizens to freedom of circulation and settlement.[4] This elaborate provision grants Canadian citizens and permanent residents the right to travel throughout the country, "to move to and take up residence in any province" (art. 6(2)a)) and "to pursue the gaining of a livelihood in any province" (art. 6(2)b)).[5] Despite its objective, it is a classic right in that it protects individuals from government and legislative measures that may effectively compromise individuals' freedom of circulation and settlement. Nothing forces these governments and legislatures to adopt any standard whatsoever to enforce the mobility rights of individuals; instead, they must abstain from interfering with the exercising of the rights of mobility.

The right granted by article 6 of the Charter is not absolute, however, because this provision relativizes the completeness of the right granted by explicitly allowing governments and legislatures to adopt, without consideration of the freedom of circulation and settlement, any general application standard, provided it does not stipulate distinctions founded "primarily on the basis of province of present or previous residence" (art. 6(3)a)). In addition, the same article of the Charter allows the adoption of standards imposing residency conditions, providing that they are imposed by legislative means and that they are "reasonable" (art. 6(3)b)). Moreover, considering that article 1 of the Canadian Charter of Rights and Freedoms applies to this article as well as to all other articles (and therefore has relativizing potential), governments and legislatures possess, despite the legal rights conferred, a relative latitude to impose some restrictions on mobility rights and consequently on the policies, standards and practices founded on residency criteria. In other words, governments and legislatures must be prudent before restricting the right to circulate and settle, but probably possess more manœuvring room than with respect to the other provisions of the Charter that are not subject to article 1. They must abstain from restricting the right within certain limits, but it should be noted that nothing forces them to adopt measures that exemplify this right.

Nonetheless, it is undoubtedly here that the provision of article 6 of the Charter and chapter 2 of the Framework Agreement are differentiated. In the latter agreement, not only is there an attempt to eliminate barriers to mobility for current and future programs, but the parties also undertake to eliminate "any residency-based policies or practices" in a host of sectors, all under provincial jurisdiction. In other words, the signers of the Framework Agreement pledged to voluntarily eliminate requirements that could have easily passed the tests of articles 1 and 6(3) of the Charter. Consequently, governments find themselves effectively agreeing to restrict their normative (and in particular, legislative) sovereignty well beyond the requirements of the Canadian Constitution in this area, with regard to criteria such as those founded on residency and, more generally, in relation to interprovincial mobility barriers.

Principle of Freedom of Movement and the AIT

The final version of the AIT was signed on September 12, 1994. It proposes a broad series of measures that oblige the governments of the signing provinces to "to reduce and eliminate, to the extent possible, barriers to the free movement of persons, goods, services and investments within Canada..." (article 100). Throughout the AIT, the parties agree to consider the circulation of individuals as one of the fundamental principles of the agreement.[6] Chapter VII of the AIT, which specifically covers the mobility of labour, contains several provisions relating to circulation and settlement of workers and professionals. It is nonetheless worth noting that these provisions are essentially formulated in terms of free trade concerns and the reinforcement of Canadian domestic markets. There is surely an important difference between the AIT provisions and those of the Framework Agreement regarding mobility, because the latter are situated within a document that pertains to the Canadian social union.

From a normative standpoint, the provisions of the AIT do not bind parties other than the signers of the agreement. However, it would probably be erroneous to claim, as we did for the Framework Agreement, that this is essentially a policy document without true legal scope, at least over the short term. On the contrary, through its wording, the AIT foresees a series of recourse mechanisms in case of violations of its terms, to settle disputes among governments or even between an individual and a government.[7] Accordingly, third parties, apart from the signers of the AIT, are given recourse with regard to non-compliance with the agreement. This is a type of stipulation for the benefit of another, conferring on third parties who are not parties to the agreement the right to exercise recourse in the case of violation of the terms of the agreement.

As for the legal formulation of the terms of the Framework Agreement regarding freedom of movement, it is important to determine whether the signing governments would prefer traditional legal standards in public law (laws, regulations) or a more contractual approach, such as that adopted in the case of the AIT. It is also important to determine whether, in essence, the new agreement would grant rights to governments (which is foreseeable) together with concerned third parties (which is less likely but cannot be excluded). It is therefore difficult at this stage to speculate on the approach that will be adopted and the subsequent impact of the application of the provisions of the Framework Agreement governing freedom of movement on the terms of the AIT. In general, however, it should be noted that traditional legal standards, such as laws and regulations, will shape the terms of the agreements that may be ratified by governments. There is a very strong likelihood that if a contractual approach is favoured it will include conflict-resolution mechanisms that encompass the signers of the agreement as well as injured third parties, if applicable.

Principle of Freedom of Movement and Bilateral Agreements Signed by Provinces

The conclusion above also applies to bilateral agreements covering freedom of movement which provincial governments occasionally sign. Similar to the AIT, these are essentially intergovernmental agreements, some of which even grant complaint rights to concerned third parties.[8] Once again, we cannot speculate at this stage on the normative approach that will be adopted by the signers of the Framework Agreement. Nor can we speculate on the impact of the application of its provisions regarding freedom of movement on the terms of interprovincial agreements to which the provinces are parties and which contain provisions relating to mobility for any given category of individuals.

Inter-Normative Difficulties

It is difficult at this stage to draw more than interim conclusions on the possible impact of the mobility section in the Framework Agreement clause on existing mobility standards. This is because of the uncertainty as to the legal avenues that will be selected to apply the Framework Agreement. In fact, the legal nature and especially the legal effects of bipartite or multipartite intergovernmental agreements remain one of the black holes in the public law system in Canada. Despite the multitude of intergovernmental agreements of all kinds prevailing in a wide array of sectors, jurisprudence is nearly non-existent on this topic. Moreover, the doctrine is not very informative in this respect. The difficulty stems entirely from the fact that by nature the agreements are closer to private law than public law. This implies that the government, whether federal or provincial, is essentially using private law to apply its policies, creating a difficult situation of inter-normativity whose contours are remarkably vague.

Lastly, there is the particular difficulty of the fact that the Quebec government did not ratify the Social Union Framework Agreement and is therefore not bound by it. Quebec's partners in the AIT and in some bilateral agreements nonetheless are bound by the document and may experience a situation where they seek to renegotiate such normative instruments in order to comply with the requirements of the Framework Agreement. In this case, the onus will evidently be on Quebec to decide whether it is appropriate to approve, indirectly in this case, the contents of a Framework Agreement to which it has not agreed. Note that this possibility remains essentially theoretical because there seems to be a practice whereby standards are not imposed on partners who have not agreed to them.[9]

Provisions of the Framework Agreement Regarding Freedom of Movement and Traditional Positions of Quebec

To attempt to measure the correspondence between the section of the Framework Agreement relating to mobility and the traditional positions of Quebec on this topic, we must begin by initially identifying these traditional positions more precisely.

Quebec's Traditional Positions Regarding Mobility

It would be an overstatement to say that mobility rights are invariably central to Quebec's constitutional preoccupations from the standpoint of political parties or successive provincial governments. However, it would also be an exaggeration to claim that these concerns have never emerged in the past. In this respect, one can assert that beyond the parties and individuals in place in the Quebec government, an analysis of the various stances reveals what can be called traditional positions on mobility rights. These traditional positions have been expressed both during large-scale debates on the constitutional future of Quebec and in debates that, in the past 15 years or so, have arisen as part of the emergence of free trade on the North American continent. In general, it is relatively vague regarding the parameters of this mobility.

Traditional positions taken during debates on the constitutional future of Quebec

During large-scale debates on the constitutional future of Quebec, successive governments and political parties have had occasion to voice their support for mobility rights. Accordingly, in 1979, the sovereignty-association project defined the free circulation of people as an "area of common activity," which the sovereignty-association treaty that Quebec signed with the rest of Canada would address in order to "maintain the present Canadian economic entity."[10]

Following the failure of Meech Lake, the Quebec Liberal Party published the report of its Constitutional Committee.[11] This document insisted on economic integration to ensure optimal economic development conditions, notably as part of a Canadian common market. It is therefore along these lines that the report proposed more specifically, regarding the mobility of individuals, that Canadian legislatures "abstain from imposing any kind of restriction on the free mobility of people, products and capital," adding that "[a]s trade and markets expand to encompass the entire globe, the Canadian economic sphere must be freed from any obstacle to the mobility of productive resources."[12]

A few weeks later, in March 1991, the report of the Commission on the Political and Constitutional Future of Quebec (Bélanger-Campeau), which was co-signed by both Premier Bourassa and then Leader of the Opposition Jacques Parizeau, revisited the same theme. It pointed out that there is a very firm consensus to the effect that Quebec must not seek to "create barriers to the free movement of persons, goods, services and capital within the Canadian economy," and that it is worth "maintaining the advantages ensuing from this freedom of movement."[13] The report proposed that if the province becomes sovereign, the main elements of the common market might be maintained in effect by harmonizing Quebec law with the prevailing federal legislation.[14] It then specified that "allowing the residents of Quebec and Canada to work freely throughout the territory would also make it easier to maintain the main elements of the Canadian common market" providing, however, that this mobility is reciprocal.[15] By implication, according to the Commission, the current right to settle and work can be guaranteed by new mechanisms.[16]

Traditional positions taken during debates on the emergence of a North American economic zone Since the mid-1980s, the idea of freeing trade within a new North American zone has gained significant ground in commercial and government circles. In 1985, the Royal Commission on the Economic Union and Development Prospects for Canada, better known as the Macdonald Commission, published its voluminous report that espoused the establishment of a free trade mechanism with the United States.[17]

The same year, the Quebec government, through its premier at the time, Pierre Marc Johnson, agreed to negotiate free trade proceedings. However, it set a number of conditions such as the desire to be involved throughout the negotiating process, the need to apply transitional measures following the implementation of the new trade system, and that Quebec could not be bound by any agreement in sectors that fall under its constitutional responsibilities unless it agreed to them.[18] Later, while answering questions before the National Assembly, Premier Bourassa had the opportunity to espouse and clarify the position expressed by his predecessor.[19] During discussions regarding the free trade agreement with the United States, the Quebec government reiterated its agreement in principle with free trade. It maintained and elaborated on its conditions, including those relating to compliance with sharing of jurisdictions and with the completeness of laws and programs in the cultural, communication and language sectors. Although nothing in this document specifically refers to the mobility of individuals and workers in the North American context, the document expresses Quebec's interest in including these services in a future agreement.[20] In a document that followed the signing of the Free Trade Agreement by Canada and the United States, then Minister of External Trade and Technological Development Pierre MacDonald stated that Quebec's priorities were respected and that the Quebec government's support of the agreement was desirable.[21]

The debate on the opportunity for Quebec to participate in the expansion of the North American trade zone with Mexico resurfaced a few years later. Then Minister of International Affairs, John Ciaccia, once again formulated the conditions under which Quebec would support the expansion process. They were more or less identical to those stated earlier during the signing of the Free Trade Agreement with the United States. The conditions centred on compliance with sharing of legislative jurisdictions and with laws and policies regarding social issues, communication, language and culture. They also stressed maintaining leeway for the government of Quebec to modernize the Quebec economy, establishing sufficiently long transitional periods and launching appropriate adaptation measures.[22] Nonetheless, this position statement was silent on issues relating to mobility of workers, apart from mentioning that some sectors of the economy such as consulting engineering have much to gain from the signing of a tripartite agreement.[23] In a subsequent document, the same ministry explained that the North American Free Trade Agreement is generally favourable to Quebec's interests because it maintains and even enhances some of the gains obtained earlier in the formulation of the Canada-US Free Trade Agreement.[24] During discussions surrounding the adoption of the two large North American Free Trade treaties, nothing particular arose regarding mobility of individuals or labour in the traditional positions of Quebec, apart from the general rule that requires full compliance with Quebec's legislative jurisdiction. Issues relating to mobility are clearly covered by this rule, which has been followed by all of the provincial governments over the years.

Traditional positions regarding the adoption of the Agreement on Internal Trade It is therefore not surprising in light of the preceding discussion that debates surrounding the adoption by Quebec of the AIT have given rise to the expression of the traditional Quebec consensus regarding the importance of free trade and its inherent issues, including individual mobility. Whereas the AIT had been signed by a Liberal government in Quebec, it was a Parti Québécois government that enacted the law that empowered the National Assembly to apply the AIT. The Minister Responsible for Canadian Intergovernmental Affairs said, during a debate on the bill, that the AIT was situated "entirely within the free trade logic of Quebec's economic dynamics," explaining that approval of the AIT directly ensued from Quebec's earlier consent to the Canada-US Free Trade Agreement and NAFTA.[25] Once again, there was a deliberate effort to repeat, on behalf of Quebec, the importance of respecting the constitutional jurisdiction of Quebec in the application of agreements such as the AIT.[26]

Comparing the Framework Agreement on Freedom of Movement and Quebec's Traditional Positions

Evidently, even if the position statements described above were issued in different contexts, they remain relatively coherent with regard to the importance of free trade and its inherent freedom of movement. Quebec's traditional positions in these areas can be summarized as follows:

- Regardless of the parties and governments in power, Quebec has constantly endorsed the principle of free trade and its requirements. Free trade of services, both within Canada and abroad, has always been considered desirable. The same is true of its corollary, the free circulation of individuals. This position, without exaggeration, can even be described as constituting one of the most dominant, firmest and most fundamental traits characterizing Quebec in the past 20 years. If the free trade principle is generally accepted and shared, this does not preclude that fundamental conditions be respected to make the free trade parameters acceptable for Quebec.
- Three broad conditions were identified that consistently seem to represent Quebec's fundamental positions. The first is respect for the constitutional jurisdictions of Quebec. This means that the definition of the parameters of the free trade programs and their implementation cannot or must not circumvent Quebec and its institutions, which must have their say and, if applicable, take action to apply mechanisms that fall under provincial jurisdiction granted by the Canadian Constitution. This fundamental position has been put forth and vigorously defended by all Quebec governments, whether federalist or sovereigntist.
- As an extension of the above position, Quebec has always demanded to keep its full legislative and normative manœuvring room in sectors that it considers crucial, such as language, culture, communication and education. Quebec has consistently refused to let these sectors, inherent to its sovereignty and distinct character, elude its control in the guise of free trade of some sort. Here again, governments and political parties

across the board have invariably maintained an approach that is characterized by consistency and vigour.

- Lastly, Quebec has always insisted on maintaining manœuvring room to enable the Quebec government to face new challenges triggered by functional transformations imposed by free trade, for example with regard to programs to support industries particularly affected by these processes.

These traditional positions identified above convey a common logic. In effect, Quebec agrees to embark on the free trade route (and by extension, that of mobility) only if it chooses this path and if its conditions and jurisdictions are respected. Consequently, while exercising its full sovereignty, it has signed and implemented the AIT (which contains provisions regarding freedom of movement) and it has signed bilateral agreements with neighbouring provinces that include mobility provisions. Similarly, Quebec has always insisted on participating in the negotiation of large multilateral trade agreements and has demanded to be in charge of their implementation in areas under its jurisdiction.

The corollary of this observation is that, again by extension of the logic of its traditional positions, Quebec would not agree to constraints being imposed on it to which it has not consented and which would not include some form of reciprocity. In fact, this situation may be imminent in the case of the Framework Agreement and its provision regarding freedom of movement (chapter 2). A gap definitely exists between this provision of the Framework Agreement and Quebec's traditional position, explained above. The preceding analysis reveals that this gap is manifested mainly in three areas, namely:

- The replacement of free trade logic by social logic as a foundation of freedom of movement. In effect, whereas Quebec has always approved of mobility as part of large trade agreements, it has never, to our knowledge, prioritized mobility within its concept of the Canadian social union. In other words, the traditional position of Quebec with regard to mobility does not reflect the new logic put forth by the Framework Agreement, mainly because Quebec simply does not have a traditional position regarding the question of mobility in a social context.
- Eliminating residency criteria in sectors where Quebec has full jurisdiction. We have seen the extent to which Quebec, in its traditional positions on free trade, insisted on protecting the sectors that it considers crucial, e.g., culture, language and communication. However, in a social

union context, decidedly provincial social sectors such as education, health, training, social services and social assistance are affected by the Framework Agreement clause. Do these sectors merit protection at least equal to those which, like culture or language in a free trade context, have led Quebec to insist on conserving full sovereignty? If the province chooses, in exercising its sovereignty, to eliminate residency criteria, at the very least this action must serve its interests. Note that even if the Canadian Charter of Rights and Freedoms at least to a certain extent eliminates residency criteria, Quebec has never agreed to this constitutional instrument, neither in 1982, nor thereafter.

- The Framework Agreement may impose mobility decisions on Quebec even if the province does not subscribe to it. Central to the fundamental position of Quebec is, as we have seen, the principle that it must remain master of its own choices. Yet, because of the very logic of the Framework Agreement, it is clear that the terms of certain instruments Quebec has already ratified must be amended by the other Canadian partners. For example, the AIT must clearly be amended to take into account new deadlines imposed for the application of chapter 7 of the Framework Agreement. One should also not rule out the possibility that Quebec's co-signers of some bilateral agreements will want to renegotiate the agreements to take into account some of the principles of the Framework Agreement. Ultimately, Quebec may have to renegotiate agreements that it has signed, owing to the effects of the Framework Agreement, even if it has chosen not to endorse this agreement.

The gap between Quebec's traditional positions regarding the mobility provision of the Framework Agreement may thus be significant. But in terms of the essence of the question, it may not be that significant if Quebec, while fully exercising its constitutional jurisdiction, believes that full mobility in the social sector is desirable.

Conclusion

FROM THE PRECEDING ANALYSIS, A NUMBER OF BROAD CONCLUSIONS CAN BE DRAWN. First, it is clear that there is a considerable gap between the initial position of the provinces regarding freedom of movement and the clause in the

Framework Agreement adopted in Ottawa in early February 1999. This gap is manifested in terms of what we have called the prevailing logic, as well as with regard to the obligations imposed on the signing governments, including the amendment of existing and future social programs.

Second, it has been shown that chapter 2 of the Framework Agreement respecting mobility goes further than the provisions relating to the topic found in existing instruments that Quebec has signed (the AIT and bilateral agreements) and others that it has not ratified (article 6 of the Canadian Charter of Rights and Freedoms). Therefore, this clause, if adopted by Quebec, would effectively impose an additional normative layer on Quebec legislators and the administration. However, most probably, the other parties cannot impose measures on Quebec without its consent.

Moreover, it is significant that the Framework Agreement clause imposes many new constraints on the signing governments. These include the fact that it is impossible for governments to create new obstacles to mobility when new social policy initiatives are launched, the obligation for governments to eliminate all policies or practices founded on residency criteria in critical social sectors such as post-secondary education and social assistance, the obligation for sector ministers to submit annual reports that inventory accessibility barriers based on residency, the constraint of full compliance with the provisions of the AIT regarding mobility of labour and the imposition of a firm deadline.

Lastly, we have seen that the terms of the Framework Agreement depart considerably from Quebec's traditional position with regard to mobility by imposing a major paradigm change. As we have demonstrated, key sectors of Quebec activities, including social programs and education, are at stake where mobility rights are concerned.

1 This text, whose only official version is in English, reads as follows:
"Freedom of Movement

- All governments support and promote the principle that Canadians are free to pursue social and economic opportunities anywhere in Canada. Mobility reflects our shared citizenship and is essential for equality of opportunity. Specifically:
- All governments are committed to freedom of movement of Canadians.
- All governments are therefore committed to eliminating unreasonable barriers to mobility while maintaining governments' ability to pursue legitimate public policy objectives.
- All governments support the labour market provisions of the AIT under the current implementation process.
- All governments are committed to promoting the mobility rights of Aboriginal Canadians by ensuring full access to, and portability of, federal social programs and benefits both on and off reserve."

See *Agreement on Internal Trade* (Ottawa: Internal Trade Secretariat, September 1994).

2 The clause in the declaration in principle of the Framework Agreement reads: "For greater certainty, nothing in this agreement abrogates or derogates from any Aboriginal, treaty or other rights of Aboriginal peoples including self-government."

3 *Finlay v. Canada (Minister of Finance)*, [1993] 1 S.C.R. 1080.

4 It reads as follows:
"6. (1) Every citizen of Canada has the right to enter, remain in and leave Canada.
(2) Every citizen of Canada and every person who has the status of a permanent resident of Canada has the right
a) to move to and take up residence in any province; and
b) to pursue the gaining of a livelihood in any province.
(3) The rights specified in subsection (2) are subject to
a) any laws or practices of general application in force in a province other than that discriminate among persons primarily on the basis of province of present or previous residence; and
b) any laws providing for reasonable residency requirement as a qualification for the receipt of publicly provided social services.
(4) Subsections (2) and (3) do not preclude any law, program or activity that has as its object the amelioration in a province of conditions of individuals in that province who are socially or economically disadvantaged if the rate of employment in that province is below the rate of employment in Canada."

5 For a discussion of the whys and wherefores of this complex provision, see Pierre Blache, "Les libertés de circulation et d'établissement," in G.-A. Beaudoin and E. Mendes (eds.), *The Canadian Charter of Rights and Freedoms*, 3rd ed. (Toronto: Carswell, 1996), p. 8-1.

6 See *Agreement on Internal Trade*, Sec. 101, par. 3 (a), (c) and (d), sec. 402 and, generally, chapter VII of the AIT entitled "Labour Mobility."

7 See *Agreement on Internal Trade*, chapter XVII entitled "Dispute Resolution Procedures," articles 1702 and following (Consultations) and 1711 and following (Initiation of Proceedings by Government on behalf of Persons).

8 See, for example, the *Agreement on the Opening of Public Procurement for Québec and New Brunswick*, March 30, 1994, section 9-4 and following; *Accord de libéralisation des marchés publics du Québec et de l'Ontario*, May 3, 1994, section 9-1 and following; *Amendements à l'accord de libéralisation des marchés publics du Québec et de l'Ontario*, May 30, 1996, section 8-11; *Ontario-Quebec Agreement on Labour Mobility and Recognition of Qualifications, Skills and Work Experience in the Construction Industry*, December 6, 1996, section 8.2 and following.

9 This practice is inspired by article 704 of the AIT.

10 Quebec Government, Executive Council, *Québec-Canada: A New Deal. The Québec*

Government Proposal for a New Partnership Between Equals: Sovereignty-Association (Quebec: Éditeur officiel du Québec, 1979), p. 57.

11 Constitutional Committee of the Quebec Liberal Party, *A Québec Free to Choose*, Report for Submission to the 25th Convention, January 28, 1991.

12 *A Québec Free to Choose*, p. 36.

13 Quebec National Assembly, *Report by the Commission on the Political and Constitutional Future of Québec*, Quebec (March 1991), pp. 10-11; also see p. 56.

14 Quebec National Assembly, *Report by the Commission on the Political and Constitutional Future of Québec*, pp. 57-58.

15 Quebec National Assembly, *Report by the Commission on the Political and Constitutional Future of Québec*, p. 61.

16 Quebec National Assembly, *Report by the Commission on the Political and Constitutional Future of Québec*, pp. 52-62.

17 Royal Commission on the Economic Union and Development Prospects for Canada, *Report* (Ottawa: Minister of Supply and Services Canada, 1985).

18 Speech by Pierre Marc Johnson, First Ministers' Conference on the Economy, Halifax, November 28-29, 1985, p. 6 in Secrétariat aux affaires intergouvernementales canadiennes (SAIC), *Québec's Traditional Constitutional Positions 1936-1990* (Quebec: Ministère du Conseil exécutif, November 1991), p. 73.

19 National Assembly of Québec, Committee on Institutions, *Journal des débats*, April 29, 1985, p. CI-153; National Assembly of Québec, *Journal des débats*, December 15, 1987, p. 10691.

20 Quebec Government, *La libéralisation des échanges avec les États-Unis: une perspective québécoise*, Quebec (April 1988), pp. 84, 87.

21 Quebec Government, *The Canada-United States Free Trade Agreement: A Quebec Viewpoint* (Quebec: Ministère du Commerce extérieur et du Développement technologique, 1988).

22 Quebec Government, *The Liberalization of Trade Between Canada, the United States and Mexico: the Issues From a Quebec Perspective* (Quebec: Ministère des Affaires internationales, May 1992), pp. 14-17.

23 Quebec Government, *The Liberalization of Trade Between Canada, the United States and Mexico*, p. 12.

24 Quebec Government, *Quebec and the North American Free Trade Agreement* (Quebec: Ministère des Affaires internationales, 1993). See also Quebec National Assembly, Committee on Institutions, *Journal des débats*, March 9, 1993, p. CI-1287 and following.

25 Quebec National Assembly, *Journal des débats*, October 16, 1996, 10:05 [Translation]. "While most governments agree to play the 'liberalization of world trade' game, it seems to us quite normal, self-evident, that the same benefits should be granted to companies that depend on the Canada-Québec economic space." *Journal des débats*, October 16, 1996, 11:10. [Translation]

26 *Journal des débats*, October 16, 1996, 10:20.

Informing Canadians — Public Accountability and Transparency

Introduction

OUR STUDY DEALS SPECIFICALLY WITH THE PROBLEM OF ACCOUNTABILITY AND rendering accounts in the Social Union Framework Agreement. Chapter 3 of the agreement will be paid special attention since it lays out a general accountability structure for all Canadian social programs. However, the theme of government accountability and transparency has marked all the negotiations on Canada's social union in various ways.

Our mandate was essentially to carry out a textual and contextual study of the documents within the prescribed analytical framework. It is not, therefore, an interpretation derived from some special theory in political science or constitutional theory. Since the author is a specialist in constitutional law, the reader may, nevertheless, see glimpses here and there of certain academic conventions proper to that discipline.[1]

Accountability and the Canadian Social Union: Some Analytical Themes

Vertical Accountability and Horizontal (Intergovernmental) Accountability

THERE IS A FUNCTIONAL CORRELATION BETWEEN THE VARIOUS CONCEPTS FORMing the subject of this study. Accordingly, the obligation to explain and justify inherent in the concept of rendering accounts ensures accountability, thus permitting the attribution of responsibility and, from there, effective political sanction. Transparency, the corollaries of which are the duty to inform and communicate, is, in itself, a precondition to rendering accounts and accountability since "If programs are not transparent, accountability will become blurred."[2] Throughout this report, we will frequently refer to accountability as the principal generic concept designating all the mechanisms for political accountability in social programs.

Analysis of the evolution of federal/provincial relations that characterizes Canada's social union requires a prefatory explanation of the distinction between government accountability *to the citizen*, which operates along a vertical axis, and accountability *between governments* within a federal state, which can be conceived of as horizontal due to its internal role within the state structure. Whereas vertical accountability is coterminous with the functioning of parliamentary representative democracy, intergovernmental accountability in an area of provincial jurisdiction requires an adjusted application of the precept of dual sovereignty within a federal state. Any Canadian social unity strategy that attempts to reinforce significantly the requirement that provinces be accountable to the central authority would be the precursor to standardization and even centralization.

To examine the issues of accountability raised by the Canadian social union project, it is necessary to differentiate two very distinct strategies or processes. The first is the fundamental distribution of powers as a systemic means of clarifying the lines of political responsibility. The second is the creation of special mechanisms that proceed from a voluntarist, highly targeted approach.

An Approach Based on the Organization of Power: Systemic Accountability

The tangle and confusion of responsibilities results in organizational impenetrability within the state that can lead to a breakdown in the democratic process. A clarification of the roles of the levels of government in the social field, especially by eliminating duplication of services, would improve accountability, since citizens would then be in a better position to know which level of government has political responsibility for financing, planning, implementing and delivering social programs. They would know from whom to request an account of such matters so that "[i]n the current Canadian context, enhanced accountability means a clarifying of the roles of the two levels of government in the social sphere."[3]

The simple rationalization of responsibilities, including the assertion of exclusive provincial jurisdiction in social matters and the right to opt out is a source of vertical, democratic accountability. That is why this dimension of the negotiations on the social union cannot be avoided in the present study, even though our mandate is focused on special, rather than systemic measures of accountability.

An Approach Based on Special Measures

While the rationalization of government roles promotes general political accountability in a parliamentary democracy, the negotiations on the Canadian social union touched on special or more complete measures for rendering accounts. The various types of special accountability procedures that are relevant to the present study are described below.

Evaluation

Setting up special mechanisms to assess outcomes encourages accountability in a context where the complexity of government action makes it difficult for the citizen to evaluate the efficiency of social programs. Analyzing these measures requires a sound understanding of the way standards are developed and applied and how to gauge their political consequences for federal diversity and provincial autonomy.

Information

The principle of information and public reporting requires that the electorate and other governments be made aware of the results, rules of operation and financing of program assessment. This obligation is linked, on the operational level, to government transparency. In the dynamic of intergovernmental relations, this concern for transparency can also be expressed as the need for visibility and political legitimization.

Consultation

Consulting with citizens and with other governments on the development and implementation of social programs spurs governments not only to report on the content of social policy projects and decisions, but also to provide justification and receive feedback.

Sanctions

Accountability is also reinforced by giving citizens or governments the opportunity to set in motion procedures for institutional control over social policy decisions. Administrative recourse for the governed, or an intergovernmental dispute resolution mechanism, would compel authorities to submit to inspection and perhaps even to criticism by others when planning and providing social programs. The public nature of decisions, reports or recommendations for dispute resolution by authorities would reinforce transparency and the opportunity to require accountability.

The Evolution of Provincial Positions on Accountability: From Saskatoon to Ottawa

It emerges very clearly from the documents we have analyzed that in various ways the theme of accountability occurred regularly during the provinces' progress toward the proposed Canadian social union. The provinces' thinking comes out in favour of provisions that promote a vision of accountability that is both systemic and specialized.

Accountability Through Rationalization of Responsibilities

The Saskatoon Consensus of August 6, 1998

In its proposals of July 15, 1998, the federal government only accords very secondary importance to avoiding overlap and promoting accountability by rationalizing responsibilities. This concern is completely absent from the statement of the major goals and principles of the social union. Ottawa is content, at best, to call for "harmonization," "on an as-needed basis," of the activities of the two levels of government when setting up joint, Canada-wide programs.[4]

This outright trivialization of systemic accountability contrasts with the provincial consensus arrived in Saskatoon, in which the provinces agreed on the need to reinforce accountability by better defining the respective responsibilities of the levels of government with respect to social programs.

Chapter 1 of the Saskatoon consensus, which will later be analyzed in more detail, proposes a procedure for exchanging information and for consulting before modifying social programs that affect the other level of government. This mechanism aims at detecting and remedying potential duplication ("to ensure that the proposed change did not duplicate effort").

Moreover, chapter 2 of the Saskatoon consensus provided that, in the context of intergovernmental cooperation in setting up or modifying Canada-wide programs in areas of provincial jurisdiction, the governments have to agree to define "clear roles and responsibilities for each order of government" and to respect "a commitment to reduce and avoid overlap and duplication." It is chapter 3, however, which makes accountability through clarification of responsibilities an urgent priority for the social union. It states that:

> The practice of Canadian federalism has, over time, confused the roles and responsibilities of the two orders of government. This confusion undermines public accountability. Greater clarification would enhance collaboration between governments and increase the public's understanding of which order of government is responsible for the delivery of social programs.

The document also states that "[a] proposed process for clarifying roles and responsibilities is being reviewed by F/P/T officials."

The Victoria Proposal of January 29, 1999

Although the federal government's thinking remained unchanged in its document of January 25, 1999, the Victoria proposal expresses a stronger attachment on the part of the provinces to a systemic approach. The provincial governments reiterated with renewed vigor their desire for greater accountability by rationalizing and distributing responsibilities. Chapter 1 identifies the Canadian values that underlie any social union and proclaims that:

> Canadians want and deserve governments working better together by clarifying responsibilities, eliminating overlap and duplication, and enhancing accountability...This agreement offers Canadians...more accountable government...

Also, in chapter 2, which lays out the guiding principles that all governments will follow when planning and implementing social policies, the provinces and territories demand recognition of their constitutional precedence in social affairs:

> Under the Constitution, provinces and territories are primarily responsible for social policy and the delivery of social programs.
>
> Governments believe strongly in increasing accountability to the public and improving the effectiveness and efficiency of the social union. To this end, governments are committed to:
>
> - reducing and avoiding overlap and duplication;
> - clarifying roles and responsibilities by assigning, where appropriate, responsibility for areas of the Social Union to one order of government or the other; and,
> - minimizing areas of joint responsibility where this would improve the effectiveness and the efficiency of the social union.
>
> Governments are committed to working together in partnership where this would result in improved services to Canadians and explaining to Canadians their respective contributions to social programs.

Thus, in order to give concrete expression to these guiding principles within an effective social union, the provinces envision various forms of implementation. They first reassert the provisions of the Saskatoon consensus on the following points:

- the advance notice and consultation procedure for modifying programs in order to prevent duplication
- the consensual approach to be adopted in relation to federal spending for new or modified Canada-wide programs, which would recognize the need to clarify responsibilities and reduce or avoid overlap and duplication.

However, the provinces added chapter 6, which provides for the creation of a ministerial mechanism for the application of a framework which defines responsibilities for new social programs and reformulates responsibilities for existing programs:

> Canadians need to know which order of government to hold responsible for specific decisions in areas of social policy. Clarifying roles and responsibilities in the management and delivery of social programs will enable Canadians to hold their governments are [*sic*] accountable for decisions they make.
>
> The considerations identified in the graphic attached will guide the development of federal and provincial/territorial roles and responsibilities in new social programs.
>
> Within two years, sector Ministers will review current federal and provincial/territorial responsibilities, using considerations below, and, where agreed, take measures to align responsibilities in accordance with them.
>
> Sector Ministers will report annually to the Ministerial Council for Social Policy Reform and Renewal, on progress in realigning roles and responsibilities. The Ministerial Council will provide an annual public report to First Ministers, summarizing the progress made by sector Ministers.

The provinces and the territories partly combine the systemic approach with specific transparency measures by requiring a public report and an outcome review of the clarification of roles and allowing the public, at that point, to judge the progress in the battle against overlap and confusion of responsibilities. This goes back to the provinces' commitment to "explaining to Canadians their respective contributions to social programs."

Because the provincial position attributes primary responsibility for social programs to the provinces, it could help contain the federal presence in this field. Defining responsibilities more clearly and curbing the proliferation of disparate policies could be interpreted as meaning, in this context, that where a provincial program exists, the federal government should abstain, or, if a province proposes to take action, Ottawa should leave the field free.

The Social Union Framework Agreement

The agreement reached between the federal government and the nine provinces pays scant attention to the theme of accountability by means of a clear definition of roles and elimination of overlap. The need to rationalize responsibilities does not appear in the underlying principles of the agreement. Nor is there any statement that the role of the provinces in the social field takes automatic precedence.

The possible optimization of roles and responsibilities is mentioned in chapter 4, "Working in partnership for Canadians":

> Governments therefore agree to:
>
> ...
>
> Collaborate on implementation of joint priorities when this would result in more effective and efficient service to Canadians, including as appropriate joint development of objectives and principles, clarification of roles and responsibilities, and flexible implementation to respect diverse needs and circumstances, complement existing measures and avoid duplication.

Also, the parties stipulate that the introduction of certain new programs will be subject to prior intergovernmental consultations and that "governments participating in these consultations will have the opportunity to identify potential duplication and to propose alternative approaches to achieve flexible and effective implementation." (chapter 5) There is no guarantee that these consultations will result in an elimination of duplication.

The similarities between the Framework Agreement and earlier federal documents (July 1998 and January 1999) and the contrast with the Victoria proposal stand out clearly. First of all, there is a striking absence in the Framework Agreement of any formal indication by the signing governments that they intend to link rationalization of responsibilities to the democratic ideal of accountability. The explicit concern that prevails in the statements reproduced above seems rather to be efficiency and effectiveness. This dilutes the political bases for limiting joint responsibilities, which could become more tolerable as soon as they no longer threaten the efficient delivery of programs.

Unlike the Victoria proposal, the Framework Agreement makes no provision for any ministerial mechanism to formally and systematically define the demarcation lines and to restructure roles in accordance with the concept of primary provincial responsibility. Far from being an imperative which should shape the future orientation of the social union in the name of democratic accountability, the clarification of responsibilities is presented as desirable in certain cases "if applicable."

Special Accountability Measures

Vertical Accountability as a Basic Principle of the Social Union

The Saskatoon Consensus The federal document of July 15 contains a chapter on "public accountability and transparency" which reads as follows:

> Interdependence and collaboration demand heightened attention to transparency, clarity and enhanced accountability.
>
> All governments agree to enhance public transparency and accountability for expenditures and results
>
> Provinces and territories will use federal funds for their intended purpose and will pass on increases to Canadians
>
> Each government will monitor and measure outcomes and report regularly to its constituents on expenditures and results achieved
>
> Sector Ministers will develop comparable measures and appropriate third-party mechanisms such as independent social audit to assist in the monitoring and measurement of expenditures and outcomes
>
> Governments will publicly recognize and explain the respective roles and responsibilities and funding contributions of each government[5]

Although the document contains several references to federal spending, it presents public accountability as a valid guiding principle for all social programs, not just those involving federal funding.

The federal proposal on this question has no exact equivalent in the document that lays the foundations for the Saskatoon consensus. This is despite the fact that the introductory provision of the consensus mentions that although these guiding principles and basic rules are not covered in any specific provision in the document, they will constitute the essential components of a framework agreement on the social union.[6]

The federal concern with vertical accountability is, however, partially echoed in chapter 1 of the Saskatoon consensus relating to intergovernmental cooperation in joint areas of responsibility or when one government's social policy decisions are likely to significantly affect another government. This provision states that "Governments could agree to measure key social policy outcomes with a view to reporting on their actions to the public." Note the hypothetical and conditional nature of this provision: these measures are part of what the provinces describe as "*possible* collaborative initiatives," and the document states that governments *could* agree on such an approach.

The Victoria Proposal The federal proposal of January 25, 1999 reiterated all the main elements of its July 1998 document, while emphasizing Canada-wide integration and the possible standardization of assessment mechanisms for programs and accountability.[7] Additional provisions were added concerning the recourse available to citizens and the possibility of addressing complaints related to access and service.

The Victoria proposal somewhat narrowed the gap between the federal and provincial positions. Chapter 5 reiterates the need for intergovernmental cooperation in areas of joint responsibility or when the decisions of one government on matters of social policy are likely to significantly affect another government. The provinces' position on this point is less hypothetical and conditional than it was in the Saskatoon consensus. In the Victoria proposal there is a firm commitment to assess program outcomes and account to the public: "Governments agree to measure key social policy outcomes with a view to reporting on their actions to the public." We should note, all the same, that the commitment, as in the Saskatoon consensus is only valid for "key social policy outcomes," that is, the most important programs.

It is however, in chapter 7 of the Victoria proposal that we find the most important innovation from the provinces' point of view. According to the terms of the chapter entitled "Accountability for Canadians":

> Canada's Social Union can be strengthened through enhancing each government's accountability to its constituents. Each government therefore agrees to:
>
> Clarify the roles of Governments and inform Canadians of the responsibilities of each government.
>
> Ensure that social programs are delivered in a fair and transparent way.
>
> Monitor and measure outcomes of their own social programs and report regularly to their constituents on how their social programs have performed.
>
> Share best practices to enable jurisdictions to develop their own outcome measures.
>
> Publicly report financial information to ensure Canadians understand the relative funding contributions of governments to programs.
>
> Publicly report on their respective commitments of providing stable and adequate funding for social programs.
>
> *Involvement of Canadians*
>
> Governments agree that Canadians should have appropriate opportunities for public input in developing priorities and objectives for social programs.
>
> Canadians should have access to fair and transparent administrative processes in social programs. Accordingly, governments agree to:
>
> - Make publicly available eligibility criteria for their social programs.
> - Have in place appropriate administrative mechanisms at the local level, that allow citizens to appeal when they believe they have been treated unfairly in the administration of a social program.

Following the federal government's example, the provinces enshrine here, as a key aspect of the social union, the general obligation for governments to assess and report program outcomes to citizens and to explain the roles and responsibilities of each order of government. These commitments apply to the entire range of social programs across the country, whether provincial, federal or joint.

Chapter 7, moreover, establishes citizens' right to participate in policy development and commits the parties to implement policies by means of a transparent and equitable administrative process.

With the insertion of this chapter, the provinces and the territories come closer to the federal position, while still indicating a different point of view on certain important aspects. They are particularly close on the following points:

- Governments must monitor and measure program outcomes and regularly report program performance to their constituents.
- Each order of government will inform constituents on their respective roles and responsibilities in and financial contributions to social programs.

- Canadians should have a reasonable opportunity to participate in defining priorities and objectives of social programs.

The provincial consensus enshrined in the Victoria proposal, however, differs from the federal proposals with regard to the following:

- According to the provinces, although governments will exchange information on best practices, all governments will develop *their own measures* for assessing program outcomes. In addition, governments may only monitor and review *their own* social programs and will only inform their constituents of these program outcomes. The federal document of January 1999 gives the provincial and federal sector ministers the task of developing appropriate means for measuring outcomes, including comparable indicators for agreed objectives, social assessments, and independent social review. From the federal point of view, the intergovernmental decision-making process extends to annual accounting mechanisms, enumerating best practices, citizens' participation and information on the roles and contributions of governments. The federal position confers unassailable legitimacy on Ottawa's standardizing role, but leaves much less room for independent provincial action within a highly integrated decision-making process and a standardizing assessment dynamic. These are not likely, in the long term, to encourage diversity in planning social programs across the country. It also gives governments less room to manœuvre on assessment measures and potentially adds to the constraints of rendering accounts by giving review power to interest groups (who are frequently fond of national standards and programs).
- While the provinces and territories commit themselves to informing citizens of the responsibilities and contributions of each order of government, the federal document states that governments will "publicly recognize" these contributions and responsibilities. The desire to assert legitimacy for both levels of government to operate in the social field, where the provinces have jurisdiction, emerges more clearly in the document prepared by Ottawa.
- The federal position commits the provinces and territories to using federal funding for its intended purposes and to pass on any increase to Canadians. This political injunction against any rerouting of federal funds by the provinces is not found in the provinces' Victoria proposal.

The closeness of the federal and provincial positions on vertical accountability as a basic principle of the social union is therefore relative. The provinces are clearly more concerned with reconciling their demands for transparency and accountability with respect for provincial autonomy and diversity in determining the means to implement these requirements.

The Framework Agreement Chapter 3 of the Framework Agreement commits the signatories to make public accountability and transparency a basic principle of the social union. The relevant provisions read as follows:

> Canada's Social Union can be strengthened by enhancing each government's transparency and accountability to its constituents. Each government therefore agrees to:
>
> *Achieving and measuring results*
>
> - Monitor and measure outcomes of its social programs and report regularly to its constituents on the performance of these programs
> - Share information and best practices to support the development of outcome measures, and work with other governments to develop, over time, comparable indicators to measure progress on agreed objectives
> - Publicly recognize and explain the respective roles and contributions of governments
> - Use funds transferred from another order of government for the purposes agreed and pass on increases to its residents
> - Use third parties, as appropriate, to assist in assessing progress on social priorities
>
> *Involvement of Canadians*
>
> - Ensure effective mechanisms for Canadians to participate in developing social priorities and reviewing outcomes
>
> *Ensuring fair and transparent practices*
>
> - Make eligibility criteria and service commitments for social programs publicly available
> - Have in place appropriate mechanisms for citizens to appeal unfair administrative practices and bring complaints about access and service
> - Report publicly on citizens' appeals and complaints, ensuring that confidentiality requirements are met.

With respect to the requirement for program assessment and public reporting, the provinces that signed the agreement essentially adopted the federal point of view. The text of the Framework Agreement contains not just the points of convergence between the federal proposals of July 1998 and the Victoria proposal but also most of the elements proposed by Ottawa that were not agreed to by the provinces in Victoria.

Let us first note that as well as undertaking to exchange information on best practices, the Framework Agreement between the federal government and the nine provinces adds that the federal government will: "work with other governments to develop, over time, comparable indicators to measure progress on agreed objectives."

There is no longer any question that each government, independently and without interference from the other order, should be able to develop its own program assessment mechanisms. This requires governments to work together to establish performance indicators for predetermined objectives that are "comparable" and therefore not likely to differ substantially. Such an approach tends to legitimize a federal normative input, to integrate assessment measures and to favour national standards for performance indicators. It may also lead to uniform objectives (since "progress" will be gauged by the benchmark of "agreed objectives"). This will permit the respective "performances" of various governments to be compared against parameters that may tend to obliterate social and political particularities in the country.

In addition, as in the federal document of January 25, 1999, the Framework Agreement commits to "use third parties, as appropriate, to assist in assessing progress in social priorities." This provision is perfectly compatible with the will expressed by the federal government, both in July 1998 and January 1999, to create independent mechanisms for social assessment and review, even though it does not go as far as laying down an intergovernmental definition of these mechanisms as Ottawa wished. This could therefore be moving in the direction of active participation by interest groups, several of which have, in the past, promoted a federal interventionism. The expression "where appropriate" might suggest that the constraint is merely relative, but one cannot escape the conclusion that the parties agreeing to a principle of possible third-party assessment can be seen as an over-complication of accountability mechanisms. This, in turn, suggests that the governments could only with great difficulty disavow any idea of "social assessment."

As with the federal document of July 1998 and the proposals of January 25, 1999, the Framework Agreement requires governments to "publicly recognize and explain the respective roles and contributions of governments," which reflects the federal government's preoccupation with more formal public recognition of equal legitimacy of the two orders of government in exclusive provincial spheres of jurisdiction.

Moreover, the Framework Agreement takes up the federal injunction against possible misapplications of "funds transferred from another order of government." While the provision is not explicitly addressed to the provinces and territories, there is no doubt for whom this message is intended.

In the Framework Agreement, Ottawa and the nine other provinces reaffirm several parts of the Victoria proposal concerning citizens' participation in developing social priorities and the transparent and fair administration of these programs. Unlike the Victoria proposal, however, the Framework Agreement does not state that the mechanisms for administrative appeal should take place "at the local level."

Moreover, the Framework Agreement adds to the constraints relating to transparency and accountability by incorporating the following elements proposed by Ottawa in its text of January 25, 1999: (1) public review of outcomes is accepted, (2) the publication of program service commitments is required, (3) complaints on access and services are authorized and (4) there is an obligation to "report publicly on citizens' appeals and complaints."[8]

Accountability in the Context of Federal Spending on Canada-Wide Programs

Before it became a fundamental principle in social policies in Canada, accountability was initially seen as a special item related to the federal spending power within fields of exclusive provincial jurisdiction.

The Saskatoon Consensus The provinces saw a need for governments to collaborate in setting priorities, objectives and basic principles for federal spending on Canada-wide programs. With this in mind, they supported flexibility and respect for the provinces' ability to reconcile Canada-wide program priorities with their special jurisdiction in the field. They appealed to the principle that, in a field of provincial jurisdiction, the provinces must consent to any federal spending on a new Canada-wide program, or to any modification of an existing program.

Two possible means of collaboration were proposed for restricting the federal spending power:

Step 1: Collaboration

1. Joint priority setting on federal cash and tax expenditures on new or modified Canada-wide programs in areas of provincial jurisdiction.
2. Joint agreement on objectives and principles for new or modified Canada-wide programs, including:
   - program flexibility which respects provincial/territorial priorities
   - clear roles and responsibilities for each order of government, and,
   - a commitment to reduce and avoid overlap and duplication.

> 3. Agreement to develop, measures and publicly report on outcomes of new and modified Canada-wide programs, consistent with each government's roles and responsibilities.
> 4. Agreements should incorporate measures to ensure the adequacy and certainty of funding.
>
> *Step 2: Flexibility*
>
> Where the collaborative approach in Step 1 does not achieve agreement, the following provisions will be invoked:
>
> 1. Any new or modified Canada-wide program in areas of provincial jurisdiction requires the consent of a majority of provinces. The consent of the territories will be sought.
> 2. The federal government will provide full financial compensation to any provincial or territorial government that chooses not to participate in any new or modified Canada-wide program, providing it carries on a program or initiative that addresses the priority areas of the new or modified Canada-wide program.
>
> Federal spending in an area of provincial jurisdiction which occurs in a province or territory must have the consent of the province or territory involved. Agreements should incorporate measures to ensure adequacy and certainty of funding.

The value of these two models of intergovernmental cooperation for any accountability study is that the first procedure could include citizens' rights to program-review and outcome-reporting procedures.

This first procedure could be described as "purely consensual" in that it postulates total or unanimous consent by the governments and best upholds the rule of provincial consent. The second procedure is "by majority," since it empowers a majority of the provinces to agree with Ottawa on priorities, principles and objectives of Canada-wide programs, either new or revised. In return, according to the rule of provincial assent, the second procedure allows a government to opt out with full compensation providing it sets up or supports a program in a field prioritized by the Canada-wide program.

Failing agreement on the application of the first procedure, the second could be used, that is, a simple majority process adhering to specific rules, without any accountability mechanism. Accordingly, no requirement for accountability and transparency can be imposed on a province under this majority procedure. This results from the fact that the right to opt out with full compensation is subject to just one condition — a provincial program in the same priority field. Ultimately, accountability mechanisms for the provinces could only be fully consensual in the field of Canada-wide programs involving questions of provincial jurisdiction.

Finally, note that in its July 1998 proposals on federal social transfers, Ottawa did not raise the question of accountability. It preferred a purely majority approach for authorizing federal interventions in a field of provincial jurisdiction. In addition, the federal government restricted the principle of majority provincial consent to new shared-cost programs, leaving the way open for any other federal initiative in a provincial field. The right to opt out with compensation was also reduced to implementing equivalent or comparable programs.

The Victoria Proposal The federal proposals of January 25, 1999 correspond with the document of July 1998 with respect to the majority rule regarding provincial consent to new federal initiatives, although the precise type of initiative subject to provincial agreement has been redefined.[9] However, the new document drawn up by Ottawa adds to the July 1998 version with regard to accountability. It now proposes the idea of subjecting governments to an "accountability framework":

> The [g]overnment of Canada and the provincial and territorial governments will agree upon an accountability framework for such new social initiatives and investments. The accountability framework will include commitments on results and performance, information-sharing, and mechanisms for public reporting and disputes settlement. All commitments under the Framework will apply.
>
> Funding will be provided to all provincial and territorial governments that meet or commit to meet the agreed Canada-wide objectives and agree to respect the accountability framework.[10]

Ottawa thus takes the position that the federal government and a majority of the provinces should have the power to require any non-participating province to "meet" national objectives defined by them and to comply with a detailed accountability framework that they have determined.

Notwithstanding this new federal position on accountability, in Victoria, the provinces' positions remained unchanged on dual procedures for restricting the federal spending power. The provision relating to accountability as a purely consensual component of the procedure still remains, although general rules of accountability and transparency are added to the provincial consensus (chapter 7). This does not necessarily result in redundancy, however. In fact, although it does not make joint planning of shared indicators or independent third-party assessment a necessity, the provision in chapter 5 of the Victoria proposal does not rule them out, as is the case in chapter 7.

The Social Union Framework Agreement The provinces that were party to this agreement rejected a fully consensual collaboration model and adopted only a majority approach that was in line with Ottawa's proposals. Majority provincial assent is required only for new programs supported by intergovernmental transfers. It is worth quoting the relevant terms of the Framework Agreement which, particularly in the case of accountability, are clearly inspired by the corresponding provisions in the federal proposals of January 25:

> *New Canada-wide initiatives supported by transfers to Provinces and Territories*
> With respect to any new Canada-wide initiatives in health care, post-secondary education, social assistance and social services that are funded through intergovernmental transfers, whether block-funded or cost-shared, the Government of Canada will:
> Work collaboratively with all provincial and territorial governments to identify Canada-wide priorities and objectives
> Not introduce such new initiatives without the agreement of a majority of provincial governments
> Each provincial and territorial government will determine the detailed program design and mix best suited to its own needs and circumstances to meet the agreed objectives.
> A provincial/territorial government which, because of its existing programming, does not require the total transfer to fulfill the agreed objectives would be able to reinvest any funds not required for those objectives in the same or a related priority area.
> The Government of Canada and the provincial/territorial governments will agree on an accountability framework for such new social initiatives and investments.
> All provincial and territorial governments that meet or commit to meet the agreed Canada-wide objectives and agree to respect the accountability framework will receive their share of available funding. (chapter 5)

Note that, in line with the terms of the federal document of January 25, there is no explicit mention of a "right to opt out." However, the possibility of supporting or implementing a provincial program that is parallel to the federal initiative does follow from the fact that "all" provincial governments complying with conditions could receive available financing, even though only a majority of provinces had agreed to participate in the federal program.

Note also that Ottawa and the nine provinces will henceforth make accountability an essential item in the intergovernmental collaboration over federal spending. But this takes place in a normative context that differs in several aspects from the positions that the provinces defended in Saskatoon and Victoria.

- The Framework Agreement, in full compliance with Ottawa's point of view, does not create a dichotomy between the consensual approach and the majority approach for implementing an accountability framework. Such a framework will be decided by the Government of Canada and the provincial and territorial governments in line with the principle of majority provincial consent. Thus a minority province that does not participate in a new federal Canada-wide initiative and wishes to support or create its own program must commit to respecting "the accountability framework" laid down by the federal government together with the provincial majority. In a departure from a key aspect of the provincial consensus, the province will not be exempt from restrictive accountability measures. This constraint opens a new dimension on the implementation, in chapter 5, of the dispute avoidance and resolution procedure laid down in chapter 6, since this mechanism can be set in motion when one province is considered as not complying with the accountability framework.
- The expression "accountability framework" used in the text of the Framework Agreement opens up a wide range of controls, including both vertical and intergovernmental accountability measures. Chapter 3 of the agreement already commits the signing parties to universal vertical accountability measures, applicable to all social programs across the country, whether provincial, federal, joint, Canada-wide or not. Consequently, it would have been useless to reiterate this general principle in chapter 5. The parties' intention is, therefore, to allow an intergovernmental rendering of accounts. The implications of potential accountability mechanisms can go beyond program reporting to citizens. Recall that the Saskatoon consensus and the Victoria proposal were explicitly limited to a commitment to cooperate with the federal government to "publicly report on outcomes of new and modified Canada-wide programs." With the Framework Agreement, the federal government and a majority of provinces will be free to give the central authority a right to monitor provincial programs which goes beyond what is required to account to its constituents for its use of public funds.
- The scope of the accountability requirement is considerably extended by the fact that accountability reporting on a non-participating

province's program will be aimed not simply at compliance with "priorities," but also the attainment of specific Canada-wide "objectives" determined by a majority, just as the federal government advocated in its text of January 1999.

Ultimately, the Framework Agreement is evidence of a significant retreat by the nine provinces, which now accept the idea that, in the case of non-participating provinces, the federal authorities may impose an accountability framework that places more restraints and potential limits on their autonomy. They have no reciprocal commitment from Ottawa that it will be accountable to them for all the federal interventions in fields of provincial jurisdiction.

Transparency and the Duty to Explain: Intergovernmental Consultation

The Saskatoon Consensus The consensus of the premiers in Saskatoon was based on a document drawn up in June 1998 by the provincial ministers responsible for negotiations. This document gave an operational dimension to the guiding principle of cooperation or intergovernmental partnership. It promoted efficiency in intergovernmental cooperation by means of transparency, explanation and even justification of social policies. Each government was obliged to advise the other order of government, in writing, of any change in social policy likely to have an effect upon that other order. What is more, this notice had to include a detailed written description of anticipated changes that would allow the other government to review the program properly:

> Each order of government could be required to give the other written notice of any major change proposed to a social policy or program in any area in which the actions of one government significantly affect another government. At the same time that notice of the proposed social policy or program change is given, written information about the change would be provided in sufficient detail to enable the receiving government to assess it adequately.

The document went further by requiring consultation with the other order of government in addition to the obligation to report:

> The government initiating the change could be required to engage in meaningful consultation, including consideration of alternative initiatives, with the other government to ensure that the proposed change did not duplicate effort or operate in a counterproductive manner. Consultation could result in further collaborative action.

The federal government's record over recent years tends to indicate that these provisions would have mainly protected the provinces against unexpected, unilateral modifications of procedures by the federal government. However, the provinces would also have been restricted regarding the management of their own social policies in a context of closely overlapping provincial and federal action.

Note that modification of Canada-wide programs in areas of provincial jurisdiction was also, under the provincial consensus, made subject to unanimous or at least majority provincial consent (with the right to opt out). If the requirement to report and consult envisioned by the provinces applies only to the modification of existing programs, this is apparently because the new federal initiatives were largely covered by procedures requiring that the implementation of Canada-wide programs receive the backing of all the provinces or of a majority (with the right to opt out).

It should also be pointed out that, in Saskatoon, the provinces kept their distance from the position, expressed in the federal proposals of July 15, 1998, that advance notice would be required for any major change in social policy. However, the federal proposals did not ask for prior consultation with the other order of government. The consultation requirement, from the federal point of view, was valid only for the implementation of new programs and policies likely to have an effect on other governments or on the social union. By limiting the reporting requirement only to "major" changes, and by excluding any consultation requirement, Ottawa showed it regarded its freedom of action as particularly important in any change of policy or established programs.[11]

The Victoria Proposal Just like Ottawa, which had merely restated the content of its July 1998 proposals in its January 1999 text, the provinces held to their position with only slight differences. First, the agreement became imperative by the replacement of the expression "should be" by "shall." If the Saskatoon consensus only planned a reporting and consulting requirement in the case of "major" policy change, the new provincial position was more general and referred to "any change proposed to a social policy or program." On the other hand, prior notice and consultation would now be required only when the proposed modification would "significantly affect" the other order of government.

The Social Union Framework Agreement Chapter 4 of the Framework Agreement reads as follows:

> The actions of one government or order of government often have significant effects on other governments. In a manner consistent with the principles of our system of parliamentary government and the budget-making process, governments therefore agree to:
>
> - Give one another advance notice prior to implementation of a major change in a social policy or program which will likely substantially affect another government
> - Offer to consult prior to implementing new social policies and programs that are likely to substantially affect other governments or the social union more generally. Governments participating in these consultations will have the opportunity to identify potential duplication and to propose alternative approaches to achieve flexible and effective implementation.

It is quite clear that this provision is mostly modelled on the federal documents. It is, in fact, even more permissive than the previous federal proposals regarding the modification of established programs by Ottawa, since there is no mention of the amount of detail this notice should include. The transparency requirement is thus weakened.

The Framework Agreement repeats the consultation requirement in the case of new programs by mentioning that consultations can serve to detect possible duplication and propose alternative solutions. On this point, the document reflects the concern expressed in the provincial consensus rather better than the federal proposals.

The fact remains that the nine provinces lined up for the most part with the federal government, which insisted on maintaining the greatest possible room for manœuvre to modify existing federal programs and policies. The logic of transparency and accountability inherent in the requirement to report, explain and justify was largely abandoned. If we pursue the hypothesis that the provincial consensus expressed in Saskatoon and Victoria aimed at containing federal unilateralism by advocating some rendering of accounts for the modification of existing programs, then this aspect of the Framework Agreement could only represent a retreat from the provincial position.

Transparency and Accountability in Dispute Resolution

Although we do not wish to analyze this component of the social union in detail, it is useful to summarize certain aspects.

The Saskatoon Consensus In its document of July 15, the federal government proposed implementing mechanisms for avoiding disputes between governments. These mechanisms had to include "joint fact-finding" as well as "requirement for intergovernmental discussions, consultations including involvement of third parties as appropriate."[12]

Although the provinces agreed, in the introductory provision of the Saskatoon consensus, on the need for a dispute avoidance and resolution procedure, they had not yet fully considered what such a mechanism would consist of and how it would operate.

The Victoria Proposal Chapter 8 of this agreement sets out the provinces' position on the nature and operation of a dispute avoidance and resolution mechanism. Where disputes occur, negotiated solutions are encouraged. This resolution can, if necessary, be assisted by the intervention of a third party who, in the first instance, would be a mediator. Should mediation break down, an individual or committee of three would be responsible for reporting and proposing a resolution. The parties should then try to reach agreement on the basis of the report.

We must emphasize that, for a government, the simple fact of being required to submit its actions to third party review and assessment is part of the dynamic of intergovernmental accountability, each party having to formally record the findings of the third party and take them into consideration in their relations with the other order of government. The provinces, however, wanted to add a powerful mechanism for vertical accountability should a stalemate between governments occur. The Victoria proposal stipulates that: "If a negotiated solution is again not reached, the report will be made public and the governments are to be advised by the report and will have to publicly justify their respective positions."

Governments are therefore required to report publicly to their constituents and justify their actions. Voters will be able to assess the record of the elected officials and attribute political responsibility as appropriate. Given the importance of social programs for Canadians, there would probably be intense political pressure to comply with the recommendations formulated in the public report.

In addition to making the electorate a direct agent in the process by giving it the ultimate sanction when governments are unable to resolve disputes, the provinces set out standards for transparency and vertical accountability to apply to the outcome of this process in every case:

> *Reporting to Canadians*
> Governments agree that the involvement of Canadians will help ensure the mechanism is effective. Canadians will be involved in a number of ways, including:
> Outcomes reporting: Ensuring that all Canadians are informed on outcomes of the dispute settlement mechanism.
> Annual public reporting: Annual reporting on the operation of the mechanism, its goal, performance and effectiveness in helping to avoid and resolve disputes. (chapter 8)

By empowering citizens to supervise the operation of this process, the provinces wished to make them watchdogs over their efficiency. The provincial governments were quite clear in their opinion that accountability was a key factor in finalizing a procedure to encourage the fullest possible compliance with commitments for federal spending, stability and adequate program funding. This strategy is probably connected with a concern for counterbalancing a certain inequality between the parties to Ottawa's advantage in a period of financial uncertainty.

The Social Union Framework Agreement This new version of the federal proposals of January 25, 1999 is more detailed in certain respects but assigns almost no importance to the question of transparency. Ottawa is content to stipulate that "Governments will report publicly on an annual basis on the nature of intergovernmental disputes and their resolution."

Compared with the Victoria proposal, the principle of transparency is highly diluted in the Framework Agreement, in which the parties come much closer to the federal model. It can first be observed that the federal government and the nine provinces adopted a formula that is generally much less restrictive than the Victoria proposal. It simply states that "sector ministers should be guided by the following process, as appropriate." Negotiations, conducted on a purely ministerial level, "will be based on joint fact-finding" as outlined in the federal document of July 15, 1998. The parties may agree to call upon a third party to assist in fact-finding or mediation. It should be noted that recourse to a third party remains discretionary, which restates the federal position but differs from the provincial position in the Victoria text, where it was required. A further difference is that there is no longer any question that the fact-finding inquiry should culminate in recommendations, as the report can only be factual.

As for transparency and rendering accounts, it was agreed that the fact-finding report and the mediator's report, where applicable, could be made public only if one of the parties so requested: "At the request of either party in a dispute, fact-finding or mediation reports will be made public."

The parties involved can, therefore, by mutual agreement, ensure that the process is conducted in complete secrecy. If the fact-finding report is indeed published, it cannot come from a third party and will contain no recommendations, which is likely to make it more difficult for the electorate to assess the facts. It must be recalled that the provinces had, in the Victoria proposal, stipulated that the report and recommendations would have to be published only in the case of a breakdown in negotiations. It also required in such a case that governments publicly justify their respective positions. The Framework Agreement does not explicitly require public justification after the report is published, although one might imagine that, depending on the terms of the report, governments may decide spontaneously to explain their position to the electorate.

The Framework Agreement makes no reference to the requirement set out in Victoria to report annually to citizens on the general operation, objectives, outcomes and effectiveness of this mechanism. The federal government and the nine provinces undertake only to report publicly "on an annual basis on the nature of intergovernmental disputes and their resolution." Consequently, information that should be made available to the electorate may be less than complete.

While the text of the Framework Agreement is less exacting from the standpoint of vertical accountability, it does add an element of intergovernmental accountability by mandating the Ministerial Council to receive "reports from jurisdictions on progress on commitments under the Social Union Framework Agreement."

Summary of the Evolution of Provincial Positions

It is useful here to summarize the discrepancy between the provinces' initial position in the Saskatoon consensus and the final result of the negotiations as set out in the Social Union Framework Agreement.

Promoting Accountability by Clarifying Responsibilities

In the Framework Agreement, the nine provinces agreed to abandon much of the Saskatoon consensus and the Victoria proposal, in which they had clearly made enhancing accountability through the rationalization of responsibilities a primary democratic goal. Instead, it was the philosophy of the federal government that prevailed, since reduction and avoidance of overlapping responsibilities, in accordance with the primary role of the provinces in social affairs, do not appear among the basic values and effective principles governing the social union. Overlapping and duplication of services are, to some degree, sanctioned by the nine provinces, who reject any special ministerial mechanism for reorganization of responsibilities for existing programs. Faced in their fields of jurisdiction with a new federal initiative other than a Canada-wide program supported by intergovernmental transfers, they only obtained the power to "identify potential duplication" and to "propose" alternative solutions (chapter 4).

Vertical Accountability as a General Principle of the Social Union: Chapter 3 of the Framework Agreement

The Saskatoon consensus differed substantially from the federal proposals of July 1998 in that it contained no provision for citizen accountability. This was largely left up to regular mechanisms for rendering accounts within a parliamentary democracy. Chapter 7 of the Victoria proposal displays a relative *rapprochement* between the provinces and the federal government concerning the general requirement that governments measure the efficiency of their programs and inform the electorate of the results of each order of government's role and financial contribution. This reconciliation was almost complete in the Framework Agreement, when the nine provinces abandoned the Victoria approach which favoured autonomy and independent government action in developing outcome measures for their own programs.

In addition to accepting an intergovernmental procedure for developing measures and objectives to legitimize federal and ultimately national standardization of programs, the provinces agreed to give a role to third parties whose intervention would not necessarily promote the maintenance of diverse policies. They supported the federal concern for "public recognition" of the role of the two governments in areas of provincial jurisdiction and willingly submitted to Ottawa's opposition to any reallocation of federal funds. In addition, the provincial governments' idea of requiring governments to report publicly on their commitments for adequate, stable funding for programs has died by the hand of the signatories of the Framework Agreement.

However, the gulf is not as wide between the Victoria proposal and chapter 3 of the Framework Agreement regarding citizens' participation in defining social priorities and the electorate's right to fair, transparent administrative recourse. In fact, in the Framework Agreement the federal government and the nine provinces make the argument for transparency and accountability that appeared in the Victoria proposal, for example, in the planning for a program review mechanism requiring governments to report publicly on appeals and complaints. It seems that the provinces lost scarcely any ground from the standpoint of their ability to plan special administrative control measures.

Accountability in the Context of Federal Spending on Canada-Wide Programs

In Saskatoon and Victoria, the provinces adopted the position that accountability mechanisms at to be fully consensual in the area of Canada-wide programs involving spheres of provincial jurisdiction. The possibility was therefore excluded that a province would be subject, against its will, to any form of accountability if it did not participate in a Canada-wide program. The Framework Agreement, however, announced a fundamental change of direction in the attitude of the nine provinces, who now agreed that the federal government and a majority of the provinces could jointly set up an accountability framework from which a non-participating province could not opt out without losing the right to financial compensation.

While the Saskatoon and Victoria documents only provided for consensual vertical public accountability mechanisms, nothing in the Framework Agreement prevented Ottawa and a majority of provinces from agreeing on an intergovernmental accountability formula that gave the federal government a genuine right to supervise the planning and delivery of social policies that lie within exclusive provincial jurisdiction. Not only did the nine provinces subscribe to the possibility of intergovernmental accountability, they also agreed to extend this accountability to monitoring the successful attainment of Canada-wide objectives set by Ottawa and a majority of the provinces.

Transparency Through Intergovernmental Consultation When a Decision Affects the Other Order of Government

The consensus expressed by the provinces in Saskatoon and Victoria could have contributed to slowing down unilateral federal action on the modification of existing programs by requiring Ottawa to demonstrate transparency to the provinces, provide them with full explanations and take their point of view into consideration before initiating any modifications. The federal authorities were concerned with maintaining manœuvrability on existing programs and only required consultation when a new program was created.

But in agreeing to the Framework Agreement, which only stipulates general prior notice without requiring consultation before modifying existing programs, the nine provinces essentially lined up with Ottawa. They will certainly benefit from the freedom to modify their own programs without compulsory consultation, but they had already agreed to give up this latitude in the Saskatoon consensus and the Victoria proposal in exchange for the right to require Ottawa to demonstrate transparency and justify any unilateral change in existing programs that might affect their social policies.

Accountability and Dispute Resolution

It emerges from the terms of the Framework Agreement that the nine provinces diluted their position on transparency and vertical accountability in dispute resolution as stated in the Victoria proposal. The report that will be made available to the public will likely not contain any recommendations on the means of ensuring compliance with the Framework Agreement, and governments will have no explicit obligation to report publicly on their inability to reach a solution. The Framework Agreement also eliminates the requirement to report annually to the electorate on the operation of the dispute resolution mechanism and its potential for promoting compliance with government action on agreed commitments.

But while the provinces have accepted a reduction in special vertical accountability measures that they could have used as a lever to moderate an unfavourable power relationship in the financial sphere, they do not totally abandon them. Under the Framework Agreement, governments will be quite at liberty to require the publication of a fact-finding or mediation report before negotiations break down. This is the kind of measure that is likely to encourage a government to account for itself publicly.

In short, it is undeniable that the change in positions from the Saskatoon consensus to the Framework Agreement saw the provinces soften their stand on several fronts in favour of the federal point of view. The need to enhance accountability through a systematic reduction of overlap has largely faded. The provinces' freedom to act independently on program evaluation was not accepted; a province must bind itself to an accountability framework imposed by the majority if it wishes to avoid participating in a new Canada-wide program without depriving its population of federal transfers; and Ottawa is under practically no obligation to account for changes in existing programs.

The Social Union Framework Agreement in the Light of Quebec's Traditional Position

Quebec's Historic Position on Accountability and Accounting

Quebec's General Position on the Organization of Powers in the Social Domain

Successive Quebec governments since the Second World War have long been opposed to federal spending on social programs in areas of exclusive provincial jurisdiction. While recognizing the freedom of other provinces to tolerate federal interventions, Quebec has always claimed the right to opt out of programs set up by Ottawa unconditionally and with full fiscal compensation. The issue for Quebec was to claim a fair share of fiscal resources, with total financial independence in relation to the federal government, in order to guarantee its ability to exercise the constitutional powers that have long been regarded as indispensable for safeguarding and promoting its specific needs.[13]

The large-scale constitutional manœuvres of 1987 and 1992 nevertheless led Quebec to accept major compromises within the context of far wider negotiations than were deemed necessary to settle Quebec's various historic claims. In 1987, the Quebec government supported section 7 of the Meech Lake Accord, which involved a constitutional change requiring the government of Canada to provide fair compensation to any province opting out of a new national shared-cost program in an area of provincial jurisdiction if the province supported a program which was "compatible with the national objectives".[14] This would have merely resulted in a very partial control of the federal spending without the opting-out province completely avoiding the restrictions arising from national objectives.[15]

The Charlottetown Accord reaffirmed this compromise in the area of shared-cost programs, while to some extent bolstering the role of the federal government through a reference to section 36 of the Constitution Act, 1982 respecting the commitments of the federal government to equalization and social and economic development.[16] The agreement, which politically committed governments to preserving and developing the social union on the basis of national standards in the health field,[17] also included a general framework mechanism for federal spending in areas of provincial jurisdiction. Through a mechanism that is applicable to all new and existing federal programs, the federal government and the provinces had to minimize overlap and respect provincial priorities while encouraging the realization of national objectives. Prior consent from the provinces and the right to opt out with compensation were not among the explicit guidelines framing the federal initiatives, although, apparently, it would have been possible, through intergovernmental political negotiations, to agree on such guidelines.[18] These provisions tended to mark out and reaffirm the principle of federal spending in areas of exclusive provincial jurisdiction.

The Charlottetown Accord provided for the negotiated withdrawal of the federal government from the field of job training and development with financial compensation to the province requesting the withdrawal.[19] This withdrawal only concerned federal programs "aimed at the province," and the province would have to ensure that these programs were wholly "compatible with national objectives" and developed jointly by the federal government and the provinces.[20]

It emerged from the Meech Lake and Charlottetown episodes that in the context of more general historic constitutional negotiations, Quebec appeared inclined to accept the right to opt out in exchange for which it would be required to set up social programs that were compatible with Canada-wide objectives developed by Ottawa, in the case of new shared-cost programs or, in other cases by an intergovernmental authority. Even though one cannot disregard the complexity of the issues, especially at Charlottetown, and although the Quebec government subsequently expressed less positive opinions of national standards or objectives, the positions adopted by Quebec in 1987 and 1992 must be considered as examples of Quebec's attitude to the organization of power in the field of social policy.

Quebec's Position Examined from the Standpoint of Accountability and Transparency

What can be said about Quebec's attitude to the question of government accountability for social programs? It must be noted that the theme of accountability and transparency has not traditionally occupied the place it does today in constitutional and political discussions on the division of powers in the social sector. However, this does not mean that the issue of accountability and transparency was totally missing from the Quebec perspective.

Intergovernmental Accountability The issue of accountability to Ottawa and of administrative controls rapidly became part of the pattern of Quebec's dissatisfaction with conditional federal transfers in areas of provincial jurisdiction. As early as 1960, the premier of Quebec linked rejection of conditional federal spending with the desire to avoid administrative controls:

> Experience shows that often these joint programs do not permit the provinces to use their own revenues as they wish nor to take local conditions sufficiently into account. Moreover, they raise administrative difficulties that are the cause of a loss of efficiency or duplication of effort and increased costs. The provinces must have in their service persons specially charged with making reports to Ottawa concerning the execution of these programs and the [f]ederal government must, in its turn, hire employees to see that the conditions laid down by Ottawa are fulfilled by the provinces.[21]

The government of Quebec preferred opting out with fiscal rather than monetary compensation in order to minimize administrative controls.[22] Control procedures evolved in line with changes in the administration of federal transfer programs. For example, during the era of the Canada Assistance Plan, the provincial government had to inform the federal government of the content of its programs prior to receiving funding, and had to send Ottawa data on expenses incurred in order to obtain the payment of funds. In the context of the Canadian Health and Social Transfer, an annual report is sent to the central administration.

Although the Meech Lake and Charlottetown accords compelled Quebec to ensure its programs were compatible with national objectives, the Quebec government did not change its attitude toward accountability. Nor did it abandon its preference for tax allowances. The relevant provisions of the constitutional accords of 1987 and 1992 did not specify the terms for payment of the "fair compensation" that provinces wishing to opt out of federal programs should receive. Nor was the provision of compensation dependent on a commitment by the province to comply with any constitutional accountability framework or an assessment of the compatibility of its programs with national objectives.[23]

Recently, because of specific agreements with the federal government in the field of employment, Quebec has agreed to implement accountability frameworks incorporating certain joint initiatives and to send Ottawa certain information. Thus, in chapter 5 of the Canada-Quebec Labour Market Development Implementation Agreement, Quebec agrees to "discuss" and "exchange" information with Ottawa on setting up, monitoring and reviewing targets, to send Canada the results of these indicators (5.2.3.2) and the data required for calculating these results. Quebec also commits to "discuss" with Ottawa the review framework that the province will develop (5.3.1), to send the federal government reviews as soon as they are approved (5.3.3), to deposit a financial statement from the Auditor-General of Quebec specifying that these funds are used in compliance with the purposes set out in the agreement (5.5), and lastly, to send Canada a detailed report on the collection and allocation of overpayments in activities targeted by the agreement (5.6). The Employability Assistance for People with Disabilities Initiative (EAPD) although not identical, follows the same pattern.

Recent practice suggests that Quebec can accept certain intergovernmental accounting formulas designed to enhance Ottawa's accountability toward its own constituents, when such formulas are seen as maintaining exclusive provincial control over all essential aspects of the programs.

Vertical Accountability Quebec governments have traditionally opposed Ottawa's intervention in the provincial social field through federal spending, not only because of its age-old desire for autonomy, but also out of a wish to rationalize responsibilities in order to exclude contradictory interventions or spending public monies twice. This struggle to eliminate overlap and confusion in programs is commonly justified as an impetus for the efficient use of fiscal resources, rather than a concern with organizational transparency and accountability vis-à-vis the electorate.[24] However, concern for the enhancement of public confidence by means of a more rational organization of programs has occasionally been voiced.[25]

By advocating the withdrawal of the federal government and the recognition of exclusive provincial jurisdictions, Quebec quite naturally supported the clarification of responsibilities in a manner that favours accountability to the electorate. The acceptance of a conditional right to opt out in the Meech Lake and Charlottetown accords does not detract from this logic. Quebec's traditional demand that the right to opt out of a federally funded program be linked to tax points rather than monetary compensation tends to militate in favour of accountability, since the government that spends public monies also collects them.

It seems that Quebec has not, in the past, advocated the implementation of special vertical accountability measures applicable to all social policies.

This survey of Quebec's position reveals that, in general, Quebec has sought to prevent intergovernmental accounting frameworks from hampering the efficiency and autonomy of its social policies. It has also demanded exclusive responsibility in the social field, which in itself promotes a clarification of roles in this field and therefore accountability to citizens.

The Framework Agreement in Relation to Quebec's Traditional Position

Accountability by Means of the Organization of Powers

The Framework Agreement is clearly a good distance away from Quebec's traditional position by virtue of the fact that, unlike the provincial consensus, it does not systematically enhance the rationalization of responsibilities and the struggle against program overlap and confusion. Moreover, it includes no commitment to set up any authority mandated to organize and carry through a revision of various government roles in the name of transparency and accountability.

This distance is especially great in chapter 5, in which the provinces' ability to opt out is restricted to new Canada-wide initiatives funded by intergovernmental transfers. This opens the door to the perpetuation of duplication of existing federal government programs, especially when coupled with new initiatives not covered by the right to opt out, which will only be subject to simple consultation (direct subsidies, etc.).

Vertical Accountability as a Basic Principle of the Social Union

Quebec's traditional position with regard to accounting to citizens has been to treat its social programs like the rest of its government policies, that is, in compliance with the full range of control and accountability mechanisms in a parliamentary democracy. Chapter 3 of the Framework Agreement diverges from this approach by introducing special assessment and reporting measures for the specific instance of social programs.

While Quebec has always claimed the right to manage its own policies with complete autonomy because of its social and cultural distinctiveness, the Framework Agreement commits the federal and provincial governments to measuring all their programs according to convergent indicators that are developed jointly and correlated to objectives agreed between governments. This type of integrationist assessment is extended to provincial programs, which is hardly compatible with Quebec's historical approach.

The Framework Agreement also advocates the official participation of third parties in program assessment, which could permit interest groups that are sometimes insensitive to Quebec's aspirations to exercise more influence over the orientation of provincial programs. In Ottawa, the provinces agreed to "recognize" and publicly explain the role and contribution of the federal government in fields of provincial jurisdiction. Provincial governments thus undertake to sanction the federal presence in their own supposedly reserved domains, which does not fit well into Quebec's traditional political discourse.

Accountability in the Context of Federal Spending Related to Canada–wide Programs

Under the terms of chapter 5 of the Framework Agreement, the federal government and a majority of the provinces could oblige a province that does not wish to participate in a new Canada-wide program not only to attain the national objectives that they set, but also to comply with an accountability framework. This framework would be Canada-wide and not adapted to Quebec's unique situation as are the fully consensual accountability measures inserted in the special agreements Quebec has entered into in the area of employment. The Framework Agreement does not allow a province that wishes to opt out of the program with full compensation to negotiate an accountability framework modelled on its specific needs.

Although under the Meech Lake and Charlottetown accords Quebec subscribed to the principle of "compatibility" between its programs and national objectives, the concept was not linked to the requirement that there be precise, applicable objectives. Nor did Quebec go as far as agreeing in advance to a national accountability framework that forced it to submit to assessment and scrutiny and to demonstrate the effective attainment of set objectives. In the past, Quebec governments have tried, instead, to minimize accounting and administrative controls by advocating fiscal compensation rather than transfers of funds.

The federal government and a majority of provinces will have all the latitude they need to negotiate rules for intergovernmental accountability giving the federal government and the other provinces a significant right to see the administration and assessment of programs, including programs of non-participating provinces. There is nothing within the accountability framework set out in the Framework Agreement to suggest that the federal role would be confined to that existing under the terms of special agreements recently signed with Quebec.

Conclusion

THE GAP BETWEEN THE STARTING POSITION OF THE PROVINCES AND THE FINAL RESULT of the negotiations appears significant with respect to the issue of accountability. In general, there appears to be a weakening of the will to foster accountability by eliminating duplication and to safeguard the provinces' freedom of action in matters of vertical and intergovernmental accountability. The federal government, for its part, emerges from the Framework Agreement without really having to account to the provinces for a large number of its interventions in their fields of jurisdiction.

The gulf seems even wider between the Social Union Framework Agreement and Quebec's historical demand to opt out of all federal initiatives as an essential condition for rationalizing responsibilities. Setting a high value on its autonomy, Quebec has never welcomed the imposition of constraints in the management of its programs through intergovernmental assessment and accountability mechanisms.

1 To the Saskatoon consensus, the Victoria proposal and the Framework Agreement we have added two federal documents to our documentation: *Working Together for Canadians: A Federal Proposal for a Framework Agreement to Strengthen Canada's Social Union*, July 15, 1998 and *Working Together for Canadians: A Federal Proposal for a Framework Agreement to Strengthen Canada's Social Union*, January 25, 1999.

2 Thomas Courchene, "ACCESS: A Convention on the Canadian Economic and Social Systems," Study conducted for the Minister of Intergovernmental Affairs of Ontario (August 1996) in *Canadian Business Economics*, vol.4, no. 4, July-September, Summer 1996, p. 6.

3 Courchene, "ACCESS," p. 6.

4 Canada, *Working Together for Canadians*, July 15 1998.

5 Canada, *Working Together for Canadians*, July 15, 1998.

6 "This document does not speak to principles, ground rules and dispute settlement, which are also key elements of a Framework Agreement on the Social Union."

7 See chapter 3, where sector ministers are given responsibility for developing a full Canada-wide framework for assessment, information and rendering accounts.

8 There is no reference in the Framework Agreement to the provision of the Victoria proposal in which governments agreed to "publicly report on their respective commitments of providing stable and adequate funding for social programs."

9 Consent would be necessary even for initiatives other than joint programs. In return, the requirement for consent is restricted only to "conditional" transfers.

10 Canada, *Working Together for Canadians*, January 25, 1999.

11 Chapter 3 of the federal document of July 1998 reads as follows: "Each government will give notice in advance of making any major social policy change likely to affect another government. Notice of the proposed change will include sufficient detail to enable the receiving governments to assess the proposed action...Government will consult one another prior to implementing new social policies and programs that are likely to affect other governments or the social union more generally."

12 Canada, *Working Together for Canadians*, July 1998.

13 See, generally, Secrétariat aux Affaires intergouvernementales canadiennes (SAIC), *Québec's Historical Position on the Federal Spending Power 1944-1998* (Quebec, Ministère du Conseil exécutif, 1998).

14 The proposed constitutional provision reads as follows: 106A (1) The Government of Canada shall provide reasonable compensation to the government of a province that chooses not to participate in a national shared-cost program that is established by the Government of Canada after the coming into force of this section in an area of exclusive provincial jurisdiction, if the province carries on a program or initiative that is compatible with the national objectives. (2) Nothing in this section extends the legislative powers of the Parliament of Canada or of the legislatures of the provinces. Strengthening the Canadian Federation, *The Constitution Amendment, 1987* (Ottawa: Government of Canada, 1987).

15 Furthermore, as Professor André Tremblay pointed out, the Meech Lake Accord confirms — or at the very least presupposes – the existence of federal spending power for provincial purposes: "The objective of the Section was not to recognize spending power or to accurately describe its boundaries, despite the fact that the Section assumes and confirms the existence of the Federal Parliament's power to set up conditional national objective based grants within provincial jurisdiction areas." A. Tremblay, *La réforme de la Constitution du Canada* (Montreal: Thémis, 1995), pp. 129-30. [Translation]

16 See new draft paragraph 106A, *Consensus Report on the Constitution: Draft Legal Text*

(Ottawa, Government of Canada, 1992).

17 See new draft paragraph 36.1, *Consensus Report on the Constitution: Draft Legal Text* (Ottawa, Government of Canada, 1992).

18 See new draft paragraph 37, *Consensus Report on the Constitution: Draft Legal Text* (Ottawa, Government of Canada, 1992).

19 See section 93B.

20 See section 93C.

21 Statement by Mr. Jean Lesage, Dominion-Provincial Conference, Ottawa, July 25-27 1960, pp. 129-30 in SAIC, *Québec's Historical Position on the Federal Spending Power*, p. 11. See also statement by Prime Minister Bourassa in 1971 at the Annual Premiers' Conference, Ottawa, November 15-17, 1971, in SAIC, *Québec's Historical Position on the Federal Spending Power*, p. 28.

22 See statement by Mr. Bourassa, in SAIC, *Québec's Historical Position on the Federal Spending Power*, p. 28.

23 Certain constitutional modifications planned in the Meech Lake and Charlottetown accords, particularly section 106(A) concerning new, shared-cost programs, would, however, have given the federal government the right to use a judicial review procedure against a province in order to rule on the compliance of provincial programs with national objectives.

24 In a brief on the constitutional question delivered at an intergovernmental conference in Ottawa on February 5-7, 1968, the Quebec government declared, "There are two main reasons behind Québec's strong insistence on regaining full control over social security: first, because the simultaneous presence of two governments in this area thwarts all effective planning, makes for contradiction between the various programs and leads to waste and administrative overlap..." in SAIC, *Québec's Historical Position on the Federal Spending Power*, p. 20. See also the statements by Minister Castonguay in 1970 in SAIC, *Québec's Historical Position on the Federal Spending Power*, p. 26 and also by Prime Minister René Lévesque in 1978, in SAIC, *Québec's Historical Position on the Federal Spending Power*, p. 29. In 1994, Prime Minister Daniel Johnson gave the same address opposing overlap created by the federal presence in fields of exclusive provincial jurisdiction; see the letter addressed to Mr. Marcel Massé of February 15, 1994, in SAIC, *Québec's Historical Position on the Federal Spending Power*, p. 37.

25 See, for example, the letter sent by Prime Minister Daniel Johnson to Mr. Marcel Massé, in SAIC, *Québec's Historical Position on the Federal Spending Power*, p. 37.

Working in Partnership for Canadians

Introduction

THE OBJECTIVE OF THIS ARTICLE IS TO EVALUATE PROPOSALS TO ESTABLISH A PARTnership aimed at improving the Canadian social union by the common front of provinces, first in the Saskatoon consensus of August 6, 1998, then in the Victoria proposal of January 29, 1999, and the final result, which was the Social Union Framework Agreement of February 4, 1999. In order to assess the extent of the changes, in the first section we will analyze the evolution of the provincial positions in these three key stages of the negotiation process by identifying the initial demands of the provinces and the results obtained at the end of the process. Some analysts believe that all these agreements are part of a process, and that the situation may still evolve unexpectedly. Nonetheless, we believe that these stages in the evolution of the provincial position on partnership are broad trends and not merely currents, and that the Framework Agreement constitutes a major milestone for Canada's constitutional and political future. In the second section, we will evaluate the gap between the constitutional positions defended by the Quebec government and the final result of the negotiations with a view toward a partnership between the orders of government in the establishment of the Canadian Social Union.

Context

THE SOCIAL AND ECONOMIC UNION PROJECT IS ONE OF THE MANY ADMINISTRATIVE attempts initiated to meet the expectations of all Canadian citizens following the constitutional failures of Meech Lake (1990) and Charlottetown (1992).

Following the federal election of 1993 that brought Prime Minister Jean Chrétien's Liberals to power, it became imperative for the provinces to better affirm their roles in the Canadian federation. The premiers took advantage of their Annual Conference to advance their common positions in several areas, for example, the establishment of a domestic common market with as few constraints as possible. They also emphasized the role of the provinces in their exclusive fields of jurisdiction, clearly identified in the Constitution, and expressed a desire to better control federal spending power in these areas.

The federal elections of 1993 and 1997 saw the recasting of power relations throughout Canada. This is because, first, Ottawa was seeking to undermine the importance of the federal-provincial conferences, contrary to past practice, and second, the premiers were seeking to make their annual conferences a medium for forging consensus in order to consolidate their political preferences. These important gatherings bring to mind the provincial initiatives of Jean Lesage and John Robarts during the 1960s, when Canada had nearly reached a breaking point.

The federal election of 1993 put Canada back a decade by bringing to power a central government that virtually turned a deaf ear to the provinces. The federal Liberals were defeated in the federal election of 1984 in part because of their uncompromising attitude which contributed toward the election of a series of Conservative governments at the provincial level in the early 1980s. In 1984 Brian Mulroney's Conservatives, who pledged to reintegrate Quebec in the federation with "honour and enthusiasm" and to end federal-provincial confrontations, were swept to power with a resounding electoral victory.

The decision of provincial leaders to better harmonize their positions was consequential. If successful, it could effectively stop the central government from proceeding with its threats of unilateral intervention. Of course, Ottawa possesses the ultimate weapon to undermine any provincial consensus: its spending power. We will see below how in the social union negotiations, the central government, led by Jean Chrétien, has not hesitated to use public funds to secure provincial compliance (with the exception of Quebec). The federal government favours budgetary measures, thus giving Canadians a view of the Canadian federation from an accountant's perspective. This is how, since 1993, the central government has set government orientations, at budget submission time, not even attempting to seek accommodation with the provincial governments. The

First Ministers' Conference is viewed by Ottawa as a forum for disagreement, whereas it is simply a forum for democratic deliberation among representatives of the political communities comprising Canada.

It is in this context that Bill C-76, submitted on February 27, 1995 and adopted on June 6 of the same year, must be situated. The bill pertains to the Canadian transfer in health care and social programs. Breaking with the federal practice of consulting the provinces in the areas under their jurisdiction before proceeding with significant changes, the central government chose to unilaterally review the methods of calculating and making transfer payments to the provinces. With few exceptions, the individuals and groups that appeared before the Finance Committee in Ottawa criticized the central government's cavalier attitude in adopting this strategy and also lamented the flagrant lack of transparency in the setting of new priorities. This is far from the willingness expressed by Ottawa — both in the Speech from the Throne and in Finance Minister Paul Martin's successive budgets — to establish, with the consensus of the provinces, the principles for a Canadian social union. It is certainly revealing of the type of partnership that the central government wishes to impose on the provinces. We will examine this partnership below by focusing on the evolution of federal-provincial relations in recent years.

From Economic Union to Social Union

The concept of social union is not well understood either in Quebec or in the rest of Canada. The idea of a Canadian social union originated at the time of constitutional discussions surrounding the federal proposals of September 1991.[1] This was on the eve of the start of the Castonguay-Dobbie Commission, which was followed by the Beaudoin-Dobbie Commission, which ultimately resulted in the Charlottetown Agreement. The Charlottetown Agreement did not address the issue of social union; instead it referred to a pan-Canadian economic union. Several elements of the English-Canadian political left saw this as a major setback in their proposal for a Canada-wide nation, and squarely opposed the Charlottetown Agreement.

In the federal proposals of 1991 there was a willingness to solicit the participation of the territories and provinces. The federal government under Brian Mulroney even suggested that a Council of the Federation be created to find ways to improve the functioning of the Canadian economic union, harmonize and coordinate financial policies and agree on the eventual role of the federal spending power in new co-financed programs. The decisions of the Council of the Federation would require the support of the central government and at least seven provinces, representing 50 percent of the Canadian population.

The idea of "intra-federalism," rather than that of a true partnership between member-states of the federation and the central government, is the essence of this working document. It must be stressed that there was no question of the federal government settling for a simple majority of provinces before proceeding with changes in areas concerning the provinces; it insisted on the support of a minimum of 50 percent of the Canadian population.

The question of social union did not commonly arise during annual conferences of premiers. It did not clearly arise until August 1996, barely eight months after the referendum on sovereignty-partnership, initiated by Quebec, to find a solution to the Canadian constitutional crisis. Just before the 1996 annual conference, the government of Ontario was preparing to present a paper drafted by economist Thomas Courchene on behalf of the Minister of Intergovernmental Affairs entitled "ACCESS: a Convention on the Canadian Economic and Social System." This paper proposed a rebalancing of the Canadian federation that could have met some of Quebec's demands. In response to fierce opposition from some provincial premiers, the Ontario government did not release it at that time, and even went so far as to claim that it did not necessarily represent the government's position.[2]

This document, partly inspired by the provincial position expressed in the 1995 *Report to Premiers*, is a useful starting point to present the provinces' vision of the future of the Canadian federation based on a partnership between the orders of government. It states that, in contrast with other federations such as Germany, Switzerland and Australia, Canada has never sought to involve the provinces directly in the functioning of the domestic market, underlining the extent to which the central government has neglected to enlist the participation of the other governments in the Canadian federation.[3]

Two of the main objectives presented in that document are the preservation and consolidation of the economic and social union. Having observed major reductions in transfers to the provinces in education and social policies since the election of the Liberals in 1993, the premiers set, as a priority, a guarantee of continuity in these areas. Note that from 1995 to 1997, transfer payments to provinces were cut by $6 billion, which forced the provinces to initiate an unprecedented reform of the health and education sectors.

Courchene's document contained several interesting proposals. First, he recommended that Ottawa's fixation with setting standards and imposing a common domestic market unilaterally be halted. The proposal advanced by Ontario suggests the formation of federal-provincial partnerships, preferably through interprovincial agreements that grant significant manœuvring room to the provinces in order to ensure a more effective domestic union. Federal-provincial partnership agreements on economic and social union should promote several principles. These were accountability, transparency, efficiency, equity, citizens' rights, subsidiarity, the federal principle, federal flexibility regarding spending power, the application of an agreement between Ottawa and the provinces as equals in which provinces would have the responsibility to have their rights fully recognized, treatment of the provinces modelled on the Free Trade Agreement, and preservation of the status quo when it was not possible to agree on changes.

The Ontario paper also discusses a two-stage process to implement the partnership formulas among the provinces and between provinces and the central government, consistent with the adoption of an interim model, followed by a more exhaustive and permanent model to attain economic and social union. The document insists that during the provisional phase the following commitments be maintained or accounted for, and that the fundamental principles identified in the Canada Health Act be preserved, that responsibility for manpower training be transferred to the provinces, guidelines for federal spending power be established, a federal-provincial agency reporting to the premiers to monitor the efficiency of the economic and social union be created and an Expert Committee to judge any submitted complaints be established.

The permanent model proposed in the Ontario document clearly gives the provinces the exclusive right to conceive and provide for health care services, social assistance and education. It suggests that the parties proceed with transfers of additional equalized tax points to meet expenditures. Such an approach would shield the provinces from Ottawa's constant threats to cut or adjust budgets as it pleases. This would have demanded a marked willingness on the part of the provinces to manage these new tax points.

The notion of a social union was revived by the federal Liberals under Jean Chrétien in their indefatigable quest for a single identity for Canada. The

Chrétien government also made a deliberate attempt to change the definition of the concept of the social union by moving the centre of gravity away from a policy founded on redistribution in favour of a distributive one. This initiative is not limited to transfer payments to provinces, it also affects private organizations and individuals, while being subject to the federal government's turbulent budgetary policy. It is therefore far from the social charter claimed by several opponents of the Charlottetown Accord. This appears to be an attempt by the Liberal government of Jean Chrétien to appropriate in its favour, albeit symbolically, a major social demand put forth by the progressive forces of the country.

Evolution of the Provincial Position on the Establishment of Partnership Practices

The Saskatoon Consensus

The Annual Premiers' conference that took place on August 5, 6 and 7, 1998 in Saskatoon set the stage for what was intended to be an arm wrestling match between the provinces and the federal government over the Canadian social union. The premiers agreed to establish a more solid partnership between the two orders of government in order to safeguard social programs whose financing had been severely diminished since the introduction of the Canadian Health and Social Transfer in 1995.

The premiers pointed out that it is essential to ensure maximum cooperation and maintain the commitment that each order of government will assume its own responsibilities. The press release issued at the end of the conference stated there was an urgent need to agree to a formula for cooperation with respect to federal financial commitments in the areas of provincial jurisdiction — including health, education and social services — and called for the creation of an impartial dispute-settlement mechanism to ensure the efficient functioning of the federation. This was an innovative, even promising element for Quebec, which could, if conflicts arose, use the new body and present arguments justifying its claims. Quebec would thus have gained an additional opportunity, if it failed to convince its Canadian partners, to bring the matter to the attention of its own population.

Believing that the objective of a more solid partnership should not be achieved to the detriment of federalism, the premiers emphasized the idea that a province may "…opt out of any new or modified Canada-wide social program in areas of provincial/territorial jurisdiction with full compensation…" providing that another program or initiative in the same priority areas as those identified in the Canada-wide program is proposed. The premiers stressed the willingness expressed by the federal government at this stage of the negotiation to recognize the provinces' right to opt out. This demand paralleled the stipulation in the Meech Lake Agreement (article 7), that "The Government of Canada shall provide reasonable compensation to the government of a province that chooses not to participate in a national shared-cost program that is established by the Government of Canada after the coming into force of this section in an area of exclusive provincial jurisdiction, if the province carries on a program or initiative that is compatible with the national objectives."[4]

The premiers, aware of the dangers of unstable federal financing, insisted that there be a balance between government revenues and responsibilities so as not to jeopardize existing programs. To avoid weakening their bargaining position, the provinces agreed not to subscribe to a framework agreement until all of the sections of the agreement had been negotiated and accepted.

To summarize, the premiers' document was reactive rather than proactive. The Quebec government nonetheless saw several of its traditional claims respected, including respect for constitutional jurisdictions, bilateralism and the right to withdraw with full compensation in its areas of exclusive jurisdiction. At this stage, Quebec did not worry about the establishment of a dispute mechanism for the attainment of recourse against convergence toward a pan-Canadian definition for new social priorities, because the right to opt out had been assured.

The Victoria Proposal

The document tabled by the provinces on January 29, 1999, *Securing Canada's Social Union into the 21st Century* revisits the provinces' requirements and sets forth new provisions in order to revitalize the initiative.

This proposal preceded the presentation of the federal budget by a few days. The provinces were preoccupied following the dramatic cuts in transfer payments in provincial domains such as health, education and social services over the previous five years. They therefore had very little time to reach an agreement on a large-scale social union project.

Regardless of what transpired in the negotiations with the provinces, the federal government was free to decide on a level of generosity, without holding a genuine public debate. Gone was the era of federal-provincial conferences broadcast by the large television networks when Canadians could watch their first ministers debate the merits of various proposals elaborated respectively by provincial and federal teams. Discussions were taking place behind closed doors.

The partnership elements in the proposal of January 29 in Victoria amount to general cooperative initiatives, the development of a policy of cooperation relating to federal spending power in Canada-wide programs, and, to a lesser extent, efforts to collaborate on a narrower territorial basis. These three sectors are framed by general, but structuring principles. For example, the five principles (comprehensiveness, universality, portability, public management and accessibility) of the Canada Health Act were reaffirmed, even if the Quebec government has never recognized federal jurisdiction in this domain. There was also a suggestion of expanding the notion of partnership by extending it to relations among orders of government, communities, volunteer organizations, corporations, unions, families and individuals. This suggests that central and provincial governments are as justified in establishing partnerships among themselves as they are with any of these organizations and citizens. The direction in which the premiers had taken the partnership up to now, i.e., that of privileging federal-provincial relations, was significantly modified.

General Cooperative Initiatives

The document included ample allusions to the need for governments to collaborate in setting-up the social union. The primary responsibility was recognized as pertaining to the provinces and territories, while specifying that the federal government has an important role to play. To facilitate policy formulation and implementation, governments agreed to give notice before making any changes and to exchange information. A government proposing a project must proceed to consult with the other partners.

For Quebec, this formal obligation presents at least two difficulties in areas covered by the social union. First, it prevents Quebec from launching new initiatives without first informing its partners in the federation and second, it seems to preclude the possibility that member-states of the federation might take independent initiatives in provincial areas of jurisdiction (e.g., drug insurance). The official reason given was that if provinces were to act without consulting the federal government (and the other provinces), there might be duplication of new programs. In short, this obligation constitutes a disincentive to provincial innovation.

Formulation of a Policy of Cooperation Concerning Federal Spending Power in Canadian Social Srograms

This is certainly the main clause in the chapter dealing with partnership. From the outset, based on the federal precedent set by the National Child Benefit, the parties to the document confirmed the possibility of Ottawa pursuing similar initiatives in other sectors of activity. Note that the idea of establishing a child benefit program in the first place originated from the provinces; the federal government then adopted it and sought to make it a Canada-wide program. For the provinces, with the exception of Quebec, this program set an interesting precedent of a jointly designed Canada-wide social initiative. At the same time they rejected the imposition of unilateral federal initiatives such as the Millennium Scholarship Fund, which Ottawa presented to the provinces as a *fait accompli*.

The provinces and territories claimed to be prepared to tolerate some asymmetry in the application of government policies. The preferred option was collaboration, which translated into the establishment of a joint table to fix monetary transfers to new or modified Canada-wide programs in areas of exclusive provincial jurisdiction. The provinces therefore recognized a federal role in the establishment of priorities and policy preferences. This represents a major problem for Quebec, since it had rejected a similar approach in the National Child Benefit program, portrayed as a model to follow. By supporting the Victoria proposal, the provinces gave some legitimacy to this type of federal initiative.

Quebec appeared to be making potential gains in the proposed partnership in cases where federal-provincial collaboration failed. This is the most probable scenario for Quebec, judging by previous experiences. First, the proposal provided for a mechanism by which the majority consent of the provinces is required (without specifying the percentage of the population support required), and second, the federal government would have to grant full compensation to provinces that chose not to support the program, providing that a program or initiative respecting the priority sectors of the newly introduced or modified Canada-wide program were put in place. This provision poses two problems for Quebec. The fact that there is no stipulation of a minimum percentage of popular support required to implement a Canada-wide project legitimized the principle of provincial equality. It would also lead to overrepresentation of the least populated provinces. For Quebec the most advantageous section of the Victoria proposal is the right to opt out, which would allow the province to define its own priorities while seeking to harmonize its policies with those of the other Canadian provinces.

Collaborative Initiatives on a Narrower Territorial Base

The object here was solely to impose limits on the federal spending power when there is federal intervention in a field of provincial jurisdiction. Such an intervention, subject to a dispute-settlement mechanism, may only take place once the consent of the province or territory affected has been secured. The dispute settlement mechanism represents a gain for the member-states of the Canadian federation, providing that the parties are adequately represented and the neutrality of the process is assured. During the conference of federal, provincial and territorial health ministers in September 1998, Quebec felt that it could benefit from the implementation of this mechanism.

In short, the Victoria proposal points to some flexibility on the part of the federal government, as well as the possibility of reaching agreements adapted to each province.

The Social Union Framework Agreement

With respect to the principles behind the Framework Agreement put forward by Ottawa and unanimously rejected by the parties represented in the Quebec National Assembly, there clearly is an emphasis on equal opportunities. This principle did not appear in the Victoria proposal of January 29 and is a significant change, because there is no mention of promoting the equality of conditions dear to the Quebec government. Paradoxically, while the federal government claims to be seeking greater equity among citizens, it stresses equal opportunities through labour mobility and similar policies. The federal government proposes, moreover, to offer appropriate assistance to those in need. This is a good intention, but actually represents an intrusion into exclusive provincial jurisdictions. This position therefore presages conflicts with provincial governments, which are responsible for social assistance. Here are two aspects (equal opportunities through labour mobility and intrusion in the field of social assistance) over which the governments of Ottawa and Quebec will find it difficult to agree.

The section on partnership, "Working in Partnership for Canadians," is quite different from the relevant section of the Victoria proposal. The three types of initiatives that, in the Victoria proposal, reinforced the partnership with the provinces are, in the Framework Agreement, placed in the chapter covering federal spending power. By a simple transposition, everything now ensues from the recognition of federal spending power, because only provinces that recognize this power would have access to the federal bounty. It is now not an option for the provinces to exercise their right to opt out with full compensation unless precise conditions are met.

In addition, Ottawa reserves the right to contribute to provincial budgets on condition that the provinces (1) endeavour to attain the Canada-wide objectives defined by Ottawa in the new initiatives (rather than in co-financed programs as was the case in Meech) in health care, post-secondary education, social assistance and social services — all sectors of exclusive provincial jurisdiction, and (2) agree to faithfully respect the accountability framework sanctioned by Ottawa and the provinces (excluding Quebec). The right to opt out, so dear to Quebec governments since the early 1960s, is presented as an inclusion right (*forcing in* rather than *opting out*). Therefore, once the central government obtains the approval of six provinces, the other provinces are bound to fulfil national objectives. The right to opt out is essentially a creation of the mind, because a government that does not support an initiative must establish a program that complies with the objectives pursued by Ottawa. It is therefore not truly possible for a province to opt out of federal initiatives unless it is ready to force its constituents to pay twice for the services dispensed. Also, by adhering to the framework agreement, the Canadian provinces (with the exception of Quebec) are approving the federal spending power that enables Ottawa to infringe significantly on recognized provincial powers.

By proposing direct transfers, the federal government is also expanding its definition of partnership to include individuals and organizations that operate in the health care, post-secondary education, social assistance and social services sectors. It is up to the provinces to detect any duplication and to report it to the federal authorities. Any changes in this area will be subject to at least three months' notice. The central government intends to use its spending power to launch new direct initiatives aimed at individuals and organizations in order to promote equal opportunities and promote mobility and the achievement of other Canada-wide objectives. The only limiting clause is that the provinces will be given three months notice and eventually, will be offered the opportunity to be consulted. As part of new Canada-wide initiatives supported by the transfers to provinces and territories, the central government agrees to pay projected available amounts on condition that the provincial and territorial governments abide by Ottawa's accountability framework, along with the Canada-wide objectives. This procedural framework is therefore highly constraining because the provinces are presented with a *fait accompli*, and it is impossible for them to inform their constituents of the real impact of decisions taken.

The federal government therefore proceeded to undertake major changes between the Victoria proposal of January 29 and the Framework Agreement of February 4, 1999. In the latter, all "partnership" agreements with the provinces, individuals or various target establishments hinge on Ottawa's goodwill and the provinces are required to officially recognize Ottawa's spending power in social domains. The federal government even suggests that the new social union is the product of its spending power. The central government is laying the cornerstones of the social union, as it conceives it, by advancing several non-federal principles, including the uniformity of programs, skirting around the provinces in the development of the overall project and getting direct access to partners (individuals, families, communities, voluntary organizations, businesses, unions, etc.), without taking into account provincial responsibilities in these areas of exclusive jurisdiction. From a better-defined partnership with the provinces in the agreement of January 28, 1999, Ottawa is opting to expand the notion to include partners with whom it would be easier to deal because they are not accountable to citizens, as are elected provincial governments.

However, the federal government insists that a more formal role be granted to the Ministerial Council, about which little is known. The partnership proposed by Ottawa seems to be one-way only, because the provinces must provide the information that leads to the implementation of joint priorities in the areas of exclusive provincial jurisdiction. Ottawa therefore has assumed the right to provide prior notice, while still being able to resort to the secrecy surrounding the budget process to avoid its commitment of prior notice stipulated in the Framework Agreement. The federal government will choose, if it deems applicable, to offer consultation before going ahead with new policies or social programs that may affect the social union. Naturally, the provinces will be free to decide whether or not to seek to influence the choices of the federal government. At any rate, the policies put forth by any of the provinces will be proposed to all the provinces in order to avoid the appearance of difference between them. This puts an end to the diversity of services offered by each of the Canadian provinces, a principle that underpins every federation.

The partnership proposal advanced by the federal government to the provinces has a duration of three years, because the governments reportedly want to conduct a formal evaluation of the Framework Agreement at the beginning of the third year. This is in fact a double-edged sword for the federal government. It may want to portray itself as the great defender of all Canadians on the eve of the next federal election, seeking to use its spending power to achieve its political objectives. But the most assertive provinces, Quebec being the prime example, might use this Framework Agreement to demonstrate that the vision embodied by the document is more heavily inspired by unitary than by federal systems.

The Framework Agreement will certainly have repercussions on Quebec-Ottawa relations. Moreover, the Health Accord,[5] which also is of three years duration and which the government of Quebec, like the other provinces, has refused to approve, will nonetheless apply to the member-states of the federation. However, the Bouchard government has found the general objectives of the draft agreement acceptable and has undertaken to fully reinvest in the health care sector additional funds granted by the Canadian social transfer following the Saskatoon consensus. Three broad objectives are pursued by the draft agreement, namely (1) to maintain, protect and improve health care, (2) to provide access to comparable and efficient health care services based on needs and not on the ability to pay and (3) to guarantee the continuity of adequate financing.

The notion of partnership used in the draft agreement poses a problem because the document refers to health as a responsibility shared between society, communities and individuals, and indicates that there is already a broad government consensus that is backed by orientations adopted by Canadian health ministers in September 1998. We know that Quebec did not approve the general orientations identified during this conference, but this does not seem to be a problem for Ottawa or the provincial capitals. The agreement poses at least two other difficulties for Quebec, because it must be interpreted both in the context of the Social Union Framework Agreement and keeping in mind that it strengthens the principles on which the Canada Health Act is based. Is this a case of sneaking through the back door something that cannot go in by the front door?

The Quebec government saw the Health Accord as a means of increasing its financial manœuvring room, especially since the promised new funds must be reinvested on the basis of provincial priorities. This policy inevitably appealed to Quebec.

General Comments

This brief look at the evolution of federal-provincial relations from the Saskatoon consensus in August 1998 up to and including the Framework Agreement of February 4, 1999 highlights Ottawa's imposition of new restrictions in spheres of exclusive provincial jurisdiction, specifically health care, post-secondary education, social services and social assistance.

Underlying the reform that led to the social union was the provinces' quest to ensure the continuity of existing social programs, guarantee financing stability, reduce duplication of services and limit federal spending power, which is frequently used to reorient provincial priorities in fields of exclusive jurisdiction. The final result is quite far from the objectives that the provinces envisioned, because they are now forced to recognize the federal spending power. Moreover, financing is linked to the budgetary process and can be reduced with little warning. The agreement has also made it easier for the federal government to meddle in provincial domains.

The Framework Agreement cannot, however, circumvent the Canadian Constitution even if its authors act as if it does not exist. Lastly, Aboriginal peoples are given lip service, merely assured of federal collaboration to find practical solutions to their pressing demands.

The Gap Getween Constitutional Positions Defended by Quebec and the Imposed Social Union Framework Agreement

It has become commonplace in Quebec to evaluate constitutional changes based on the traditional demands made by governments in power in Quebec, be they federalist or nationalist. This has the advantage of demonstrating the common stands taken by governments of different stripes. This approach has two weaknesses: it does not allow proper identification of new areas of intervention and it reveals little about the evolving nature of federalism itself and the forces at work. However, knowing that a given traditional demand by Quebec has not been respected is an essential starting point, even if it does not sufficiently elucidate the broad trends that are characteristic of changing power relations.

In this section we present the foundations of the Quebec and Canadian positions in constitutional matters, along with the avenues explored by the Quebec government to protect its constitutional rights and affirm its vision of federalism.

The Key Pillars of the Quebec Position

At the heart of the Quebec vision of federalism lie six major elements: dualism, provincial autonomy, respect for provincial jurisdiction, accountability, equality of conditions and social cohesion. These elements constitute the backdrop for Quebec-Canada relations since the mid-1940s.

Dualism

The first pillar on which the Quebec vision of federalism is founded is certainly the coexistence of two founding peoples with their specific traditions, lifestyles, institutions and cultures. It is on this principle of dualism that the theory of the pact between English and French Canadians was built. This pact underlies the very origins of Canada.

The thesis of dualism has been constantly affirmed by Quebec governments. It has also on occasion been put forward by Ottawa, for example, by Lester B. Pearson at the creation of the Laurendeau-Dunton Commission in 1963. But it was judge Thomas-Jean-Jacques Loranger who, in the early 1880s, contributed most to formulating the pact theory. Judge Loranger summed it up in three main propositions:

1. The Canadian Confederation is the result of a pact between the provinces (British colonies) and the Imperial Parliament;
2. The provinces adhere to the federative pact with their former constitutions and their legislative powers that they agreed to partly divest in favour of the central government, while retaining the right to full enjoyment of the non-transferred powers; and
3. The powers of the provinces are the residue of the powers prior to Confederation, and must not be seen as powers conferred by federal authorities.

This vision of Canada resulting from a pact between the member-states and, by extension, the founding nations, has been invoked in a document published by the Royal Commission on Aboriginal Peoples in 1993 that stipulated the inherent rights of first nations.[6] This principle, which is sometimes misunderstood if not totally ignored, is nonetheless the one that has enabled French and English Canadians to co-exist in the vast territory of North America. Respect for this duality has been manifested in many ways over the years; suffice it to mention the Macdonald-Cartier coalition at the origin of Canadian Confederation, the principle of alternating leaders in the Liberal Party of Canada and the Laurendeau-Dunton Commission in the mid-1960s. More recently, the Pepin-Robarts Commission (1977-1979), the 1991 report by the Spicer Commission and the 1998 Supreme Court reference regarding Quebec's right to secede have confirmed the solidity of this thesis as a foundation of the Canadian federation.

Respect for the principle of dualism has nonetheless not prevented successive governments in Quebec from displaying openness to asymmetrical application of constitutional preferences in Canada, providing the contracting parties agree.

Provincial Autonomy

Provincial autonomy is the second pillar of the Quebec constitutional position, and has been ever since it joined the Confederation. This principle emphasizes the idea that Quebec must be granted significant manœuvring room in the federal framework if it wishes to protect and improve the political, cultural and social living conditions of its citizens. This principle has been expressed with varying intensity during the history of Quebec. Premiers Honoré Mercier, Maurice Duplessis and Jean Lesage all defended the idea of greater autonomy for Quebec in the Canadian federation in order to best respond to the expectations of citizens and the political community.

The principle of provincial autonomy is clearly established in the report by the Royal Commission of Inquiry on Constitutional Problems (the Tremblay Report, 1956), Quebec's constitutional response to the report of the Royal Commission on Dominion-Provincial Relations (Rowell Commission, 1940). The Tremblay Report insists particularly on fiscal autonomy as a response to Quebec's demands, as the following quote illustrates: "there can be no federalism without autonomy of the state's constituent parts, and no sovereignty of the various governments without fiscal and financial autonomy."[7] The authors of the Tremblay Report believed that the two orders of government must exercise their responsibilities by fully respecting the sociological reality of two founding peoples, on which each order of government bases its legitimacy.

The Tremblay Report endorsed the principle of subsidiarity by establishing that the government that is situated closest to citizens and the established organizations be the one that assumes the responsibilities. The notion of subsidiarity has been used in another sense in recent years in the context of the European Union. To legitimize their quest for a larger entity, Jacques Delors and other European thinkers simultaneously hailed "downward subsidiarity" in response to critics of centralization and "upward subsidiarity" to propose more efficient action plans.

This concept, essentially perceived as decentralizing, has nevertheless had several manifestations. Note, however, that the Ontario government document that should have been submitted during the Annual Premiers' Conference in August 1996 interpreted the notion of subsidiarity in its original sense, thus converging with the meaning that the Quebec government has always given it. Note also that the Quebec government has never officially embraced the notion of subsidiarity, aware that it may be interpreted differently by the other parties involved and open the door to a new sharing of powers that might prove unfavourable for Quebec.

Respect for Provincial Jurisdiction

In tune with the leading experts on federalism, in particular Kenneth C. Wheare, Quebec's constitutional position has always been founded on the idea that the member-states of the federation and the central government must be able to fulfil their functions in their respective fields while avoiding overlap and duplication. This nonetheless presumes substantial coordination among the orders of government.

The idea of exercising one's constitutional powers without interference has always been a mainstay of the Quebec vision of the federal project to which Quebec political representatives voluntarily subscribed in 1867. This was without renouncing the powers that were not included in the BNA Act of 1867, as defended by the dualist thesis.

For most of period between Confederation and its replacement by Ottawa with the Supreme Court in 1949, the Privy Council in London and the premiers of Quebec and Ontario formed the main ramparts when Ottawa thought it could meddle in areas of provincial jurisdiction. The Privy Council in London acted to ensure that Ottawa respected the sharing of powers as part of the federal principle of non-subordination of powers, stipulating that none of the two orders of government can be subjected to the other in their exclusive areas of responsibility.

Quebec has firmly expressed its willingness to exercise its provincial jurisdictions both internally and externally based on the Gérin-Lajoie doctrine (named after the former minister of education under Jean Lesage), especially since the early 1960s. Overall, there is formal recognition of Quebec's right to affirm its international presence in its areas of jurisdiction, such as culture, education and social policies. This has occasionally led to disputes between Quebec and Ottawa, with the latter perceiving such initiatives by the Quebec government as acts of overt defiance.

Accountability

The notion of accountability refers to the government's obligation to answer to its constituents by displaying the greatest possible transparency. This notion is essential for the efficiency of any federation, because it precludes attempts at direct action by governments in all areas that do not fall under their jurisdiction. Underlying the question of accountability is the use of the federal spending power. This is the subject that has been most criticized by all Quebec premiers since the Royal Commission on Dominion-Provincial Relations in the late 1930s. Politicians of all stripes — from the Union Nationale leader Maurice Duplessis; to Liberals Robert Bourassa, Claude Ryan and Daniel Johnson; and sovereigntists René Lévesque, Pierre Marc Johnson, Jacques Parizeau and Lucien Bouchard — have expressed aversion to its use. Claude Ryan's beige paper in 1980 is very eloquent on this topic.[8] The Meech Lake and Charlottetown Accords also proposed to control the federal spending power by imposing guidelines to foster greater respect for power sharing.

Equality of Conditions

With the advent of the Quiet Revolution and the concomitant rise of the welfare state, Quebec, more than any other member of the Canadian federation, affirmed its willingness to pursue equity objectives rather than simply accepting liberal principles inspired by voluntarism. In order to compensate for the historical imbalances that disproportionately benefited English Quebecers, the Quebec government proposed a vast catch-up program in the sectors of education, health care and social services and transportation, among others, to equip Quebec with first-rate economic, political and social infrastructures.

The process of "catching-up" set in motion in the early 1960s in Quebec quickly engendered a social vision founded on the equality of conditions rather than equality of opportunities. This does not mean, however, that the Quebec government has completely turned its back on so-called liberal economic policies in the past 40 years. Rather, it has favoured economic and social policies that emphasize redistribution of collective wealth. It is worth noting that the referendum of October 30, 1995 pitted the advocates of a redistributive social vision (the forces in favour of sovereignty) against those whose priorities lay with an economic vision founded on the market economy (those seeking to maintain the status quo).

Social Cohesion

The Quebec government has consistently strived to formulate policies that provide the greatest possible cohesion in the development of a specific national political community in North America. Premier Robert Bourassa's decision to make French the only official language of Quebec in 1974 and the enacting in 1975 of the Quebec Charter of Human Rights are two examples. Along the same lines are the adoption in 1977 by René Lévesque of the Quebec Charter of the French Language, and Jacques Parizeau's desire to make French the common language of all Quebecers. More recently, there was the decision ensuing from the Summit Conference on the Economy and Employment in March and November 1996, and the initiative of Premier Bouchard to establish a new family policy founded on the establishment of a $5-a-day day-care system in order to provide maximum manœuvring room to parents who want to return to the workforce. This constant quest to establish better-anchored social bonds has been expressed time and time again. It is in this context that federalists, autonomists and sovereigntists have all demanded more powers for Quebec.

Head-on Collision Between the Principles Defended by the Quebec Government and Those Advanced by the Central Government

We will now evaluate the extent to which the principles defended by successive Quebec governments, both federalist and sovereigntist, were rejected or supported by the central government. In essence, we examine the treatment of the same six principles of dualism, provincial autonomy, respect for provincial jurisdiction, accountability, equality of conditions and social cohesion with regard to the

Social Union Framework Agreement reached between nine provinces, territories and the central government against the will of the Quebec government.

Dualism

The Social Union Framework Agreement utterly disregards the principle of dualism that gave rise to Canada. Ironically, however, its rejection by the Quebec government has had the positive effect of expressing anew the principle of Canadian duality and a firm willingness not to depart from this founding principle of the Canadian federation. This view goes against the political forces outside Quebec, who want to substitute duality with the principle of provincial equality. The objective here is clear: make Quebec a province like the others in the Canadian federation.

It is no coincidence that the formula provided for undertaking Canada-wide initiatives stipulates that they cannot be taken without the consent of a majority of the provinces (i.e., a minimum of six provinces, representing in the worst case scenario barely 15 percent of the Canadian population). Ottawa is using its spending power to modify the responsibilities established by the Constitution, thus calling into question the foundations upon which the Canadian federation was built.

Provincial Autonomy

The central government, by means of its spending power, is seeking to ignore the federal principle of provincial autonomy by imposing Canada-wide objectives on member-states that want to be excluded from the Framework Agreement. The imposition of a uniform Canada-wide vision is intended not to encourage innovation but to constrain the provinces to evolve within the same framework, thus reducing the range of possibilities. The Framework Agreement constitutes an unprecedented assault on provincial autonomy, which is viewed by the central government as counterproductive. It seems that Ottawa is blaming provincial autonomy for blocking individual mobility and running counter to equal opportunities. In the Framework Agreement, Ottawa uses the term "equitable treatment" to justify the implementation of similar public policies, suggesting that the existence of asymmetrical social policies would lead to inequity.

For Quebec's part, successive governments have staunchly defended the right to provincial autonomy. Despite repeated federal assaults to make it disappear, Quebec governments have seen it as an important avenue for innovation and for affirming Quebec's status as a political community.

In this respect it is worth mentioning the impact of the European Union, with its economic and social integration projects, on the living conditions of Europeans. We know that the member-states of the European Union have shrinking manœuvring room to enact policies, and that these policies have tended to sink to the lowest common denominator. This helps improve the market economy but at the same time generally erodes the living conditions of the population.

Respect for Provincial Jurisdiction

The Social Union Framework Agreement hits power-sharing head on in that it allows the central government to infringe (with the consent of the provinces apart from Quebec) on areas of exclusive provincial jurisdiction. There is nothing in the agreement that leads one to envision a policy of give and take. Only the central government emerges as a political winner, while the provinces, at best, see their revenue increase slightly after having been reduced significantly following the establishment of the Canadian transfer in health care and social programs.

Moreover, with regard to respect for jurisdictions, the central government has successfully introduced new roadblocks by imposing on provinces the obligation to inform Ottawa, even before undertaking any new initiatives in their exclusive jurisdictions that may have an impact on another government. This is far from the basic principles of federalism that assume respect for the preferences of each order of government. Here again, this is a constraining initiative that may have a highly negative impact on citizens and governments that wish, for example, to put in place forward-looking redistribution policies to implement programs that reinforce the social bonds among members of a specific political community.

The central government is taking the lead and is seeking to make social policies a shared responsibility by using its spending power as a means of persuasion, without regard for the Canadian Constitution. Armed with a sizeable financial surplus, the central government is calling the shots, imposing its priorities, infringing on areas of constitutionally recognized provincial responsibility and forcing parties that wish to exercise their right to opt out of new programs to stick to Canada-wide objectives established in advance by Ottawa.

Accountability

The notion of accountability is central to all federal systems because it guarantees to citizens that their representatives are obliged to answer for their actions.

It is therefore important that the roles of each order of government be clearly defined. Is this the case in the Framework Agreement of February 4, 1999?

The declarations by the leaders of the main political parties in Quebec are strikingly similar on the dangers that the Framework Agreement sets in motion with respect to the principle of accountability. The leader of the Liberal Party of Quebec, Jean Charest, believes that "federative partners" could have seized the opportunity to better define the respective roles and responsibilities of the federal government and the provinces in sectors covered by the agreement. He further maintains that they should have clearly recognized the preponderance and the supervisory role of the provinces where their fundamental jurisdictions were most evident or risked being most affected.[9] Nothing in the agreement indicates that Ottawa wishes to make the provinces fully accountable. Note that the three months notice on new Canada-wide initiatives that Ottawa proposes to give to individuals and organizations in charge of social assistance and social services, health and post-secondary education erodes the responsibility of provincial political authorities, who are primarily accountable in these jurisdictions. The idea that Ottawa can intervene through new Canada-wide programs by making direct unilateral contributions to voluntary organizations, businesses, students, families, unions, individuals, communities, etc. in provincial domains covered by the Framework Agreement is far from guaranteeing respect for the principle of accountability and runs counter to federative principles. By seeking to interfere in the areas of exclusive provincial jurisdiction, the central government is paving the way for every possible form of duplication and runaway bidding. At its peril, Ottawa is embarking again on competitive federalism, an era generally identified with the Trudeau years.

Equality of Conditions

The Framework Agreement represents a break with the preponderant position in Quebec, since the early 1960s, on equality of conditions. The central government, partly influenced by neo-liberal ideas prevailing in the provinces west of the Outaouais, is now the great defender of the principle of equality of opportunities, whereas between 1968 and 1993 it had deliberately defended the values of a *just society* that were dear to the political formation.

The Framework Agreement rejects all government policies that may affect the mobility of Canadians, even if these policies take into account the reasonable limits existing in all democratic regimes and are specified in the Canadian Charter of Rights and Freedoms of 1982. Compliance with reasonable limits is presented as insufficient because the Framework Agreement specifies that the policies established must concomitantly abide by the principles underlying the Framework Agreement itself. This means that the Framework Agreement takes precedence over the Constitution Act of 1982! All governments, without exception, have three years to comply.

The Framework Agreement does not take into account the particular conditions in each province. One would have expected that the negative impact of the pursuit of the principle of mobility for Quebec society be taken into consideration. Instead, there is a general policy shift condemning all measures that may impair mobility, knowing full well that such policies will inevitably have negative effects on the Quebec economy. It is based on this argument that the Quebec government, strengthened by a large consensus among decision-makers, signed the agreements with Ottawa on manpower training and immigration.

Social Cohesion

The pursuit of an objective as inclusive as mobility — the central government went so far as to make it an essential element of Canadian citizenship — calls into question Quebec policies in areas as diverse as education (differentiated tuition fees, Quebec financial assistance to students), immigration (eligibility criteria), health (home care, community services and drug insurance) and the family (national child benefits). All provincial policies, according to the Framework Agreement of February 4, 1999 must abide by the underlying principles. Note, however, that because Quebec did not sign this agreement, it will be politically difficult for Ottawa to impose the terms and obligations on Quebec.

The only avenue that Quebec has to shield itself from federal impulses would be to demonstrate before the Supreme Court of Canada that its policies and practices are reasonable. There is every indication that the Framework Agreement dramatically erodes the powers of the Quebec government within the current federal system. It would be difficult for the province to implement innovative measures such as those described in the inaugural throne speech of the 36th legislature of the Quebec National Assembly. How can the Quebec government launch a parental leave program that respects the criteria of mobility and equal opportunities if other governments do not wish to do the same? How can it maintain and add to its $5-a-day day-care policy without being taken to task by the other provinces and the central government? Under the framework agreement, the provinces have three years to eliminate distinctions based on residency. How can the Quebec government subsequently launch new programs, programs that, by definition, are established based on residency criteria?

Instead of encouraging new initiatives, the central government is constraining the provinces within their own areas of jurisdiction, calling into question the very raison d'être of federalism that militates in favour of respect for diversity as a means of integration. The central government has chosen to encourage uniformity, denying member-states of the federation the right to diversity. Ottawa sees this right as a discriminating element that must be eliminated.

Conclusion

The proposed rebalancing of the Canadian federation in the Framework Agreement of February 4, 1999 raises fundamental questions for the Quebec government. It is a cause for concern that the central government is imposing its presence on all provincial and territorial governments in areas in which it has no constitutional jurisdiction. The six pillars of the Quebec position have been systematically called into question by the Framework Agreement. Dualism and provincial autonomy are squarely rejected by the agreement. Regarding respect for provincial jurisdictions, the agreement demands that provinces subscribe to the existence of federal spending power within their own areas of jurisdiction, despite the fact that they have long and frequently expressed the wish to abolish this power or at least better control it. Efforts on the part of both orders of government in the past few years to make accountability a fundamental principle of the government of Canada are also called into question by the Framework Agreement because it opens the door to new duplication. The principle of equality of conditions defended by successive governments in Quebec is simply rejected as running counter to the principle of equal opportunities. This principle, for its part, is depicted as reducing differences between the political preferences of national, regional and provincial political communities in Canada. The objectives pursued by the Quebec government to provide its population with strong social bonds that could give the Quebec political community greater cohesion are simply seen as contrary to the homogenizing vision pursued by the central government.

The Quebec government therefore finds itself in a tighter vice than ever in the Canadian federation. It must consequently rely as much as possible on its own political levers to affirm its difference. The Quebec government might, if it deems it appropriate, call on the consultation and dispute-settlement mechanisms laid out in the Framework Agreement. However, even if this grants Quebec an additional forum in which to discuss its position, there are no guarantees as to the final result. Lastly, the Quebec government, despite evident risks, may be forced to appeal to the Supreme Court of Canada to have the right to establish its own priorities in its areas of jurisdiction recognized and to obtain equitable compensation, if applicable.

1 Government of Canada, *Shaping Canada's Future Together* (Ottawa: Minister of Supply and Services, 1991).

2 Thomas Courchene, "ACCESS: a Convention on the Canadian Economic and Social System," Study conducted for the Minister of Intergovernmental Affairs of Ontario (August 1996) reproduced in *Canadian Business Economics*, Vol. 4, no. 4 (July-September, Summer 1996), pp. 3-26.

3 Ministerial Council on Social Policy Reform and Renewal, *Report to Premiers* (December 1995).

4 *Strengthening the Canadian Federation: The Constitution Amendment, 1987* (Ottawa: Government of Canada, 1987), p. 16.

5 *Health Accord*, February 3, 1999.

6 *Partners in Confederation: Aboriginal Peoples, Self-Government, and the Constitution* (Ottawa: Royal Commission on Aboriginal Peoples, 1993), p. 23.

7 See, David Kwavnick (ed.), *The Tremblay Report, Report of the Royal Commission of Inquiry on Constitutional Problems* (Toronto: McClelland & Stewart, 1973), p. 215.

8 See, Quebec Liberal Party, *A New Canadian Constitution/Constitutional Committee of the Quebec Liberal Party* (Montreal: Liberal Party of Quebec, 1980).

9 *La Presse*, February 16, 1999, p. B3.

Federal Spending Power

Introduction

I DO NOT BELIEVE I HAVE TO SPEND A GREAT DEAL OF TIME ON THE RESPONSIBILITIES OF the Canadian Secretariat for Intergovernmental Affairs which involve, on the one hand, the preparation of studies and documents necessary for the participation of the government in the negotiation of intergovernmental agreements and, on the other hand, advising government and entering into bilateral or multilateral discussions and talks at the intergovernmental level in order to ensure that such negotiations are successful.

It seems legitimate to me to wonder whether the current government has been provided with sufficient information and support to closely follow the Social Union Intergovernmental dossier and, whenever necessary, to take part in it. The few documents at my disposal and the information received allow me to state that, with respect to spending power, the government's political branch was provided with fairly complete information. I will use the major portion of a public document to support my point of view: *Québec's Historical Position on the Federal Spending Power 1944-1998.*[1]

Historical Position of Quebec on the Federal Spending Power

There is an essential point of which some commentators seem to have lost track: Quebec's historical position on constitutional questions or on intergovernmental issues is not going to become outdated or obsolete with the passage of time, globalization or the increasing interdependence of peoples and governments. Preserving Quebec's identity and distinctiveness and protecting the powers of the National Assembly are based on fundamental principles that are the basis of the political actions of the government of Quebec. These positions taken by various Quebec governments cannot be otherwise, unless we want to renounce our identity and autonomy.

In order to create an analytical framework within which to understand Quebec's rejection of the Social Union Agreement, I will draw upon some characteristics and information already presented in other contexts.

The Quebec government has always tried to comply with the 1867 Constitution, which assigns exclusive powers to the federal and provincial governments. But, with its spending power, Ottawa can unilaterally launch spending initiatives based on shared-cost programs that it has fully financed or direct payments to individuals or institutions in areas that are entirely within provincial jurisdiction. Left almost without judicial supervision, the spending power means that the federal government can unilaterally change to its advantage the Canadian Constitution, especially to ensure its own visibility.

Whatever the administrative method selected by the federal government (fully financed federal programs or direct spending), its effect on provincial authority is the same: intrusion and encroachment in fields of provincial jurisdiction and on the definition of provincial priorities, and disruption of provincial programs. At the budgetary level, the impact is especially awkward if shared-cost or block-funded programs are involved — the province, not wanting to lose money and see its citizens' taxes used to finance the program in other provinces, therefore agrees to spend in the targeted sector under conditions dictated by the federal government. If the federal contribution is reduced, the province will have to increase its own spending to meet federal conditions or standards. If the federal program is based entirely on federal funding or operates on the basis of payments (in cash or tax credits) to individuals or institutions, the effect is just as negative because it involves overlap or duplication and forces the province to readjust or change its programs or policies.

The reason for this federal dysfunction is the mismatch between governments' fiscal resources and their constitutional responsibilities. Since the Second World War, the federal government has had tax revenues that significantly exceed its responsibilities under the division of legislative jurisdictions. As long as this issue is not settled, the crisis in Canadian federalism will continue. Now that spending power has become the keystone of federalism, the prospect of this question being settled seems rather remote.

Many serious problems ensue from the federal spending power. All Quebec premiers, including the current premier, have been aware of them, and senior public administrators have probably explained them repeatedly to their political principals. These include:

- Lack of compliance with the 1867 Constitution because exclusive provincial powers have become competitive powers subject to federal standards
- Monitoring of provincial powers and orientation of their applications by the federal government
- Corruption of Canadian federalism in which the federal government is now established as the upper, incumbent or unitary government
- Impediment to the introduction of asymmetrical and flexible federalism, because spending power is used as a policy standardization instrument (especially in social matters) and to deny Quebec's distinctiveness
- Increased legislative centralization, subordination of the provinces and decline of provincial autonomy
- Sterilization of shared legislative jurisdictions
- Multiplication of all kinds of programs with overlap, contradiction, piggybacking, conflict and wasted money and energy
- Obligation that the provinces change their priorities and readjust their programs
- Obstacles to efficient provincial planning and budgetary control, especially when the federal government unilaterally opts out of program funding
- Disincentive to fiscal responsibility and government accountability because in many cases it is impossible to know who is responsible for a government initiative or action
- Negation of the subsidiary status principle, which states that the government that is closer to the citizens is in the best position to deal with problems
- Lack of provincial faith in the written Constitution because federalism based on spending power is outside the Constitution and outside judiciare supervision

In this context, Quebec's defensive reaction is understandable. Quebec has insisted on compliance with monitoring of the federal spending power according to the 1867 Constitution. It has consistently demanded fiscal balance or matching of fiscal resources with legislative jurisdictions (responsibilities). Because this demand has been ignored, Quebec has had no choice but to denounce encroachments or intrusions in its fields of jurisdiction and state its will to determine its own priorities, because it is in a better position than is the federal government to meet the needs of its citizens in the fields granted to it by the Constitution of Canada. In reality, this constant refrain by premiers of Quebec has not succeeded in preventing the federal government from launching dozens upon dozens of initiatives or programs. The consequence has been invasion of and glossing over provincial fields of jurisdiction by the federal government since 1950.

The best means Quebec has found to mitigate the effects of this invasive federal presence has been the opting out formula, together with financial or fiscal compensation. By and large, over the past 50 years, each time the federal government has used its spending power to launch an initiative or program in Quebec's fields of jurisdiction, the premier at the time has asked the federal government to allow Quebec to opt out and manage its affairs and be compensated for the amounts it would have spent if the initiative or program had applied to the province. No premier has ever departed from this traditional and constant position.

The problem is that these requests to opt out with compensation have rarely received the approval of the federal government, which is clearly documented in the publication prepared by the Secrétariat aux Affaires intergouvernementales canadiennes, *Québec's Historical Position on the Federal Spending Power 1944-1998*. Quebec won a few points in the early 1960s (subsidies to universities, education allowances, students loans, pension plan and funding for programs established in 1964-77), but the opting out formula has rarely succeeded since then. When opting out is denied, the province is bullied into participating and letting things take their course. Otherwise, it would be depriving its citizens of federal funding and simultaneously funding the service or program in the other provinces. This author has strongly denounced the federal spending power that establishes a domineering and predatory federalism.[2]

Even though Quebec's position is basically defensive and is not a profound departure from the 1867 Constitution's position, it is not shared by the other provinces or the federal government. The other provinces see it as an attempted assault against the federal regime or an outmoded and anachronistic theory of federalism put forward by Quebec separatists or constitutional experts from the dinosaur age. Many, and perhaps even most provinces, feel at ease with the federal spending power and do not see the need to restrict its use.

Very often, if not almost always, Quebec goes it alone in the field of federal spending, regardless of what government is in Quebec City. The episode of the Millennium Scholarship Fund is an example of this fundamental problem, which is a manifestation of practically irreconcilable concepts or approaches to Canadian federalism.

Quebec Had to Participate in the Social Union Agreement Negotiations to the Extent that its Positions Were Favourably Received

Negotiations for this agreement started in February 1998 and Quebec was not an active participant at the beginning. The proposed agreement involved major issues. The provincial governments had to protect social programs and ensure their stability, permanence and soundness against unilateral decisions by the federal government to discontinue funding them. Over the preceding few years all provinces had been hit by drastic federal cuts in cash transfers to the provinces in the fields of health care, social assistance and education. The provinces' prime objective to preserve and promote social programs and protect themselves against the uncertainty and fluctuations in federal funding is understandable in this context. The Canadian social union had to be improved.

However, this commendable objective is only one aspect of the undertaking. For Quebec, the other aspect was the delimitation of the federal presence in establishing, planning, funding and implementing social programs, something that Quebec has always claimed as its primary and exclusive jurisdiction. When the premiers created, at their 1996 annual conference in Jasper, a Federal-Provincial-Territorial Council on Social Policy Renewal, the mandate of which included the issue of a national child benefit as well as the role of provinces in defining national standards, Quebec could not subscribe to it. Quebec could not participate in a procedure that would sanction the legitimacy of the federal presence in its spheres of exclusive jurisdiction. The premier thus took this opportunity to repeat one of Quebec's central claims, that the federal government should withdraw from the social policy field, and insisted on Quebec's right to set its own priorities out of its own taxes.[3] The other provinces spoke of "rebalancing" the roles and responsibilities of Ottawa and the provinces (in fields of provincial jurisdiction), while the Quebec premier defended the integrity of provincial authority against centralization:

> The Government has neither the intention nor the mandate to abandon any dimension of Quebec's constitutional jurisdiction, regardless of whether the operation envisioned is of a constitutional or administrative nature...Quebec governments, regardless of their option regarding Quebec's status, have long sought to strengthen these jurisdictions to favour control by the Quebec people of its social, economic and cultural development. [What the provinces are offering us is centralization, a retreat, a denial of the historic progress of the Quebec people...]
>
> Quebec cannot commit itself to a rebalancing process with general orientations and specific measures that lead to the abandonment of fundamental demands based on the defence of its jurisdictions and their gradual erosion by intergovernmental and administrative means. [What is being offered to Quebec is the creation of a Canadian government that is more powerful, a Canada that is more centralized and less respectful of the wishes of the Quebec people.][4]

Prudence demanded that Quebec not get actively involved in these talks but follow their progress from a distance.

During the August 1997 Annual Premiers' Conference in St. Andrews, Quebec insisted on its position with particular force because it had just been compelled by the federal government to accept the National Child Benefit (an important element of family policy) without the right to opt out. In addition, the other provinces agreed with the concept of an intergovernmental mechanism to develop national standards for social programs jointly with the federal government:

> Quebec intends to maintain control over its social policy directions and choice of priorities, as its government recently showed with its family policy, with the implementation of its pharmacare program and with an alimony payment collection system. The Quebec government is the best positioned government to meet the specific needs of Quebecers.
>
> An intergovernmental mechanism to formulate national standards applicable to social programs would thus pose a direct threat to Quebec's existing prerogative[s] and responsibilities in defining and managing its social policy, exercised under its exclusive jurisdiction in this field. The fact is that such a mechanism would impede Quebec's leeway, i.e. its current capac-

ity to set its own policy directions, priorities and terms for social programs financed by Quebec taxpayers.

Another consequence of such a mechanism would be the admission that the federal government has responsibilities in defining social policy that are not recognized in the Constitution. It would lend legitimacy to the federal government's long-standing claims in this field, which are clearly at odds with the constitution.[5]

This was the appropriate response, and in terms of legitimate government action, Premier Bouchard did not have the mandate to depart from the guidelines that reasonably well-informed citizens expected from their premier.

A few months later, Premier Bouchard told the First Ministers' Conference in Ottawa that the Quebec government would be willing to participate in a task force on the social union if the provinces accepted three major conditions advanced by various Quebec governments regarding the federal spending power:

1. The participants must express an interest in the recognition of a province's unconditional right to withdraw with full compensation in respect of any measure or matter likely to affect an area of provincial jurisdiction and agree that the definition of this right of withdrawal will be a key objective of talks on the umbrella agreement.
2. During the discussions on such an umbrella agreement, all participants, including the federal government, must agree to a moratorium on any new federal government initiative or measure likely to affect an area of provincial jurisdiction...
3. The Quebec proposal must in no way be interpreted as direct or indirect recognition of federal spending power or any federal role whatsoever in the realm of social policy. Moreover, Quebec reaffirms its historic position concerning respect of its field of jurisdiction.[6]

This proposal was rejected.

In March 1998, the Federal-Provincial-Territorial Council on Social Policy Renewal met to start negotiations on a possible social union framework.

The following month, the ministers responsible for negotiations met in Toronto and the Quebec Minister for Canadian Intergovernmental Affairs, with the prior explicit agreement of the Cabinet, repeated Quebec's position as stated in December 1997 by Premier Bouchard:

[Quebec believes that the development, planning and management of social programs are under its sole jurisdiction...The Quebec government is closest to the Quebec people and best placed to respect its aspirations and meet its needs and priorities. For these reasons Quebec has always demanded that it be allowed to opt out, with full fiscal or financial compensation, of any initiative by the federal government financed by its spending power. Quebec

> believes that it must be the sole architect of social initiatives that it defines in accordance with its way of doing things and with its specific reality...]
>
> [Quebec's] position is clear: Quebec requests that the umbrella agreement on the social union recognize its historic position by providing for an unconditional right to opt out with full compensation in respect of any new initiative or new federal program, whether jointly funded or not, in the sectors of social programs within the jurisdiction of the provinces. [This position is in compliance with the guidelines which the Quebec government adopted last December regarding the way it is to carry out its Canadian intergovernmental relations.
>
> Without the possibility of such unconditional opting out with financial compensation, Quebec could not in any way take part in any Social Union Framework Agreement project negotiated between the federal government and the other governments. Not to recognize the right of Quebec to opt out with financial compensation of any federal initiative in the field of social policies is to refuse to clearly recognize Quebec's specific reality, its distinct character. It confirms that the recognition of the unique character of Quebec proposed by the Calgary Declaration is purely symbolic.
>
> The guaranteed right of opting out with full financial compensation is an inescapable condition of the participation of Quebec in negotiations concerning a possible social union project.][7]

Although this author could not obtain documentation on this topic, it is likely that the provinces, with the exception of Quebec, continued their discussions. Two months later, they succeeded in defining "a common position on the question of the limitation of the federal spending power, which is close to Quebec's historic position."[8] A consensus had been reached. This consensus developed among the provinces and materialized in June 1998 at the interprovincial meeting of ministers responsible for negotiating the social union agreement.

In June 1998, the conditions had therefore been met for Quebec to take an active part in the negotiations related to a social union project.

The Saskatoon Consensus: A Promising and Acceptable Position

IT IS THEREFORE IN THIS CONTEXT THAT PREMIER BOUCHARD WENT TO SASKATOON in early August 1998 for the 39th Annual Premiers' Conference. This was the context of an opening up by the provinces (not by the federal government) to Quebec's demands. (The federal government conveyed its proposal to the provinces on July 16, 1998.)

The conference press release contained a number of principles that promised a favourable outcome to the negotiations:

- Willingness of premiers to protect social programs
- Willingness of governments to work together, in compliance with their constitutional jurisdiction, to ensure solid and durable social services
- Provincial/territorial consensus on the position in preparation for negotiations with the federal government
- Recognition of the incomplete but promising nature of federal proposals
- Existence of areas of convergence due to negotiating progress

The essential points of the press release clearly included Quebec's fundamental claims in the constitutional field:

> Premiers noted that...collaborative arrangements on federal spending in areas of provincial/territorial jurisdiction, and a fair dispute resolution process are essential to a balanced and fair partnership...
>
> Premiers noted that the federal proposals contain provisions for opting out. Premiers emphasized that the flexibility afforded to provinces/territories through the ability to opt out of any new or modified Canada-wide social program in areas of provincial/territorial jurisdiction with full compensation, provided that the province/territory carries on a program or initiative that addresses the priority areas of the Canada-wide program, is an essential dimension of the provincial/territorial consensus negotiating position.
>
> ...
>
> Premiers emphasized that Canada's Social Union, and the programs that Canadians value most, particularly health care, must be supported by renewed fiscal arrangements that balance provincial/territorial program responsibilities with revenues.
>
> Premiers concluded their discussions on the Framework Agreement negotiations by reiterating the negotiating ground rule that no element of the Framework Agreement is agreed to until everything is agreed to.

There were four major possible gains for Quebec's negotiators:

1. An intergovernmental cooperation formula on federal spending power: in essence, the premiers were looking for critical limits to this federal power
2. The provincial right to opt out of any new or modified social program with full compensation, provided the province opting out offers a program in the same field — this was better than the Meech Lake Accord, which applied only to new programs
3. Fiscal arrangements to ensure a balance between provincial tax revenues and their legislative jurisdiction — this was probably the most promis-

ing element and the most likely to harmonize and civilize relations between Ottawa and the provinces

4. The fundamental character, "for the negotiations," of the rule requiring that the framework agreement be an integrated and indissociable package — the provinces would accept no element of the agreement without a satisfactory agreement on the whole package.

In joining the common front of the provinces while confirming "the fundamental all or nothing rule for negotiations," Premier Bouchard did much more than express his satisfaction in finding that the new parameters of the social union negotiation complied with the guidelines of Quebec's position. He gave his agreement in principle to Quebec's participation in the negotiations and accepted the fundamental rule (subject of course to Cabinet approval and confirmation of this procedure and especially its authorization of future participation of ministers or the premier). Even the federal government understood that "[t]he Premier of Quebec joined the discussions on August 7."[9]

Subsequent government statements to the effect that Quebec would participate in federal/provincial/territorial social union negotiations were merely part of the follow-up to Premier Bouchard's decision in principle made on August 7 to participate in the negotiations. All the premiers of the other provinces must have understood the Saskatoon communiqué as including Quebec's commitment in principle to participating in the social union discussions.

In conclusion, the communiqué states positions and a fundamental rule for negotiations. It obviously leaves some leeway for negotiating, since it is understood by the premiers that no element of the framework agreement project will be dropped as long as the agreement has not been accepted as a whole. But all in all the Saskatoon communiqué was extremely promising for Quebec.

The Victoria Proposal: The Best Position for Quebec

NEGOTIATIONS CONTINUED IN SEPTEMBER AND OCTOBER AND WERE INTERRUPTED during the Quebec election campaign. During this campaign, the Quebec premier confirmed Quebec's participation in the social union negotiations. Following the election, negotiations resumed in December 1998 and Quebec took an active part in them. Each attending minister received prior approval from the Cabinet, which also approved the position taken by the Quebec negotiators.

In preparing for negotiations with the federal government, Quebec then had to develop and clarify a joint position. The result of the joint front was the document: "Securing Canada's Social Union into the 21st Century, Draft Paper for Discussion Purposes only" dated January 29, 1999, the Victoria proposal. As well put together as this document was, the negotiating position it contained proved to be fragile only a few days after its adoption. In short, the joint position of the provinces did not hold very long. This suggests that our provincial partners did not have an unshakeable commitment to the joint position and had adopted it somewhat reluctantly without the deep conviction that inspired the Quebec delegation.

Following are the major characteristics of the joint position:

- It aimed to reflect Canadian values;
- It aimed to ensure the permanence, stability and funding of social programs and the accountability of governments;
- It aimed to match the tax and financial resources of provinces and their constitutional obligations;
- It reiterated the prime provincial responsibility for the creation of social policies and the implementation of social programs. It also mentioned the importance of the federal role in the social union;
- It aimed to clarify the roles and responsibilities of both government orders and to reduce duplication;
- It insisted on the necessity for adequate, stable and foreseeable financial arrangements; and
- It emphasized working together in partnership.

Chapter 5 affects the subject of this study and I will examine it more closely now. This chapter proposes both cooperative initiatives and approaches.

Collaborative Initiatives

The provincial governments postulated that, in sectors of shared responsibility and even in the case of actions of one government in its own fields of jurisdiction that significantly affect another order of government, the means of managing common interests must be improved. For this purpose, the provinces proposed a series of initiatives to support approaches to deal with federal power. It may be useful to recall that these proposals later re-emerged, in part, in the Social Union Framework Agreement (and the federal government ignored them in the federal budget):

- Advance Notice and Information Sharing
  Each order of government shall give the other written notice of any change proposed to a social policy or program in any area in which the actions of one government significantly affect another government. At the same time that notice of the proposed social policy or program change is given, written information about the change will be provided in sufficient detail to enable the receiving government to assess it adequately.
- Mandatory Consultation
  The government initiating the change shall be required to engage in meaningful consultation, including consideration of alternative initiatives, with the other government to ensure that the proposed change did not duplicate effort or operate in a counterproductive manner. Consultation could result in further collaborative action.
- Joint Priority Setting
  Governments agree to set joint overarching priorities. Where appropriate, governments also agree to broad goals, objectives and strategic directions for those priorities identified.
- Outcome Measurement and Public Reporting
  Governments agree to measure key social policy outcomes with a view to reporting on their actions to the public.

Cooperative Approaches to Spending Power in Canada-wide Social Programs

The provinces agreed to cooperate to reach a consensus when federal spending on Canada-wide programs falls within fields of provincial jurisdiction. They believed that the notion of flexibility in developing and implementing programs is an essential component of social programs. The ability of the provinces to address priority aspects of Canada-wide programs was deemed essential for the effective operation of the social union. The consent formula is necessary to pursue the cooperation described in step I:

Step I – Cooperation

- Joint priority-setting on federal cash and tax expenditures on new or modified Canada-wide programs in areas of provincial jurisdictions.
- Joint agreement on objectives and principles for new or modified Canada-wide programs, including:

> - Program flexibility which respects provincial/territorial priorities,
> - Clear roles and responsibilities for each order of government, and,
> - A commitment to reduce and avoid overlap and duplication.
>
> ◆ Agreement to develop, measure and publicly report on outcomes of new and modified Canada-wide programs, consistent with each government's roles and responsibilities.
>
> ◆ Agreements should incorporate measures to ensure the adequacy and certainty of funding.
>
> Step II – Flexibility
>
> Where the collaborative approach in Step 1 does not achieve agreement, the following provisions will be invoked...

It should be noted that the flexibility step was actually less flexible than the first step. It involved more monitoring of the spending power and more protection of provincial rights than the first step, which was ill-defined, consensual and deliberative. Let us examine the two fundamental principles of the second step, which offered provinces the protection and leeway that Quebec had always sought:

> Any new or modified Canada-wide program in areas of provincial jurisdiction requires the consent of a majority of provinces. The consent of the territories will be sought.
>
> The federal government will provide full financial compensation to any provincial or territorial government that chooses not to participate in any new or modified Canada-wide program, providing it carries on a program or initiative that addresses the priority areas of the new or modified Canada-wide program.

The above statements concern Canada-wide programs resulting from the federal spending power, which do not consist of Canada-wide programs only. Quebec, which has always considered it necessary to subject all federal spending in fields of provincial jurisdiction to the prior consent of the province or provinces concerned, found in the following text a positive response, contained in the Victoria proposal: "Federal spending in an area of provincial jurisdiction which occurs in a province or territory must have the consent of the province or territory involved."

Comments

- The Victoria joint position met Quebec's consistent demands
- It applied to any initiative or any federal measure in Quebec's fields of jurisdiction

- Consent of the provinces was required to change an existing program or launch a new program
- Failing an agreement, the joint position recognized the right to opt out with compensation to the province that did not participate in the program if it had a program that met the range of priorities of the federal program
- For the first time in Canada, the other provinces recognized and accepted Quebec's argument and position
- It integrated the best Quebec position, which was that presented by Robert Bourassa during a constitutional conference in Ottawa on August 21, 1992. Premier Bourassa's proposal was heavily covered by the media, and included the following statements:

> Essentially, Quebec is not looking for massive jurisdictional transfers: It is looking for compliance with the 1867 Constitution.
>
> It is difficult to speak of power sharing without first protecting provincial powers against the intrusions of the federal government through its spending power. It would be useless to obtain new powers if the provinces do not also obtain the management of all initiatives in their fields of exclusive jurisdiction...In all the areas of jurisdiction of the provinces, Quebec asks that:
>
> (1) the federal government may only use its spending power after an agreement with the provinces which want it;
>
> (2) current terms and conditions of the exercise of the spending power be negotiated within a given period of time, upon the request of a province and in the areas that it may want to identify;
>
> (3) failing a formal agreement in either case, any province be granted complete withdrawal of the federal government, together with appropriate and permanent compensation when it commits itself to implement a measure compatible with freely agreed upon national objectives that would be defined at the Annual Premiers' Conferences.[10]

The Victoria proposal is very comparable with Bourassa's proposal, which was rejected out of hand by the federal government and the provinces. There are nevertheless some differences between the two documents (which are more apparent than real):

- *Existing* federal programs were clearly targeted by the Bourassa proposal, but the Victoria proposal included them only when they were modified.
- Bourassa's proposal would have made it necessary to renegotiate the terms and conditions of existing programs at the request of a

province. Such renegotiations could have led to the acceptance of a consent formula involving seven provinces representing at least 50 percent of the population of Canada, and eventually to the acceptance of the rule of "consent by a majority of provinces" laid out in the joint position.

- A consent formula concerning existing programs would certainly have been applicable to new programs.
- Bourassa's proposal made opting out subject to implementation by the province of a measure compatible with national objectives that are freely agreed to and defined by the First Ministers' Conference. The Victoria proposal subjects opting out to a less constraining condition, i.e., the implementation of a program or initiative "that addresses the priority areas of the new or modified Canada-wide program."

In short, except for the expression "consent of a majority of provinces," which required qualification, the Victoria proposal and Bourassa's 1992 autonomist position are equivalent.[11] Bourassa's proposal remains an excellent point of reference.

On this point, the addition of Robert Bourassa's proposal and the Victoria proposal would have improved the 1987 Meech Lake Accord, which only dealt with new shared-cost Canada-wide programs (Meech subjected opting out to a point that seems to be more demanding than the Victoria joint position, i.e., "the province carries on a program or initiative compatible with the national objectives"[12]).

The Social Union Framework Agreement: Diametrically Opposed to the Saskatoon Consensus and the Victoria Proposal

Chapter 5 of the Social Union Framework Agreement is called "The Spending Power – Improving Social Programs for Canadians." Quebec did not sign this administrative agreement, which was reached at the executive level. It has been noted that the "framework" in question is not very binding. The legislative branch of the signatory governments can freely set it aside, since the federal Parliament and provincial legislatures are not bound by intergovernmental contracts or agreements. However, governments entertain reasonable and legitimate expectations that conventions and agreements between executives will be respected.

The Framework Agreement is based on certain principles (chapter 1) to which governments are "committed" "within their respective constitutional jurisdictions and powers." Two of the principles outlined in the first ministers' commitments are relevant to this study: "Ensure access for all Canadians, wherever they live or move in Canada, to essential social programs and services of reasonably comparable quality" and "Ensure adequate, affordable, stable and sustainable funding for social programs."

At first sight, these principles are incontrovertible. Their application in the agreement will imply the dogma of unified social programs and the consecration of the spending power.

The Framework Agreement expresses or represents the federal position. An explanation of why the Victoria proposal was dropped will be presented later.

Social Transfers to Provinces and Territories: Tribute to the Federal Spending Power

The first paragraph of chapter 5 praises the federal spending power in terms that suggest that there are no problems. It states that the use of the federal spending power under the Constitution has been essential to the development of Canada's social union. In fact, it could have said that the social union could have developed otherwise without recourse to a federal power that changes the country's Constitution. Nevertheless, the document is accurate when it states that the spending power has often been used to erect the system described in the Framework Agreement ("transfer money to the provincial and territorial governments" and "support the delivery of social programs and services by provinces" in order to "pursue Canada-wide objectives"). But pursuing federal objectives in areas of provincial jurisdiction does not necessarily militate in favour of such a system erected on the basis of the spending power.

To put it plainly, the first paragraph of chapter 5 trivializes all the excesses of the spending power and all its intrusions into provincial fields.

The second paragraph of chapter 5 is written in the same spirit and pursues the ode to shared-cost or block-funded programs in provincial fields. They are described as "Conditional social transfers" that "have enabled governments to introduce new and innovative social programs, such as Medicare, and to ensure that they are available to all Canadians." This type of language praises both the federal role and the universal nature of programs authorized by the federal presence.

The rest of the paragraph pursues this process of recognition of the spending power ("When the federal government *uses* such conditional transfers, whether shared-cost or block-funded") and states that the federal government should proceed in a "cooperative manner that is mindful of the provincial...governments and their priorities." [my emphasis].

In fact, this text and what follows it sanctions the perfect legitimacy of the spending power and ways of operating that give a free hand to the federal government to do what it wants and raid provincial fields. The prime minister did not fail to highlight the federal gain in a press release issued on February 4, 1999 when he mentioned a "new approach to the federal spending power that enshrines its essential role in the Canadian social union."[13]

Funding Predictability: Consultation and Prior Notice (Without Meaning)

The section entitled "Funding Predictablity" includes two commitments or obligations on the part of the federal government: the obligation to consult before renewing or modifying existing social programs and the obligation to include due notice provisions in any new social transfers to the provinces.

Consultation

The text states that "the Government of Canada will consult with provincial and territorial governments at least one year prior to renewal or significant funding changes in existing social transfers to provinces/territories, unless otherwise agreed."

The obligation to consult:

- is applicable starting February 4, 1999
- involves any renewal or significant fund changes in existing social transfers to the provinces

- applies to all existing social transfers, whether shared-cost or block-funded (health care, education, social assistance) and programs fully funded by the federal government (e.g., the federal program concerning the university research centre network)
- applies "unless otherwise agreed"

Prior Notice

The federal government has to include due notice provisions in any new social transfers to the provinces. Therefore, the federal government is committed to include due notice provisions concerning any renewal or change in the statutes and programs that provide for new social transfers (whether shared-cost or block-funded).

Comments

The obligation to consult mentioned here belongs more to the political than the legal field. Formulated in ill-defined terms, it does not provide for the mode or scope of such consultation. Consultation must take place "at least one year prior" to such changes. But, starting February 4, 1999, for any renewal or significant funding changes in existing social transfers, there is at the very least a political obligation for the federal government not to proceed with such transfer renewals or changes without prior consultation with the provinces about its project. The word "consult" here certainly implies providing sufficient information to the provinces about the federal project and the reaction of the provinces over the following year. During the consultation period, the moratorium should apply. Yet, the federal government did not comply when it announced the reform of the criteria for the Canadian social transfer sharing in its budget of February 1999.

There is a problem with such commitments at the level of approval of such non-compliant cases. Since the agreement comes under the administrative level, and Parliament (including the legislatures) has paramount authority in this case, statutes, including budget statutes, prevail over the agreement from a legal point of view.[14] In constitutional law, it could be argued that, on this point (the commitment to consult), the Framework Agreement includes a constitutional convention, and that actions that infringe on it are "unconstitutional" within the meaning of a Supreme Court decision.[15] But one of the conditions of the existence of such an alleged constitutional convention, that of compliance with precedents, is rather difficult to establish.

New Canada-Wide Initiatives Supported by Transfers to Provinces/Territories: Illusory Protection for the Provinces

The Limited Cooperation Regime in the Definition of Federal Policies

It must be stressed that new federal initiatives include all initiatives in health care, post-secondary education, social assistance and social services that are funded through transfers to the provinces, whether they are shared-cost or fully funded federally. With respect to these initiatives, which are under provincial jurisdiction, the Government of Canada is committed to

- Work in cooperation with all provincial and territorial governments to determine Canada-wide priorities and objectives; and
- Not initiate Canada-wide programs without the consent of a majority of the provinces

This means that the federal government may launch any shared-cost program or any federal funding measure that is within provincial jurisdiction with the agreement of only six provinces, irrespective of their population. It may also set Canada-wide priorities and objectives for any new federal shared-cost or block-funded program involving a transfer of cash to the provinces. The text is not very clear about the obligation to agree on priorities and objectives according to the majority rule (the majority rule appears at the level of the creation of the initiative). However, the majority consent formula that appears at the end of the text of both commitments mentioned above would also govern the definition of priorities and objectives of the programs. At least, this is how it is understood by the author of the document (the federal government), which also recognizes that the new regime includes "by far the largest proportion of provincial/territorial program spending, including what provincial and territorial governments have identified as their top priority – health care."[16]

Several commentators have criticized this notion of "the consent of the majority of the provinces" and have rightly denounced the democratic flaw contained in it. Essentially, the federal government could convince six small provinces representing 15 percent of the Canadian population to launch a new program, set its conditions and objectives and impose them on the majority of the population, which might not want it. As a matter of principle, such criticism seems well founded, but in reality the federal government would hesitate to implement a project that was disliked or rejected by the major provinces.

However, many criticisms could have been avoided if the agreement had combined the requirement of a majority of the population with that of a majority of the provinces.

This omission should not be used as a *casus belli*. The Quebec government itself proposed in 1976 that any exercise of the spending power be subject to the approval of a majority of the provinces.[17] Twenty years later in the Speech from the Throne, the federal government committed itself to refrain from using its spending power to create new programs in areas of exclusive provincial jurisdiction without the consent of a majority of the provinces. The idea was therefore not entirely new when the premiers adopted it in their Victoria proposal.

The problem does not lie in the deficiency of the consent formula. The general framework of the agreement welcomes the federal government into areas of provincial jurisdiction with open arms, gives it considerable freedom of action and initiative with the most anti-federalist instrument of intervention available, locks the provinces into their own domestic affairs and will not let them get out of the federal headlock that will result from this model. In real life, the provinces are going to have to participate in the discussions on priorities and objectives and are, in the normal course of things, going to accept the federal money, the programs and their norms. The very rare dissenters will have no other choice but to follow, because their right to do it alone or to opt out is an illusion. In short, the proposed regime is more closely related to an authoritarian centralist regime than to a flexible federalist regime.

To conclude, these remarks may well be relegated to the exclusive realm of political theory, because in the reality of government operations, at this point it is difficult to imagine new federal initiatives being funded through transfers to the provinces.

Moreover, the federal government does not have to abide by the mechanism of the required consent of a majority of the provinces that applies to shared-cost programs. It can easily ignore its own commitments and proceed differently and unilaterally, as was so clearly shown in such files as the National Child Benefit, the Millennium Scholarship Endowment Fund, the Canada Foundation for Innovation and the funding of research and research centres.

Theoretical Right of Provincial Governments to Determine the Detailed Program Design and the Mix Best Suited to Their Needs

I read with considerable surprise the statement on the theoretical right of provinces to determine the program design and mix best suited to them: "Each provincial and territorial government will determine the detailed program design and mix best suited to its own needs and circumstances *to meet the agreed objectives*." [my emphasis]

This is simply begging the question, since the right of the provinces to determine the detailed program design and mix best suited to their needs and circumstances must be exercised "to meet the agreed objectives." Since these objectives are likely to be federal objectives endorsed by a simple majority of provinces, the right or leeway of the provinces is quite illusory because they must first meet the agreed objectives. I will show below that meeting the agreed objectives is a pressing necessity, because the commitment to meet Canada-wide objectives is the *sine qua non* for receiving federal funding.

From now on, it will be difficult, in the field of Canadian constitutional law, to speak of provincial autonomy in domains set aside in the Constitution for the provinces. If one province were to opt for a program that suited its needs and circumstances but did not meet the objectives agreed upon (between the federal government and six provinces), it would be penalized to such a degree that its only option would be to faithfully meet the Canada-wide objectives as they are defined.

Opting Out Formula or Right to Compel?

Of all Quebec's claims over the last 50 years, the right to opt out with compensation from federal programs funded by the spending power is one of the most important and consistent. This is not only because this claim is based on an autonomist measure that is peculiar to federalism, but also because it expresses Quebec's distinctiveness. The Framework Agreement is especially harmful in this respect, since it ignores and rejects Quebec's consistent claims and confirms that Canadian federalism is unable to renew itself to accommodate the needs of a distinct Quebec.

Right of a Province to Reinvest Federal Funds That Are Not Required: Conditions of Exercise

According to the agreement, any provincial government that does not require the total transfer to fulfil the agreed objectives because of its existing programming would be able to reinvest any funds not required in the same or related priority area.

The right or possibility for a province to "reinvest" part of the federal transfer (i.e., the amounts that the federal government would normally spend in the province and transfer to it) is subject to several conditions:

(a) The province must have its own programming (programs, measures, initiatives, policies, etc.)

(b) This programming must enable it to meet the agreed upon Canada-wide objectives

(c) The portion of the federal transfer that is not required to fulfill the objectives must be "reinvested" (not "spent") in the same *priority area* or in a "related" priority area

The plan to monitor the spending of public funds by the provinces outlined in the text is not really equal to the opting out formula, which allows for both flexibility and distinctiveness. If, for the sake of discussion, we want to call this "right to reinvest" an opting out right, we would have to agree that such an opting out right does not exist if a province does not have a program. In this case, the province must create one and meet the agreed objectives before it can reinvest the portion of the transfer it does not require (not very likely) in the same priority area. On the other hand, if the province is already in the race for "agreed" objectives, the odds are that these will be at the upper extreme of the province's objectives, so that the right to reinvest is nothing but an illusion or a utopia. In all cases, the provinces must do "the same thing" before they can access the right to "reinvest" in the same priority area. To claim, therefore, that the agreement recognizes the capacity and liberty of the provinces to implement social programs suited to their needs would indicate a rather careless reading of the agreement.

Obviously such a mechanism of constraint in federal-provincial relations could not be accepted. It would lead to control and supervision by the federal government of activities that are under provincial jurisdiction, and the provinces would have to render accounts. Is their programming adequate to meet Canada-wide objectives? Have they sufficiently met the national objectives in any given case? What portion of the federal transfer is available to them to reinvest in the same or related priority area? Is the related priority area selected by the province allowable?

This is so restrictive, controlling and stifling that it would not leave much room for flexibility and distinctiveness. Thus, the uniformity of social policies that is typical of unitary regimes becomes a fundamental feature of the Canadian political organization. This agreement proves to be much more controlling and constraining than the Meech Lake Accord, which provided a true opting out formula and only demanded that the provincial measure be compatible with the national objectives. It contains more constraints than did the February 1996 Speech from the Throne, in which the federal government committed itself to give the provinces the right to opt out "provided they establish equivalent or comparable initiatives." One can look to the 1992 Beaudoin-Dobbie Report to imagine a system that so much resembles a mandatory supervision regime used by parole boards in criminal law.[18]

Other Conditions to Obtain Federal Transfers

At the end of the item dealing with new initiatives supported by transfers to the provinces, the agreement sets two additional conditions for provinces to meet in order to receive funding.

- Their government must meet or commit to meet the agreed Canada-wide objectives
- Their government must commit to respect the accountability framework

The accountability framework does not exist yet, but what we know of it again reinforces the constraining and rigid character of the model.[19] In the Framework Agreement, the signatories committed to agree on an accountability framework concerning "new social initiatives and investments" (chapter 5). The provinces will therefore be associated with the development of an account-rendering mechanism for spending from federal transfers, and will of course have to comply with this mechanism to receive a share of the available funding. This is one more step toward provincial subservience to the new laws born of a partnership with the federal government in areas of exclusive provincial jurisdiction.

The first condition mentions the obligation to meet agreed national or Canada-wide objectives or a commitment by the province to meet them. This new institutional or contractual mechanism does not accord with the fundamental principle of provincial autonomy. Not only is this interference in provincial spheres by the federal government with its programs, but the new code of conduct will demand that the provinces commit themselves to meeting the national objectives in order to receive funding.

These new approaches or new procedures originate in an undesirable concept of Canadian federalism. Nevertheless, any experimenting with new approaches or procedures could well be hypothetical or virtual, because the federal government makes little use of new initiatives funded by transfers to the provinces, instead preferring direct federal funding.

Direct Federal Spending: Royal Road to the Invasion of Provincial Fields

The Social Union Framework Agreement is one of the great victories of the federal intergovernmental machine. For Quebec, whose duty it was not to append its signature, I hesitate to speak of a failure. This would presuppose, to a certain degree, that its current or past premiers, as well as the public administration, had failed in their analyses, establishment of files, operational support and intergovernmental negotiations. This was not the case. The implications of the developments in early February cannot be measured according to deficient concepts of gains or losses. I will return to this later. For the time being, before strategic and more political considerations can be stated, we must complete the analysis of the "Direct federal spending" item.

Under the title "Direct federal spending," the document endorses spending power as direct transfers with a definition that is trivializing and legitimating: "Another use of the federal spending power is making transfers to individuals and to organizations in order to promote equality of opportunity, mobility, and other Canada-wide objectives."

The spending power is presented as normal and justified because it aims at promoting equal opportunity, mobility and other federal objectives. The text does not mention *agreed upon* Canada-wide objectives but simply "Canada-wide objectives," in other words, federal objectives that are defined unilaterally by the federal government. We know that this element of the spending power is increasingly becoming the preferred federal instrument to intervene in the fields of health care, post-secondary education, social assistance and social services. This is clearly shown by certain federal initiatives, in particular, the National Child Benefit, the Canada Foundation for Innovation, the Health Transition Fund, the Millennium Scholarship Fund and the funding of research and research centres.

Yet the rule of conduct that the agreement assigns to the federal government when it launches "new Canada-wide initiatives through direct transfers to individuals and organizations" in the above-mentioned fields seems extremely simple and even lightweight:

- The federal government "will, prior to implementation, give at least three months notice and offer to consult," and
- Governments participating in these consultations will have the opportunity to identify potential duplication and to propose alternative approaches to achieve flexible and effective implementation

This system is not binding and does not set out guidelines for this element of the spending power:

- The federal government has no legal obligation to give notice and consult since the budget legislation that funds spending initiatives is not under the control of the political commitment assumed by the federal government.
- The obligation to give at least three months due notice is meaningless since neither the addressee of the notice nor the contents or form of the notice are given. A three-month general notice issued in the Gazette Canada would suffice.
- The commitment to *offer to consult* is so poorly defined that it is meaningless. The federal government does not commit itself to consult the provincial governments. It commits itself to "offer to consult." For example, an offer to consult made to some hand-picked governments or to a few individuals, services or accommodating organizations would be quite sufficient: This type of consultation is a sham.
- The opportunity given to individuals or organizations to identify potential duplication and propose alternative approaches does not mean very much either, since such consultation can take place privately and the expressed advice does not bind the federal government.
- This alleged supervision of the spending power here is far from what Quebec has consistently asked for (prior consent and withdrawal) and what the provinces agreed to in the Victoria proposal. Opting out with compensation has been completely erased.
- This very informal way of proceeding will facilitate the federal social programs that ensure federal visibility, but will continue to disrupt provincial priorities and policies.
- The provinces do not need to stick to objectives or any accountability framework: it does not apply here.

Implications of Agreement: Decline of Provincial Areas of Jurisdiction and Increased Federal Uniformity

THE TEXT OF THE FRAMEWORK AGREEMENT IS OBVIOUSLY MARKED WITH THE FEDERal seal and can in no way be compared with the Saskatoon consensus (August 1998) or the Victoria proposal (January 1999). Seen from the point of view of Quebec's positions, chapter 5 of the Framework Agreement is a step backward and produces a situation that is worse than the *status quo*. Indeed, it contains a monitoring of the spending power that is so flexible that the federal government will find few, if any, restraints. For the first time in the history of intergovernmental relations, the provinces, with the exception of Quebec, have confirmed and recognized the legitimacy of the spending power and have given Ottawa the green light to intervene in all areas of exclusive provincial jurisdiction.

The document cannot be compared with the Meech Lake Accord, which went as far as to include a true opting out formula with compensation and had been very careful to add a safe clause to avoid any recognition of the spending power and any extension of federal power. The Meech Lake Accord did not give Ottawa *carte blanche* to meddle in provincial matters through social programs funded by transfers to individuals and organizations. Nor did it give the federal government the possibility, with respect to social programs funded through transfers to the provinces, to come to an agreement on new programs, priorities and objectives with six small provinces, whose contribution to funding would be small, and impose them on the other provinces.

The Framework Agreement puts in place all the levers and instruments for centralization and for reducing Quebec's distinctiveness. The federal government is crowned top government and the provinces will become its branches or franchises. It will practice a sham joint management with the provinces, but the model adopted is actually closer to a unitary government. It will be able to impose its priorities and its programs in all sectors on the provinces and on all organizations: hospitals, community centres, health services, high schools, research centres, universities, school boards, libraries, etc. Nothing will escape its ability to intervene.

The worst part of this model is the inability of the provinces to do otherwise and protect themselves. They will have to participate and comply. They will have no veto right and no real right to opt out of a program with compensation. They should at least have obtained paramount or overriding authority to define and manage social programs adapted to their populations and to their own reality. This is not at all the case.

The dogma of uniformity will prevail and any concept of flexibility, adaptation and distinctiveness will have to give way to Canada-wide standards and objectives. The provinces will regret the small margin of manœuvre they have given themselves. They have now imprisoned themselves inside the shackles of Canada-wide standards, priorities, conditions and objectives, to which will be added a framework of accountability and account rendering.

For Quebec, the agreement sounds the death-knell of an asymmetrical Canada and of anything that might resemble a regime of special or specific treatment. For Quebec this document marks the end of the opting out agreements of the 1960s and special agreements such as those involving immigration or manpower (1991 and 1997). It is hard to see how the fundamental principles or underlying philosophy of the Social Union Framework Agreement could allow a repetition of these agreements. The agreement also buries Quebec's claims regarding spending power: it is closed for three years and it is applicable now. It can be renegotiated in three years, but by then it will be too late to recover the ground lost and insist upon our traditional positions. There is a risk that it will become permanent.

The federal Constitution has been weakened by these intergovernmental manipulations and clearly slipped toward centralization. The field of social policy, which Quebec has always considered to be its exclusive responsibility, has been reclassified and is now in the class of joint or shared responsibilities, with clear federal supremacy. The powers of the National Assembly are therefore reduced: In the field of social policy, the social union agreement is in large measure what the Canadian Charter was with regard to the powers of the National Assembly (except that the courts will not ensure that the agreement is carried out). In short, the National Assembly will find it difficult to claim that Quebec is master of its own domestic affairs. The "predatory" federalism, identified by Robert Bourassa, has now been given a clean bill of health.

Canadian federalism has lost one opportunity to renew itself other than through centralization. It has ignored a rare and previously unheard of province-wide consensus that could, if it had been accepted by Ottawa, have sent a message of hope to the Quebec autonomist federalists who look for shared accommodation, pooling, and respect for Quebec distinctiveness. The confrontational climate between Quebec and the government of Canada can only persist. Certain commentators might say that it is because of the Quebec premier's "separatist" label that an agreement that corresponded with the joint position could not be obtained, but this claim does not have much validity when one recalls that Premier Bourassa had suffered an even more bitter failure with a proposal that resembled the Victoria consensus.

The inescapable conclusion here is that the Quebec premier could not and should not have signed such a deal. In not signing, he recognized nothing and did not create a damaging precedent. He also did not risk incurring financial losses for Quebec. On the other hand, if he had signed, our premier would have agreed with directions that are substantially unacceptable, inadmissible and obviously irreparable. There is no question of Quebec subscribing to a permanent and structuring presence of the federal government in its own fields of jurisdiction, thereby renouncing its own identity. Premier Bouchard did not sign because Quebec's values and the concepts on which they are based are still relevant, comply with its fundamental interest and continue to inspire the construction of modern Quebec. Globalization cannot involve the repudiation of a process of national assertion and the acceptance of uniform policies that do not protect and promote Quebec's distinctiveness.

Strategies for Action

Before concluding this study, I will briefly examine some strategies for action. The events of February 1999 (the Framework Agreement and the federal budget that fails to comply with respect to social transfers) should not remain without response. Quebec must consider a range of judicial and political means to protect its areas of jurisdiction, achieve fiscal autonomy (matching tax resources and responsibilities) and ensure the federal government meets its own commitments and complies with the Constitution.

Before starting this discussion on strategic matters, it would be useful to attempt to explain what occurred between January 29 and February 4, 1999, despite the fact that the information remains very incomplete. It appears that everything had been decided prior to the February 4 meeting, and that the about face of the provinces was already complete. The First Ministers' Conference was something along the lines of a simple role-playing exercise. For the third time in 19 years (1981, 1990 and 1999), the provinces did not honour their signatures and said no to Quebec. Jurisprudence cannot explain this phenomenon, which is strictly political. This result can be put down to intergovernmental manœuvring where pressure, veiled threats, promises of money and the very interest of players were the forces at play. Short-term budgetary considerations (the federal money available for health care was the price paid for the provinces accepting the federal document) obviously prevailed over any willingness to harmonize relations with Quebec and accept its claims. In other words, the provinces failed to find the strength to oppose the dominating federalism proposed by Ottawa. In a few hours, they abandoned their own position and lined up behind Ottawa, without any negotiation and knowing that all Quebec political parties were against it.

This, therefore, is a Canadian federalism that radically diverges from the Quebec approach. Its provincial partners accepted a strong federal government that speaks for them and develops uniform social policies. They did not find choosing the model of a unitary government too repulsive. It is within such a context that I will say a few words to outline the strategic order.

The judicial weapon does not seem to me the best weapon to return the known or agreed practices of the federal spending power to a size that better complies with the 1867 Constitution. The known overlaps and the Framework Agreement that perpetuate them do not lend themselves to any significant judicial review. The attitude of the courts toward the exercise of the spending power has been disappointing. The Supreme Court has already stated, in response to a province that claimed that the essential principle of federalism required that Parliament not interfere in provincial areas of jurisdiction through its spending power:

> It was said that, in order to protect the autonomy of the provinces, the Court should supervise the federal government's exercise of its spending power. But supervision of the spending power is not a separate head of judicial review. If a statute is neither *ultra vires* nor contrary to the *Canadian Charter of Rights and Freedoms*, the courts have no jurisdiction to supervise the exercise of legislative power.[20]

The federal spending power enjoys considerable recognition by the courts, which validate federal statutes that set national objectives or impose spending conditions of federal monies by the provinces. *The YMHA Jewish Community Center of Winnipeg Inc. v. Brown*[21] and *Finlay v. Canada (Minister of Finance)*[22] decisions support the use of federal power because the Supreme Court found quite acceptable in the *Finlay* decision a federal law "designed to encourage provinces to develop programs consistent with national objectives."[23] In *Eldridge v. B.C. (Attorney General)*[24] the highest court of the land conceded that the health care field belonged to the exclusive jurisdiction of the provinces, but that:

> This has not prevented the federal Parliament from playing a leading role in the provision of free, universal medical care throughout the nation. It has done so by employing its inherent spending power to set national standards for provincial medicare programs.[25]

A few additional references will illustrate the judicial point of view concerning federal power:

- *Friends of the Island Inc. v. Canada (Minister of Public Works)*: "The spending power is an agreement to give another party funds to do something that the federal government could not do."[26]
- *Shubenacadie Indian Band v. Canada (Human Rights Commission)*: "The federal spending power is within the legislative authority of Parliament, even when exercised in relation to provincial matters, and does not amount to regulation."[27]

The Court quotes Professor Hogg:

> This [the Canada Assistance Plan decision] is a rather clear affirmation both of the Parliament's power to authorize grants to the provinces for use in fields of provincial jurisdiction, and the power to impose conditions on the recipient provinces.[28]

- *Brown v. B.C. (Attorney General)*:

> The Canada Health Act is an exercise of the federal spending power. While it structures the arrangements of federal funding of provincial health plans, it cannot regulate the province's health powers. Although both statutes have to do with the provision of health care benefits, the specific matters dealt with by the two statutes are quite different.[29]

◆ *Associated Respiratory Services Inc.* v. *B.C. (Purchasing Commission)*:

> Health is a matter within the legislative jurisdiction of the provinces but should not be confused with the spending power...Professor E. A. Driedger has published an informative article titled the "Spending Power." In reaching the same conclusion as Professor Hogg, he makes the point that the power to spend should not be confused with the exclusive power to make laws enumerated by ss. 91 and 92 of the British North America Act. Professor's Driedger's thesis is that the exercise of the spending power is not a constitutional or legislative issue. It is a political issue...With power respect, I agree with Professors Hogg and Driedger's observations and conclusions.[30]

These judicial precedents suggest the scope or restricted force of judicial arguments before such "political issues," to use the expression used by Mr. Driedger, former federal Deputy Minister of Justice. The chances of successfully contesting the federal spending power and conditions of its use agreed upon in February 1999 before the courts are slight. This observation takes into account the prevailing ideology of judges that will be called upon to render a decision. I am fully aware that the federal government did not, in its last budget, meet the political commitments it had assumed in the agreement. On this point, I have already noted the political character of such commitments. Anyway, it is always risky for one party to allege rights or advantages conferred by an agreement or convention that it has not signed but contested. For the time being, the agreement applies.

1. Secrétariat aux Affaires intergouvernementales canadiennes (SAIC), *Québec's Historical Position on the Federal Spending Power 1944-1998* (Quebec: Ministère du Conseil exécutif, 1998).
2. A. Tremblay, *La Réforme de la Constitution au Canada* (Montreal: Thémis, 1995).
3. See press release, "Programmes sociaux: le Québec refuse la proposition des provinces de centraliser à Ottawa les pouvoirs du Québec en matière sociale," August 23, 1996.
4. Press release, "Rebalancing federal and provincial roles and responsibilities," August 23, 1996, p. 2, in SAIC, *Québec's Historical Position on the Federal Spending Power*, p. 45. The text in brackets has been translated.
5. "Canada's Social Union, Québec's Position," Document tabled by Mr. Lucien Bouchard at the Annual Premiers' Conference, St. Andrews, August 6-8 1997, pp. 1-2 in SAIC, *Québec's Historical Position on the Federal Spending Power*, pp. 45-46.
6. Statement by Mr. Lucien Bouchard, First Ministers' Conference, Ottawa, December 12, 1997, in SAIC, *Québec's Historical Position on the Federal Spending Power*, pp. 46-47.
7. Statement by Mr. Jacques Brassard, Minister Responsible for Canadian Intergovernmental Affairs, Toronto, April 17, 1998 in in SAIC, *Québec's Historical Position on the Federal Spending Power*, p. 47. The text in brackets has been translated.
8. SAIC, *Québec's Historical Position on the Federal Spending Power*, p. 47.
9. Stéphane Dion, "Social Union: Canadians Helping Canadians," Notes for an Address to the Women's Canadian Club of Toronto, Toronto, Ontario, December 10, 1998.
10. Jean-François Lizée, *Le naufrageur* (Montreal: Boréal, 1994), p. 362. [Translation]
11. Bourassa's 1992 proposal could be compared with the proposals Pierre Marc Johnson and Daniel Johnson made in 1985 and 1993, respectively. See the study by the SAIC, *Québec's Historical Position on the Federal Spending Power*.
12. *Strengthening the Canadian Federation: The Constitution Amendment, 1987* (Ottawa: Government of Canada, 1987), p. 17.
13. Press release, "The New Social Union," February 4, 1999.
14. *Reference re: Canada Assistance Plan* (B.C.), [1991] 2 S.C.R. 525
15. *Reference re: Resolution to Amend the Constitution*, [1981] 1 S.C.R. 753.
16. S. Dion and A. McLellan, "Collaborative Use of the Spending Power for Intergovernmental Transfers: The Race to the Top model," February 5, 1999.
17. Interprovincial Meeting of Ministers of Intergovernmental Affairs and Attorneys General, Edmonton, August 1976.
18. Canada, *A Renewed Canada: Report of the Special Joint Committee of the Senate and the House of Commons* (Ottawa: The committee, 1992).
19. See Dion and McLellan, "Collaborative Use of the Spending Power for Intergovernmental Transfers."
20. *Reference re: Canada Assistance Plan* (B.C.), [1991] 2 S.C.R. 525.
21. [1989] 1 S.C.R. 1532
22. [1993] 1 S.C.R. 1080.
23. *Finlay v. Canada* (Minister of Finance), [1993] 1 S.C.R. 1080, p. 1126.
24. [1997] 3 S.C.R. 624.
25. *Eldridge v. B.C.* (Attoney General), [1997] 3 S.C.R. 624, par. 25.
26. *Friends of the Island Inc. v. Canada* (Minister of Public Works), [1993] F.C.J. 78, par. 228.
27. *Shubenacadie Indian Band v. Canada (Human Rights Commission)* [1998] 2 F.C.198. (T.D.), par. 47.
28. *Shubenacadie Indian Band v. Canada (Human Rights Commission)*, par. 48.
29. [1997] B.C.J. N° 1832 (B.C.S.C.), par. 51.
30. *Associated Respiratory Services Inc. v. B.C. (Purchasing Commission)*, [1992] 70 B.C.L.R. (2d) 57 (B.C.S.C.), p. 67.

Dispute Avoidance and Resolution

Introduction

THIS STUDY EXAMINES CHAPTER 6 OF THE SOCIAL UNION FRAMEWORK AGREEMENT, entitled "Dispute Avoidance and Resolution." The chapter will be compared with the relevant clauses presented by the common front of provinces on August 6, 1998 (the Saskatoon consensus), then on January 29, 1999 (the Victoria proposal). A similar comparison will then be made with Quebec's traditional position on this issue. The ultimate purpose of this study is to highlight any new constraints on the Quebec government.

We interpret chapter 6 critically using the English and French versions. This is a crucial and delicate step because the text is intricate. We will pay special attention to the context of the chapter, taking into account the agreement as a whole and the constitutional problems surrounding it.

Based on this analysis, we will examine the dispute resolution procedures promoted by the preparatory texts and Quebec's traditional positions, not in and of themselves, but inasmuch as they differ from the final result, the Social Union Framework Agreement. Both positive and negatives differences will be assessed. We will also examine the impact from Quebec's perspective.

Characteristics of the Dispute Avoidance and Resolution Mechanism in the Social Union Framework Agreement

The Framework Agreement consists of seven chapters, but chapter 7 is of a transitory nature. One could say that the whole agreement leads to chapter 6. For the purposes of this analysis, we will proceed from the specific to the general.

Content of Chapter 6

The dispute avoidance and resolution procedure described in chapter 6 of the agreement is not a single, enclosed system. The text describes irresolutely an ideal, desirable procedure. In the first and third paragraphs, it states that mechanisms "should" have certain qualities and the described process "should" guide the sector ministers. In other words, chapter 6 does not exclude the possibility that a process other than that it sets up could validly be used. One would expect, however, that any adaptations that emerge will respect the organization of the chapter, which establishes a non-binding mechanism based on intergovernmental cooperation, sector implementation and transparency.

Non-binding Nature of the Mechanism

Despite the fact that chapter 6 deals with disputes, it attempts to avoid the imposition of solutions on the governments involved in those disputes. Its principal method is to place the emphasis on the preliminary phases of the dispute resolution process.

In the preliminary phase, conflicts are averted by means of prevention. Significant importance is placed in the chapter on the concept of prevention: it is dominant in the title and it is the subject of one of the three items in the third paragraph, the principal paragraph of the chapter, which describes the process. It is mentioned systematically, and it is given prominent place in the Ministerial Council's role described at the end of the chapter. The dispute resolution process also depends on the preliminary, negotiating phase. In fact, if negotiation fails, the dispute cannot be resolved. No subsequent measure is provided in case of a deadlock. The process described cannot result in a decision that settles the dispute.

It is true that there is one step following negotiation. This is the possibility for any government to "require a review of a decision or action one year after it enters into effect or when changing circumstances justify," under the section entitled "Review provisions." The corresponding French title presents a problem of interpretation: "require" is unilateral, while a "clause" involves an agreement. The word "provisions" in English does not dissipate every trace of ambiguity. Does this item mean that this portion of the text constitutes "provisions" (or "clauses" in French) of the agreement itself, or does it mean that review requirements become the "provisions" (or "clauses" in French) of any agreement (or text)? In any case, the right to review confirms the non-binding character of the dispute resolution process in the agreement. If one party "may require" a review in the future, it means that this party is not satisfied with the result of the process. But if a government "may require a review of a decision or action," it cannot require that it be changed in any way. In referring to a review, the item and the context reveal that the other party remains entirely free.

Is it possible for the process described in chapter 6 to at least end up with an impartial opinion that could be imposed by its moral authority? The fourth paragraph of chapter 6 provides that each government involved in a dispute "may consult and seek advice from third parties" at any stage of the process. The advice of third parties solicited in this way would not necessarily play an impartial role and may well be neutralized by advice solicited by the opposite party. The intervention of third parties also appears in the portion of the text that describes the process at the crucial phase of negotiation. At this stage, operations are carried out jointly or separately by the parties involved in the dispute, but "Governments involved may seek assistance of a third party for fact-finding, advice, or mediation." Then there is a provision that "At the request of either party in a dispute, fact-finding or mediation reports will be made public."

Since the fact-finding report will be the "joint" work of the parties in the dispute and the parties will have the "opportunity to comment on the report before its completion," it is not very likely that it would constitute, in and of itself, a position in favour of one party. Could it be otherwise in a "mediation report"? In theory at least, the role of a mediator is broader than that of a conciliator. This is because the mediator may offer settlement proposals to the parties. However, it is difficult to imagine that a mediation report could present the mediator's proposals in such a way that they would *de facto* constitute the morally binding position of a wise man. In fact, confidentiality is the essence of the obligations of the mediator.[1] And the party that has the most to lose in the release of an embarrassing mediation report can prevent it. The Framework Agreement does not compel any government to go along with mediation. And a government can always agree to go along on the condition that the mediator does not have the mandate to make proposals or to include them in his report.

Necessary Cooperation

Chapter 6 is designed in such a way that the parties must work collaboratively for the process to work. Should one of the parties in the dispute refuse to cooperate, an impasse occurs and it cannot be overcome.

Chapter 6 opens with the idea that governments are committed to "working collaboratively" to avoid and resolve intergovernmental disputes among them. This general idea is implemented in the process that is specifically described in the third paragraph. At the prevention stage, we see that the governments are committed to "working together" through "information-sharing," "joint planning," "cooperation" and "advance notice," among other things.

The crucial stage of "negotiations" places no less emphasis on cooperation. First, negotiation includes by nature an element of cooperation in the search for a solution to the dispute. Then, the initiatives described as part of the negotiation process — fact-finding investigations and the resulting written report — are "joint." Furthermore, among the general objectives listed as early as the first paragraph, we find willingness to "resolve disputes in a non-adversarial way." As we have already seen, the specially chosen way is mediation. But mediation is not mandatory. Therefore, each party must accept it in every case. Moreover, mediation can only proceed as long as each party continues to concur. As soon as this necessary cooperation stops, there is no rescue mechanism provided for in chapter 6.

When, despite all efforts and good faith, the parties in a dispute cannot agree, something other than mutual consent must take over. In principle, mediation cannot play this role. The reason is that mediation cannot produce a decision (this is also true of conciliation). The parties to the Framework Agreement did not want any recourse to arbitration, which would enable a third party acceptable to the parties to make a decision. By stating "in a non-adversarial way" (*à l'amiable* in French), the English version is clear on this subject.

In my opinion, the objective of "ensuring democratic accountability by elected officials," stated at the beginning of chapter 6, is not sufficient justification for this choice. The agreement could have provided for an arbitration process ending with an unenforceable verdict. Even a mechanism that allowed an impartial third party to give its opinion would have been able to deal with a lack of cooperation by the parties. The "advice" of third parties mentioned in the same paragraph in chapter 6 does not meet this criterion. The details provided in the description of the process indicate that this "advice" is required by one or the other party in the dispute, for its own benefit.

The only remaining possibility is to consider the proposals in the mediation report as an enlightened impartial opinion. The confidentiality obligation and the mediation agreement should prevent such a result from occurring. Anyway, the purpose of mediation is to have the parties find a solution to their problem themselves rather than to present them with one.

Sector Implementation

As indicated in the subtitle, the Framework Agreement is an accord "between the Government of Canada and the Governments of the Provinces and Territories." These central bodies could have created a single dispute avoidance and resolution mechanism in which they played the leading role. But chapter 6 suggested a basic plan that the sector ministers must implement.

Terminologically, the chapter is not very coherent. It goes from governments to sectors — and back again — very readily. For instance, the third paragraph entrusts "sector ministers" with responsibility for the process, provides for "sector negotiations" based on "joint fact-finding," then states that the "fact-finding" report will be submitted to "governments" that will have the opportunity to comment, and then goes on to say that "governments" may seek the assistance of a third party for "fact-finding"! However, these vacillations are immaterial, because ministerial solidarity is the essence of the British parliamentary system prevailing in the federal government and all the signatory provinces. What a government wants, its sector ministers will also want. And what sector ministers do will have been authorized in some way or other by their government.

Beyond terminology, therefore, the structure and thread of chapter 6 clearly indicate that the dispute resolution process must be implemented at the sector level. This contribution of the sector ministers seems to play in two ways.

First, each sector would be responsible for setting up (through intergovernmental cooperation) its own special dispute resolution process. For example, the Framework Agreement makes it possible to create three distinct mechanisms for health care, post-secondary education, and social assistance and social services. This results first from the third of the objectives listed at the end of the first paragraph of chapter 6, that "sectors design processes appropriate to their needs." This also results from the introductory sentence at the beginning of the third paragraph, which substantiates the idea that sectors may adapt the process described in the agreement.

Second, it is at the sector level that the dispute resolution mechanism will be applied on a case-by-case basis. When chapter 6 outlines the steps concerning a given case, it includes them in the mandate of "sector ministers," specifically under the crucial title "sector negotiations." The whole third paragraph of chapter 6, and especially the second item of this paragraph, reflect this pattern. For instance, the chapter only deals with fact-finding and mediation, i.e., special disputes, within sector negotiations. We do not believe that the formula in the fourth paragraph, which refers to each government involved in a dispute, could affect the sectorial approach that emerges otherwise.

Transparency as a Political Incentive

Nothing in chapter 6 of the Framework Agreement can force a party to water down its position if it does not want to do so. This does not mean that the mechanism is ineffective. The governments are banking on political pressure to add teeth to the way disputes are resolved.

The key element here concludes the item dealing with sector negotiations, and reads: "At the request of either party in a dispute, fact-finding or mediation reports will be made public." This element stands out because it shatters the collaborative philosophy that otherwise characterizes the chapter. It is actually the only place in the chapter that allows for the possibility of a party imposing its will on the other party during the dispute resolution procedure itself. (As we have seen, the "review" comes after the process has ended.) The fact that reports will be made public means that the people will be allowed to judge the respective positions. The party in the dispute that takes a hard line or does not negotiate in good faith would be at a disadvantage in the court of public opinion. It might have to review its attitude in a more or less short term. But the possibility that reports may have to be made public could also have some prior effects in that the parties would probably adopt positions that can be defended in the public arena. This will increase the chances of a non-adversarial resolution.

The fact that reports may be made public may well jar, from a technical point of view, yet it fits well with the philosophy of chapter 6, which recommends "transparent" mechanisms that ensure "democratic accountability by elected officials" and provides that "governments will report publicly on an annual basis on the nature of intergovernmental disputes and their resolution."

Chapter 6 in Perspective

Chapter 6 appears to apply to the whole of the Social Union Framework Agreement. We believe actually that it is even intended to go beyond the agreement. For instance, the second paragraph of the chapter states:

> Dispute avoidance and resolution will apply to commitments on mobility, intergovernmental transfers, interpretation of the Canada Health Act principles, and, as appropriate, on any new joint initiative.

However, the second sentence of the chapter uses mysterious terms that are found nowhere else in the agreement. It reads "Respecting existing legislative provisions..." (In French, "*En ce qui a trait aux dispositions législatives existantes...*" This is an awkward reference to the last point of the second paragraph of chapter 8 of the Victoria proposal, which stated that dispute avoidance and resolution should "respect existing legislative provisions.")

Because chapter 6 governs the whole agreement (and even more), we must examine whether its context confirms the characteristics we have found.

Context of the Social Union Framework Agreement

The Framework Agreement may be examined statically or dynamically. We will first examine what it explicitly says to find out to what extent it allows us to identify the scope of the dispute resolution mechanism. We will then compare the characteristics of this mechanism with the interests of the governments involved.

Reinforcing Basic Characteristics The Framework Agreement stresses cooperation, but we must find out to what extent it preserves the right to act unilaterally. This problem involves the first two characteristics we identified in chapter 6. Since the dispute resolution mechanism is not binding, it can be expected that the same will apply to the substantive clauses.

The cooperative approach is at the very heart of the whole Framework Agreement. As early as the preamble, the governments claim that they want to "work more closely together," and at the very end of the text they add that they will "jointly undertake" other work. The title of chapter 4 is "Working in Partnership for Canadians," and the first item is dedicated to "Joint Planning and Collaboration." In chapters 3 and 5, there are mentions of the commitment to "work with other governments" or "agree" to find comparable indicators, priorities and Canada-wide objectives and an accountability framework. Chapter 5 states that the federal government "should proceed in a cooperative manner" when it uses conditional social transfers.

It is within this context that we must determine whether any opportunities for unilateral action remain. Chapter 4 ("Working in Partnership for Canadians") includes an item based on notices and consultation, for cases when the initiatives of one government may have "significant effects" on other governments. Likewise, chapter 5, which deals with the federal spending power, prescribes consultation and due notice. In the case of direct federal spending, no other requirement is mentioned. Nothing here could deflect a government's will.

In chapter 5, on the other hand, the consent of a majority of the provinces is required for new Canada-wide initiatives that are supported by transfers to the provinces. This requirement is weak: the six less-populated provinces represent 15 percent of the population — yet their agreement would suffice. The commitment to this in the Framework Agreement is firm. The obligation to pay to the province its share of the funding available is also firm, but conditional.

The list of sectors targeted by the agreement is outside the chapter on dispute resolution. Those that are mentioned twice in chapter 5 are also found in chapter 2 dealing with mobility. But in chapter 2, training is also targeted. Nevertheless, the avoidance mechanism does apply to mobility, as stated in the second paragraph of chapter 6.

Finally, the Framework Agreement confirms the willingness to depend on transparency and public opinion. The whole of chapter 3 is directly dedicated to this theme. And feedback from the people is mentioned in chapter 7.

All in all, the characteristics of the dispute avoidance and resolution process we have identified are confirmed, and even reinforced, in other chapters of the agreement. It remains to be seen how they are likely to operate in real life conditions.

Dynamics of Interests Involved Disputes that are covered by the chapter 6 process will not necessarily involve the federal government against all the provinces, or even the federal government against a single province. In my opinion, this is true for both disputes dealing with mobility (chapter 2) and with the federal spending power (chapter 5). After discussing these, we will deal with the case of Quebec, which did not sign the agreement.

The mobility of all Canadians may be restricted as much by federal as by provincial policies. However, since the Framework Agreement deals with questions that are related in principle to provincial jurisdiction, the mobility restrictions it addresses will almost by definition be imposed by one or more provinces, not by the federal government. Moreover, "residence-based" barriers (i.e., imposed by a province) are the major targets. In other words, within the framework of chapter 2, the government challenged, or defendant, will always be a provincial government.

If the federal government were not a party to the commitments on mobility, one or more provinces could trigger the dispute avoidance and resolution process. But the provinces are not always more likely to complain in the case of the principal problem addressed by chapter 2, residency-based barriers. The fact that a province imposes a residency period (instead of a simple residency condition) may not bother the other provinces, inasmuch as the citizens excluded are not their residents. Now that the federal government is a party to commitments concerning mobility, challenges in this field will be more frequent. Ottawa is the natural sponsor of Canada-wide values. (Jean Chrétien added mobility to the agenda in his January 25, 1999 response to the premiers.) It is conceivable that in this field the federal government will always be concerned, independent of whether a province complains. If all provinces impose the same residency condition, the dispute that might ensue would pit them against the federal government. But the typical dispute will involve a single province that imposes a condition or makes a condition more drastic. This province may have to face the other provinces, as well as the federal government.

A similar analysis can be made about the other problem explicitly mentioned in chapter 2: mutual recognition of occupational qualifications. We will analyze below the impact of the Agreement on Internal Trade.

In the case of chapter 5 and in contrast with chapter 2 of the Framework Agreement, the federal government will be the defendant during any dispute. At worst, it will have to face all the provinces. It is more likely that only one or a few provinces will be dissatisfied. And the other provinces may choose to support Ottawa's position.

All in all, the challenges should be more impressive and holding the fort will therefore be more difficult under chapter 2 than under chapter 5.

In this context, what will be the impact of the dispute resolution procedure? If the dispute involves mobility, the province challenged may take advantage of the fact that it cannot be forced to capitulate, but it will feel real pressure because of its commitment to cooperate and the necessity to show consideration for public opinion. If the dispute involves spending power, Ottawa may take advantage of the fact that it cannot be forced to yield, but it will feel some political pressure.

Quebec's situation is special here because it has not signed the Framework Agreement. Technically, the dispute resolution mechanism triggered by some measure involving mobility cannot be used against it. And it cannot use that mechanism to counter the exercise of the federal spending power. However, such obstacles may be more apparent than real. The Framework Agreement did not abolish the right to attempt to settle disputes outside its framework. Whether as a plaintiff or as a virtual defender, Quebec could therefore propose in a given case that the dispute be submitted to a process of the same nature — and the other parties could agree with this, especially because they encourage intergovernmental cooperation.

In my opinion, it is at another level that Quebec's situation is truly special. Quebec's vision of federalism has often been different from that of the rest of Canada. Independent of the question of whether an agreement applies formally to Quebec is the fact that the province is more likely to be facing, whether as the challenger or the defendant, a composite adversary that includes the central order of government and some, if not all, of the other provinces.

Legal and Constitutional Context

The very existence of chapter 6 of the Social Union Framework Agreement and certain of its characteristics are explained by the fact that the agreement does not have the force of law.

To give a clear example, the Meech Lake Accord, after controlling up to a point federal spending power, did not have to set up a dispute resolution procedure. If the Accord had been approved, its clauses would have been part of the Constitution and would have been applied by the courts. In the same way, if a federal statute imposed limits to the spending power, the courts could compel the federal government to comply with them so that no special dispute settlement mechanism would be necessary. Because the Social Union Framework Agreement is not part of the Constitution, of a federal statute, or even of a federal regulation, such a mechanism is required.[2]

Chapter 6 could have set up a process that had a constraining effect as a political commitment, but the process could not have been binding in law. On the one hand, the clauses of the Framework Agreement have no contract value because a government cannot interfere with the free exercise of state functions.[3] On the other hand, a government could always decide, with the support of its parliament, to change or contradict what it agreed to in the agreement.[4] The Framework Agreement recognizes this fact when it states under the second title of chapter 4 that commitments are made in "a manner consistent with the principles of our system of parliamentary government and the budget-making process."

From this perspective, the cooperative nature of the mechanism provided by chapter 6 involves a certain realism: true confrontation in this field could not be remedied by the law.

If the agreement cannot be located in strict legal terms, one might think that it borders on constitutional convention. A constitutional convention is a political agreement. The courts do not apply such conventions, but they may take them into account in interpreting laws. And they agreed at the time of the patriation of the Constitution to decide whether such a convention existed.[5]

For all practical purposes, this means that if a party in the Framework Agreement does not comply with the Agreement, another party may ask the courts to find out whether there is a violation. If the courts made such a ruling, the challenged party would feel quasi-legal pressure to change its behaviour. This happened at the time of the patriation of the Constitution. Obviously, Quebec cannot claim to be involved in a constitutional convention since it did not sign the agreement.

Comparison with Previous Positions

We will first examine all previous provincial positions that relate to the Social Union Framework Agreement as reflected in work preparatory to the agreement. We will then examine Quebec's traditional positions.

Provincial Common Front

The project to control the federal spending power in social fields took shape in 1997 at the Annual Premiers' Conference in St. Andrews. Quebec did not take part in the federal-provincial negotiations that followed because it demanded prior recognition of the right to opt out with compensation. But the provinces' joint position soon interested Quebec, which joined the consensus during the Annual Premiers' Conference in Saskatoon in August 1998. We will examine the text of this consensus first. We will then discuss the Victoria proposal, the version of the provincial common front that immediately preceded the conclusion of the Social Union Framework Agreement.

Saskatoon Consensus

The consensus of the 10 provinces reached at the Saskatoon Conference consists of two pages and ten paragraphs. The text does not have the protolegal form of the Social Union Framework Agreement. One can see that another document is needed to complete it and that it is only a "negotiating position." We will examine this text using the same method as we did for the Social Union Framework Agreement.

Two passages in the Saskatoon consensus deal with the dispute settlement mechanism. These are the sixth and eighth paragraphs.

In seeking to determine whether in the French version a non-binding mechanism was being sought at that time, we note that the consensus refers to "*une procédure impartiale de règlement des disputes afin d'instaurer un partenariat équilibré et juste*." Since the word "*impartiale*" qualifies the "*procédure*," it does not necessarily mean that the intervention of an impartial third party was contemplated. It could simply mean that the desired procedure should not favour one party over the other. The eighth paragraph simply refers to mechanisms to "régler équitablement" conflicts when they occur, so this assumption is still viable. In both of these places, the English terminology does not necessarily imply an impartial third party: "fair dispute resolution process" and "both prevent disputes, and resolve them fairly when they arise."

If, however, we examine some of the work preceding the provincial common front, we find that the intended "*équitable*" process included a mechanism similar to that found in the Agreement on Internal Trade (AIT). This mechanism, which we will examine later, allows the constraining intervention of an independent and impartial "special group."[6]

The second characteristic we identified in the Framework Agreement is also found in the Saskatoon consensus. The latter considers "new mechanisms to *prevent* and resolve disputes," and "new *cooperative* mechanisms that both *prevent* disputes and resolve them fairly when they arise" [our italics]. However, apparently nothing in the Saskatoon consensus refers to sector implementation or transparency. The second paragraph only states that it involves "health, education and social services."

With respect to the context of the statements relating to the dispute settlement, two points are worth mentioning. First, the Saskatoon consensus is clearly based on the search for "partnership" and the willingness to try "working together." Second, this willingness is part of a dynamic that is somewhat different from that suggested by the Framework Agreement. The whole Saskatoon text adopts the perspective of the relationships between "the two orders of government." This can be seen in the first two paragraphs of the consensus, but also in the text that refers systematically to the "federal" positions. The play of interests that results from the Framework Agreement, as we have seen, is not so simple.

The Victoria Proposal

Contrary to the Saskatoon consensus, the form of the Victoria proposal of January 29, 1999 is comparable with that of the Social Union Framework Agreement. The Victoria proposal exists only in English and consists of eight chapters, the last of which is dedicated to the dispute settlement mechanism. We will now examine it before placing it in the appropriate context.

The Content of Chapter 8 Chapter 8 of the Victoria proposal includes a crucial step that the Framework Agreement did not adopt, which would have provided the constraining character regarding moral authority. This additional step in the event that mediation does not resolve the dispute consists of asking one to three individuals to prepare a report containing settlement recommendations. The governments that are parties to the dispute must then hold new negotiations based on the report. The Victoria proposal was obviously counting on the considerable weight of an impartial opinion. It states that the two parties to the dispute jointly select the author of the report; when three persons are charged with preparing the report, each government selects one and then the two select a chair. If the negotiations that follow the production of the report fail, the report is made public.

The Victoria proposal is less dependent on the cooperation of the parties in the dispute. Admittedly chapter 8 is committed to cooperation. It stresses dispute avoidance and provides for negotiation as the primary dispute resolution mechanism. While preserving the principle of "non-adversarial" settlement, it anticipates deadlocks and provides a solution.

First, recourse to mediation is not optional but mandatory. The document states that the mechanism set up "will consist of the following three steps." The third step starts with mediation: "governments will seek the assistance of a mediator..." Later, if mediation fails, the additional step consists not of producing a "joint" factual report, but a report by an impartial third party, with recommendations. This step is also mandatory.

Otherwise, there is no real sector implementation of the dispute settlement process in the Victoria proposal. Contrary to the Framework Agreement, sectors are not mentioned at the beginning of the chapter on dispute resolution in the Victoria proposal. Sector ministers are only involved in one of the three options in the second step, at the level of the first negotiation. Generally, chapter 8 of the Victoria proposal seems incompatible with the creation of mechanisms that differ from one sector to the other.

The Victoria proposal mostly counts on transparency and the political pressure it is likely to generate. First, one of the general objectives at the beginning of the chapter provides recourse to third parties "while ensuring democratic accountability by elected officials." Later, in the case of failure, the third step ends with the publication of the impartial third party's report, and the text adds, "the governments are to be advised by the report and will have to publicly justify their respective positions." Finally, immediately after this passage, there is a section entitled "Reporting to Canadians," which states that transparency "will help to ensure the mechanism is effective."

Chapter 8 in Context We will first identify the major elements of the Victoria proposal that may help us understand the actual scope of chapter 8.

Regarding the (relatively) binding character of the dispute resolution mechanism, the most striking part of the Victoria proposal is the objection by Newfoundland to any steps beyond the mediation stage in disputes about the Canada Health Act.[7] For such an objection to be worth mentioning twice, it must have referred to an "additional step," as we have called it, but with teeth.

The cooperative (up to a point) nature of the mechanism is manifested in many ways in the Victoria proposal. The proposal is based on partnership and on the idea of "working together." Chapter 5, one of the most extensive chapters, is entitled "Working Together in Partnership" and is completely dedicated to intergovernmental cooperation.

Chapter 6 of the Victoria proposal does contain the seeds of a sectorial approach with respect to the clarification of responsibilities between both orders of government.

The sectors targeted are the same as in the Framework Agreement. But the first chapter of the Victoria proposal also mentions employment insurance. Chapter 8 does not seem to apply to this sector. Nor, incidentally, does it apply to the Agreement on Internal Trade, for which chapter 3 maintains the "current implementation process." However, chapter 4 of the Victoria proposal devotes an item to equalization, and concludes that its clauses "could be subject to the dispute settlement mechanism." The conclusion of chapter 5 states that these prescriptions "should be subject to the dispute settlement mechanism." Chapter 8, at the very end, is more categorical regarding application, but there is a note indicating that it is only a first draft.

The Victoria proposal repeatedly emphasizes transparency and accountability, and chapter 7 is dedicated to this theme.

On the dynamic level of the interests involved, the Victoria proposal is mostly designed from a bilateral perspective. It frequently refers to the "levels of government," it imposes several obligations directly on the "federal" government and it opposes the federal government against the "provinces and territories." This polarization of one level of government against the other is reflected in the dispute resolution process, where it seems inconceivable that a provincial government could join the federal government against another provincial government. For instance, in steps two and three of the process described in chapter 8, it is frequently repeated that negotiations are bilateral and that they involve "the two" governments that are parties to the dispute.

The binary nature of the Victoria proposal is also reflected in the insistence it places on clarification of the roles and responsibilities of both orders of government. Chapter 6 is dedicated to this theme and refers to a table in the appendix, where it appears that the "cooperative" involvement of both orders of government only applies to what is not exclusively under the jurisdiction of one of them. As is indicated in chapter 7, clarifying the various roles and responsibilities contributes to improving the accountability of governments.

Assessing the Gap Between the Starting Position and the Final Result

Despite the laconic character of the Saskatoon consensus, it can be said that in the social union negotiations it banked on four points: control of federal spending power in the fields of health care, education and social services; the binary nature of the power relationship; federal-provincial cooperation; and the dispute resolution procedure. From this viewpoint, the federal government probably found itself too much of a target for its taste. Through various means it succeeded in extricating itself.

First, with the addition of mobility to the negotiation, the provinces themselves became targets. This new front had limited scope in the Victoria proposal and was not subject to the dispute resolution procedure. In the Framework Agreement, the chapter dealing with mobility took on importance and became subject to the dispute resolution mechanism.

Then, the confrontational dialectic between the two orders of government was defused at two levels. Terminologically and conceptually, from Saskatoon to Victoria to Ottawa, there are more clauses dealing with "governments" in an undifferentiated manner and fewer clauses based on the two orders of government. Moreover, the deflection of frictions to sector ministers that had its seed in the Victoria proposal becomes a central characteristic of the final agreement. Furthermore, intergovernmental cooperation was pushed as far as it could go: in the final agreement, even faced with a relentless dispute, there was practically no other choice but to agree to every step.

With respect to dispute resolution, the mechanism outlined in the Victoria proposal was watered down, even adulterated, in the Framework Agreement. The provision for an impartial third party report and recommendations which, once published, would have been difficult to ignore as a fairness ruling, was eliminated. The approach involving two parties facing each other in a real case was replaced with a dialogue of participants at various levels.

Quebec's Traditional Positions

In a paper produced in 1991 by the Secrétariat aux affaires intergouvernementales canadiennes (SAIC) entitled *Québec's Traditional Constitutional Positions 1936-1990*,[8] most of Quebec's policy statements involved questions that are governed or should be governed by the formal Constitution. Like the Meech Lake Accord, the Constitution is by nature open to application by the courts, so no resolution mechanism has to be provided for disputes resulting from it.

However, the document also mentions interventions dealing with constitutional practice, including the exercise of federal spending power and "intergovernmental policy." This is the field of the Framework Agreement. It would seem, however, that until 1990 Quebec did not mention the institution of any dispute settlement mechanism in this field. To look at Quebec's traditional positions, we must instead examine the dispute resolution process found in intergovernmental accords. We will then examine the special case of the Agreement on Internal Trade, to which the Framework Agreement refers.

Intergovernmental Accords Signed by Quebec

The following accords include a dispute resolution mechanism: The Ontario-Quebec Agreement on Labour Mobility and Recognition of Qualifications, Skills and Work Experience in the Construction Industry (1996); the Agreement on the Opening of Public Procurement for Quebec and New Brunswick, revised in 1994; and the Agreement on the Opening of Public Procurement for Quebec and Ontario, signed in 1994, and amended in 1996 and 1997. The mechanisms in question are entirely different from those found in the Framework Agreement. We should add that these agreements deal with much more definite topics and involve advanced technical parameters.

The first difference between these agreements and the Framework Agreement is that the disputes dealt with in the framework of these agreements involve interested third parties who lay charges. These are usually workers or suppliers. The contentious files are therefore opened and closed or settled based on a particular problem. Disputes mentioned in the Framework Agreement are more diffuse and do not involve parties other than governments.

The second difference is that, in contrast with the Framework Agreement, these agreements make it possible to reach a decision concerning the dispute. Charges are processed by a coordinating committee made up of designated members appointed by governments and this committee may render a decision, agree or report to the ministers responsible.

Third, the agreements on public procurement also make it possible to create a committee of experts whose report may end with the necessity of accommodating the injured supplier. This is obviously a truly impartial intervention in the dispute.

It is true that mechanisms set up like this are not strictly binding. A government may always refuse to follow up on a decision or final report. But it would expose itself to retaliatory measures. And the fact that it is possible not to yield does not change the nature of a decision or conclusion.

The characteristics we have identified in the process of the Social Union Framework Agreement are so different that it would be pointless to push the comparison further. Specifically, the social union mechanism is political from the start and banks on accountability. Also, it systematically ensures that no committee can replace the government involved or render any opinion or recommendation on how the dispute should be settled.

The Special Case of the Agreement on Internal Trade

The Agreement on Internal Trade (AIT), which all provinces signed in 1994, is of particular interest in our study because the federal government is also a party to it and the Framework Agreement refers to it. This reference, at the end of chapter 2 of the Framework Agreement, mostly (if not exclusively) relates to chapter 7 of the AIT entitled "Labour Mobility."[9]

Because chapter 6 of the Framework Agreement states that its dispute resolution mechanism applies to commitments concerning mobility while the AIT has its own mechanism, it can be said that the clauses of chapter 7 of the AIT are subject to two mechanisms. Actually, there are three, because chapter 17 of the AIT itself offers two procedures, one to settle disputes between governments and the other to settle disputes between an individual and a government.

The procedure in the AIT to deal with disputes between an individual and a government is similar to those we just mentioned about the intergovernmental accords and the conclusions we reached apply perfectly to it.

The procedure in the AIT to deal with disputes between governments involves the same type of dispute as those that could occur within the context of the Social Union Framework Agreement. Essentially, once the preliminary conditions have been exhausted, section 1704 of the AIT makes it possible, at the request of one party, for a "special group" to be created with the mandate of examining whether the agreement has been violated. This special group is independent and impartial. It is expected that the conclusions in its report will be implemented. Should this fail, the report may be published and retaliatory measures taken.

This procedure has been used once and had a considerable impact. On June 12, 1998, a special group produced its report concerning a dispute between Alberta and Canada, in which it concluded that the federal Manganese-based Fuel Additives Act violated the terms of the AIT. The report had an impact on international trade: Ottawa lifted the import ban on MMT and paid $13 million in compensation to Ethyl Corporation, the American company that triggered the NAFTA dispute settlement procedure.

The dispute resolution mechanism of the AIT is very extensive and, at the level of the "special group," ends in an adversarial system in which the parties try to convince an independent and impartial third party of the merits of their position. This process is diametrically opposed to the one in the Social Union Framework Agreement.

Conclusion

QUEBEC HAS NOT SIGNED THE SOCIAL UNION FRAMEWORK AGREEMENT, AND IT IS worth asking whether its manœuvrability within the Canadian federation has been affected. From the point of view that specially concerns Quebec, it is difficult to see what it may have lost or won. The dispute resolution process in the Framework Agreement depends so much on intergovernmental cooperation that it cannot be counted on. The political conditions under which Quebec and its opposites try to cooperate in given cases will remain the determining factors.

If the dispute resolution mechanism is too weak to affect Quebec's strategic perspectives, what about the provisions in the rest of the agreement? In my opinion, the Social Union Framework Agreement tends to increase the centralization of power in Canada. Practically all the issues it deals with are under exclusive provincial jurisdiction. The agreement legitimizes federal interventions in these fields. Specifically, the first two paragraphs of chapter 5 are a paean to federal spending power in provincial jurisdictions. The cooperative federalism introduced by the agreement and its dispute resolution mechanism consists of permitting the federal government to cooperate in provincial sectors. The federal sectors remain a private preserve that is jealously retained by the dominating doctrine, firm precedents, and Ottawa's legislative, governmental and administrative policies.

It is true that on various points, as we have noted, the Framework Agreement goes further than does the Meech Lake Accord. The essential guarantee — the possibility of ensuring that commitments will be met — is contained in the Meech Lake Accord but is not in the Framework Agreement. The latter provides no way of forcing the federal government to abide by its commitments: it can interpret clauses as it wishes, without any risk of being contradicted by a duly mandated impartial body. And it can apply them as it wishes, including at the dispute avoidance and resolution stage.

1 See Nabil N. Antaki, *Le règlement amiable des litiges* (Cowansville: Éditions Yvon Blais, 1998), p. 263ff.

2 For more information on the fact that a federal-provincial agreement is not legally binding, see *Re Lofstrom*, (1972) 22 D.L.R. (3d) 120 (C.A. Sask.); the *Reference Re: Anti-Inflation Act*, [1976] 2 S.C.R. 373, pp. 432-35; *Manitoba Government Employees Association v. Government of Manitoba*, [1978] 1 S.C.R. 1123; and *Marina L'Escale Inc. v. Commission municipale du Québec*, [1996] R.J.Q. 644 (C.S.), on appeal.

3 See *Rederiaktiebolaget Amphitrite v. The Queen*, [1921] 3 K.B. 500; *Birkdale District Electric Supply Co. v. Corporation of Southport*, [1926] A.C. 355, p. 364; *Pawis v. The Queen*, [1980] 2 F.C. 18; and *Laurentide Motels v. Beauport*, [1989] 1 S.C.R. 705.

4 *Reference Re: Canada Assistance Plan* (BC), [1991] 2 S.C.R. 525.

5 *Reference Re: Resolution to Amend the Constitution*, [1981] 1 S.C.R. 753, *Reference Re: Objection to a Resolution to Amend the Constitution*, [1982] 2 S.C.R. 793.

6 See Thomas J. Courchene, "ACCESS: A Convention on the Canadian Economic and Social Systems," Study conducted for the Minister of Intergovernmental Affairs of Ontario (August 1996) in *Canadian Business Economics*, Vol. 4, no. 4 (July-September, Summer 1996), pp. 22-23; and Patrick J. Monahan, "To the Extent Possible: A Comment on Dispute Settlement in the Agreement on Internal Trade," in Michael Trebilcock and Daniel Schwanen (eds.), *Getting There: An Assessment of the Agreement on Internal Trade* (Toronto: C.D. Howe Institute, 1995), pp. 211-18.

7 See note at the end of the Victoria proposal.

8 Secrétariat aux affaires intergouvernementales canadiennes (SAIC), *Québec's Traditional Constitutional Positions 1936-1990* (Quebec: ministère du Conseil exécutif, 1991).

9 Agreement on Internal Trade, Ottawa, Internal Trade Secretariat, September 1994.

The Agreement on the Canadian Social Union as Seen by a Quebec Federalist

The agreement on the Canadian Social Union reached in Ottawa on the 4th of February 1999 between the prime minister and the premiers of all the provinces and territories except Quebec has given rise once again to sharp disagreement between the Quebec government, led by Lucien Bouchard, and the federal government, led by another Quebecer, Jean Chrétien.

Each time a debate of this nature arises, it is important to remember that even if both leaders hold a legitimate mandate to speak and act on behalf of Quebec, the premier of Quebec and the prime minister of Canada are far from representing the full spectrum of political reality in Quebec. Between the sovereignty movement as represented by the Parti Québécois and the hard-line federalist school led by Jean Chrétien, there exist in Quebec different intermediary positions. Among them, the most important is that which advocates the growth of Quebec within a renewed Canadian federation. On the Quebec political scene, this position is represented by the Quebec Liberal Party. But it also finds important echoes in larger constituencies. In certain aspects, it appeals to the many voters who support one of the federal parties. In other aspects, it also reaches out to those who are "soft nationalists."

The movement to renew federalism has had its highs and lows. On four occasions, in 1970, 1973, 1985, and 1989, it came to power under the leadership of Robert Bourassa. On four other occasions, in 1976, 1981, 1994, and 1998, it was defeated by the Parti Québécois. Despite the losses it suffered in the last two provincial elections, the movement to renew federalism remains strong in Quebec. Many polls have shown that it is still the preferred choice of a large majority of the Quebec population. Having been identified with this political movement — first as a journalist from 1962 to 1978, then as a political actor from

1978 to 1994, and now as an independent observer free from the responsibilities and constraints of office — I would like to explain how I reacted to the agreement reached on the 4th of February 1999 (thereafter the Framework Agreement).

A Deplorable Rupture

BEFORE ANALYSING THE CONTENT OF THE FRAMEWORK AGREEMENT, I WOULD LIKE TO express my disappointment regarding the circumstances which appear to have surrounded its signature. Having in no way participated in the discussions which preceded the Framework Agreement, I cannot offer a definitive judgement on this matter. As well, a clear judgement is difficult because in the months before the meeting in Ottawa, the population was given little information about the nature of these discussions.

According to the version of Lucien Bouchard and his Minister of Intergovernmental Affairs, Joseph Facal, it appears that after staying away from these discussions, the Quebec government decided — at the Annual Premiers' Conference in Saskatoon in August 1998 — to make common cause with the leaders of the other provinces and territories after certain essential elements were agreed to by the various parties (Saskatoon consensus). Among these elements was the commitment of the premiers to defend the right of a province "to opt out of any new or modified Canada-wide social program in areas of provincial/territorial jurisdiction with full compensation, provided that the province/territory carries on a program or initiative that addresses the priority areas of the Canada-wide program."

This commitment can be interpreted in various ways, as is the case with many political compromises. It is important to understand that it entailed concessions from all parties, including the Quebec government. It was notably the first time, to my knowledge, that a Parti Québécois government declared itself ready to accept the principle that the right to opt out should be accompanied by a commitment from the province involved to put into place a program or measure in the same area as the national program. Until very late in the negotiations in January 1999, the text that Quebec supported defined a common position of all the provincial and territorial governments. But the text that everyone approved (the Victoria proposal on the 28th of January 1999) was abandoned one week later, and replaced by another text that improved matters for certain provinces, but was unacceptable to Quebec. As a result, despite its having committed itself to specific conditions in a common front with the other provinces and territories, Quebec was abandoned by its partners at the crucial hour of decision.

This is the version of events put forward by the Quebec government. On the main points, it has not been challenged. If it is a fair portrait, it represents the third time in the past twenty years that Quebec has been abandoned by its partners after having decided to make common cause with them. This happened when the negotiations were underway to repatriate the Constitution. In April 1981, eight premiers, including René Lévesque, signed an agreement. In November of that year, the premiers of the seven other provinces accepted a position that was very different, and as a result Quebec was excluded. The second abandonment occurred during the Meech Lake process. In 1990, three years after all the first ministers had signed an agreement, two provincial premiers reneged on their provinces' commitments and the agreement fell apart. This most recent abandonment is without doubt less serious because the Framework Agreement is only of an administrative nature and can be revised in three years. Nonetheless, its nature is such as to increase Quebecers' mistrust of the commitments made and the rules of fair play used by the political leaders of the other provinces.

Some have attempted to minimize the importance of this abandonment by suggesting the Parti Québécois would never have let its premier sign an agreement on the Canadian social union. Those who argue in this way seem to ignore that the leader of the Quebec Liberals, Jean Charest, also declared he would have refused to sign the Framework Agreement, judging it to contain shortcomings and ambiguities that "could a priori interfere with jurisdictions of the National Assembly" and "eventually imperil certain specific interests of Quebec."[1]

I turn now to a detailed examination of the Framework Agreement.

Principles and Objectives

In the first section, entitled "Principles," the Framework Agreement lists a series of elements which are easy to support. This support, however, could have been facilitated with a clearer introduction and a fuller and more detailed definition of each objective. The preamble would have afforded an excellent occasion to define more clearly what makes up the Canadian union. It would have presented an opportune moment to restate that one of the original elements of the Canadian federation is the unique character of Quebec, and to underline that this characteristic should be taken into consideration in matters dealing with education, health and social services.

It would also have been an occasion to restate the guidelines concerning the division of powers between the federal Parliament and the legislative assemblies of the provinces and territories in the areas of education, health and social services, if need be mentioning in passing certain areas of disagreement. Unfortunately, neither this nor any other section of the Framework Agreement develops these ideas.

Greater precision would also have been useful in formulating the general objectives set out in the "Principles" section of the Framework Agreement. For example, one can easily agree that all Canadians should be equal before the law. It does not necessarily follow that all Canadians are purely and simply equal. This important difference is glossed over by the signers of the Framework Agreement. One can hope that all Canadians participate actively in the social and economic life of the country, but is it really the role of governments to "promote the full and active participation of all Canadians in Canada's social and economic life"? Governments should not create obstacles to this participation and should eliminate — by legislative means and good management of state affairs — difficulties that hamper citizen participation. But the initiative for this participation must rest primarily with citizens themselves and with civil society, rather than with governments.

Mobility

In the second section, "Mobility within Canada" the defined objectives are generally worthy of support. Every citizen should enjoy the liberty to move around and live anywhere inside a country with a federal system of government. To the extent that the criteria of admission to programs or services restrict this mobility, it is highly desirable that such barriers be eliminated. However, sweeping commitments which give rise to complicated constraints should be avoided until the real problems have been identified, and realistic timetables for their elimination have been established.

For example, the Framework Agreement calls upon governments to "eliminate, *within three years*, [emphasis added] any residency-based policies or practices which constrain access to post-secondary education, training, health and social services and social assistance unless they can be demonstrated to be reasonable and consistent with the principles of the Social Union Framework." It even requires "by July 1, 2001, full compliance with the mobility provisions of the Agreement on Internal Trade." (This 1994 agreement between the federal government and the governments of the provinces and territories deals with, among other matters, the mutual recognition of the qualification standards for the practice of trades and professions.)

The objectives pursued are commendable. Given the large number of programs which exist in these areas and the important differences between Quebec and the other provinces in these matters, however, it is doubtful that full compliance can be achieved within three years. I also doubt that, in the areas directly linked to its distinct character, Quebec will be willing to cede to an outside authority its constitutional jurisdiction in education, health and social services. It would be more realistic to promote greater mobility through procedures which stress a rigorous identification of problems, the exchange of information, and reciprocity in concrete measures.

Above all, it will remain for the governments to agree on what constitutes an obstacle to mobility. This could be more difficult than it appears at first glance. To take but one example, one may honestly believe that charging tuition fees at a higher rate for students from other provinces who wish to undertake post-secondary studies in Quebec is an obstacle to the mobility of these students. But one can legitimately argue that Quebec has maintained particularly low levels of tuition and that the advantages stemming from a low-tuition policy should be reserved for Quebec students, and consequently that it is not unfair to require students from other provinces to pay fees based on a Canadian average.

I do not approve of the Quebec government's decision to charge higher tuition fees to students from other provinces, because the negative impact of this measure on the province's image far outweighs the limited economic benefits that the Quebec treasury receives. But there must be room for honest differences of opinion of this nature. If it becomes necessary that each case be sifted through a pan-Canadian filter, as the Framework Agreement states, the sovereignty of the provinces in their areas of jurisdiction could be seriously diminished.

Accountability

THE THIRD SECTION, "PUBLIC ACCOUNTABILITY AND TRANSPARENCY," COMMITS EACH government to follow closely the performance of its policies and programs, measure the outcomes, publish regular reports, and publicize eligibility criteria to the social programs under its responsibility. The Framework Agreement also commits governments to share information with one another and work together to put in place "comparable indicators to measure progress on agreed objectives."

As with many other commitments in the Framework Agreement, these seem to be acceptable. They can be interpreted as leading to increased cooperation between governments, in the full respect of the jurisdiction of each and minimal bureaucratic entanglements. If this interpretation prevails, the Framework Agreement could deliver positive results. Given acceptable agreements, Quebec is willing to go quite far in the direction of collaboration. Since the early 1990s, for example, Quebec has played an active role, by updating the interprovincial performance indicators for primary and secondary education and by signing a 1994 national protocol "assuring the mutual recognition of post-secondary education credits."[2]

It is necessary, on the other hand, to be on guard against an alternate interpretation which will be put forward by the apostles of wholesale planning. They are to be found not only in Ottawa, but in certain provincial capitals. These people will take advantage of any small opening they can find in the text of the Framework Agreement to propose expensive and complicated new mechanisms for gathering and interpreting statistics. This will inevitably lead to the federal bureaucracy's seeking to exercise greater control.

If this alternate interpretation prevails, provincial initiatives will become more and more contained within bureaucratically cumbersome standards and administrative guidelines, over which the provinces have less and less control.

In the accountability section the governments also commit themselves to put into place consultative measures to promote that participation of citizens in developing social policies and examining the results obtained. This discourse is attractive at first glance. But upon analysis it is fraught with ambiguity. The participation of citizens in the development of policies must be achieved, in a liberal democracy, by various means that do not depend on the benevolence of governments. These include the many activities of voluntary associations and lobby groups, the work of political parties and, in a more general way, the debates stimulated by the written press and the electronic media.

What, one may wonder, will these new proposed consultative mechanisms achieve in a context which already provides many avenues for participation? One government may find it appropriate to set up consultative structures in order to govern; another may prefer to rely on methods based on the responsibility of elected officials; yet another may prefer direct democracy. It is not clear why a commitment to practise one style of public administration over another should be included in an intergovernmental agreement on social union.

Intergovernmental Partnership

THE FOURTH SECTION, DEALING WITH INTERGOVERNMENTAL PARTNERSHIP, SHARES THE same flaw as previous chapters. It is both too vague and too ambitious. A serious partnership project must be based on a clear recognition of the responsibilities and jurisdictions of each partner and on the precise identification of matters on which the partners wish to act jointly. The Framework Agreement barely mentions these requirements; instead, it is written in vague language open to multiple interpretations which one could easily invoke to justify all and any future federal intervention in social policies.

The concept of partnership, as stated in the Framework Agreement, seems to exclude any future revision of the existing division of responsibilities. It seems to take for granted that each partner will remain entrenched in its present role. The partnership will thus apply to future governmental initiatives. Stated in simple terms, the commitments described in this section are rather slight. They require, for example, that governments give one another advance notice of a major change of a policy or program. In the absence of further details, this commitment has little meaning. If, however, it were to be interpreted in a more constraining way, it might be incompatible with the obligations of governments towards their respective constituents and parliaments.

The federal government is committed to offering each province or territory an agreement it has concluded with one province or territory, while taking into account the particular situation of each. This provision expresses a laudable concern for fairness. Given the rigid orthodoxy that might govern its implementation in federal circles, however, this commitment might render difficult, or even impossible, particular adjustments which only Quebec, among the ten provinces, feels necessary.

The Federal Spending Power

THE MOST CONTROVERSIAL SECTION OF THE FRAMEWORK AGREEMENT DEALS WITH the federal spending power. I am not inclined to question this power in principle, for two reasons. First, the spending power is an essential feature of a sovereign state. Second, in the past, this power was necessary — or very useful to say the least — in situations of serious economic and social difficulty, and in promotion of equal opportunity for all Canadians.

For example, recall the Great Depression of the 1930s. How can one forget the powerlessness of governments in the face of the misery that then hit the industrialized world. Acting upon the recommendations of numerous commissions and studies that advocated more efficient public policy against the major risks of an industrial society (such as unemployment, expensive family responsibilities, insufficient education, sickness, accidents, poverty in old age), the Canadian government — like that of many other countries — made a commitment during the Second World War to better protect its population against poverty as soon as the war ended. The welfare state was born.

In Canada, due to a constitutional change, unemployment insurance was placed under the jurisdiction of the federal government. With the support of a vast majority of the population, Ottawa, over the next quarter-century enriched the old-age pension plan, and instituted new programs like family allowances, medicare, and an occupational pension scheme, and sought to revamp social assistance. The leadership of the federal government during the last half-century allowed Canada to establish a wide-ranging social security net. This would have been impossible without the federal spending power.

There are, however, difficulties — and these are not mentioned in the Framework Agreement — linked to the spending power. As the recent exercises in fiscal restraint by both Ottawa and the provinces have demonstrated, the Canadian social net put in place since the Second World War is very expensive.

The manner in which federal cuts were imposed was also the source of many disputes between Ottawa and the provinces — in particular between Ottawa and Quebec. Ottawa often imposed priorities that differed from those of the provinces; the provinces had to accept them and submit to conditions set by Ottawa to have access to federal financing.

The economic difficulties of the 1990s have forced the federal government to reduce its financial commitments towards the social programs it funds (Employment Insurance, old-age pensions) and reduce considerably the funds made available to provinces for their own programs, which are financed partly through federal transfer payments. It was quite reasonable, given this context, that the provinces sought to review the spending power — not the existence of the spending power, but the rules governing its use.

Quebec was for a long time the only province to insist on a more restrictive framework governing the spending power. Aware that Anglo-Canadian opinion has generally favoured leadership on the part of the federal government with regards to social policy, Quebec has insisted since the 1960s on a right to opt out of Canada-wide federal programs, with financial compensation. More recently, other provinces and territories have also insisted on this right. The provinces and territories seemed united on this question until January of this year. However, the final discussions in February resulted in adoption of a text quite different from that on which the provinces and territories had agreed a week earlier. Many elements of the Framework Agreement illustrate a tilt toward the federal perspective on the spending power.

Transfers to the Provinces

1. In the subsection on transfers to the provinces, Ottawa agrees not to establish any new program in the areas of health, education and social services until it has received the agreement of a majority of the provinces — that is, agreement of at least six provinces. Since a majority of the provinces can be attained with a mere 15 percent of the population, and since the smaller provinces are more inclined to rely on federal government support, this requirement will be relatively easy to satisfy. The objectives of a new program established with the agreement of a number of provinces representing a small proportion of the population could subsequently be imposed on all provinces as a condition of their access to grants related to the said program. In practice, this new system will closely resemble what we have known until now.

2. The Framework Agreement requires both the federal government and provinces to "give one another advance notice prior to implementation of a major change in a social policy or program which will likely substantially affect another government." This commitment appears promising. However, as seen in Paul Martin's last budget, the federal government is hardly bound by this requirement. A major change affecting the calculation of payments to the provinces in regards to the Canada Health and Social Transfer was introduced without advance notice. This change accelerates the transition to equal per capita transfers among provinces, and adversely affects Quebec. Even though the federal government's wish to allocate transfers on this basis has been known for a long time — and Ottawa had started this adjustment in 1996 — this latest change was imposed, according to Quebec, without prior notice and without consideration of the view expressed two weeks earlier by the provinces. Bernard Landry further claims this change will have an adverse effect on social assistance programming.[3]

3. Provincial participation in a national program has always been subject to certain conditions which aim to guarantee that the funding obtained be used for the purposes outlined in the program. While it was hoped that the Framework Agreement would have led to greater flexibility, it instead leads to more constraints. The accountability framework, to which the participating provinces will be subject, will be jointly defined by the federal government and the provinces. The federal government will have a powerful bargaining tool to tighten constraints when it judges it necessary.

4. In the case of programs financed by transfers to the provinces, the Framework Agreement opens the way to the practice of opting out. When compared with the text approved by the provinces and territories on the 28th of January, we note, however, that the Framework Agreement is more restrictive in its provisions for opting out. The right to opt out will be possible only in the case where a province already has in place a program equivalent to the new program. As noted by Joseph Facal, "as long as Quebec does not have an existing program, there is no valid right to opt out."[4]

Transfers to Individuals and Organizations

The right to opt out, as defined in the Victoria proposal, applied both to federal programs involving transfers to provinces and to federal programs involving transfers to individuals and organizations. Sharply critical of the creation of the Millennium Scholarship Fund, the Quebec government made this provision a necessary condition for adhering to an interprovincial consensus.

However, according to the Framework Agreement, this provision was cast aside. The Framework Agreement requires that the federal government give the provinces "at least three month notice and offer to consult" before launching "new Canada-wide initiatives funded through direct transfers to individuals or organizations for health care, post-secondary education, social assistance and social services." There ends its benevolence.

Apart from these slight restrictions, the federal government considers that it has the authority to undertake at will initiatives such as the Millennium Scholarship Fund, fiscal benefits for specific groups of citizens or grants to organizations working in areas which are clearly under provincial jurisdiction. Through tax credits and fiscal benefits, the federal government may, if it so wishes, play an ever larger role in the area of social policy.

Jean Chrétien, Stéphane Dion and David Cameron have, in various written and oral statements, argued that the Framework Agreement's restraint on the federal spending power is more advantageous for the provinces than that of the Meech Lake Accord. This assertion does not hold upon close examination of both texts.

In the Meech Lake Accord, the spending power provision was surrounded by a number of other provisions which went a long way toward meeting the demands of Quebec, most notably a constitutional provision explicitly recognizing the distinct character of Quebec society. No such mention is made in the Social Union Framework Agreement. No mention is even made of the paragraph in the Calgary Declaration referring to the "unique character" of Quebec.

Second, in the Meech Lake Accord, the spending power provision was constitutional in nature. In the Framework Agreement, provisions regarding the spending power are of an administrative nature, and last only three years.

Third, in the case of opting out of a Canada-wide program, the Meech Lake Accord required that "the province carries on a program or initiative that is compatible with the national objectives."[5] This was deliberately written in general terms to allow sufficient room for a flexible interpretation compatible with recognition of Quebec's distinct character. The Social Union Framework Agreement does not have the same flexibility.

Finally, David Cameron asserts that the Framework Agreement goes further than Meech in that it not only deals with transfers to provinces, but also transfers to individuals and organizations.[6] As we have seen above, the said provisions serve only to confirm and strengthen the powers and responsibilities claimed by the federal government in these areas.

Resolution of Disputes

THE FRAMEWORK AGREEMENT'S SIXTH SECTION DISCUSSES "DISPUTE AVOIDANCE AND resolution." With regards to social policies, and in particular the implementation of programs, disputes will inevitably arise between the federal government and the provinces, and among the provinces. The dispute between Alberta and Ottawa concerning the interpretation of certain provisions of the health insurance system is the best-known example. The Framework Agreement recommends that governments co-operate among themselves to avoid disputes and resolve disputes in a non-adversarial way when they arise. Despite these good intentions, it makes sense to provide for a dispute resolution procedure in the event that direct negotiations among concerned governments fail.

The first choice is to decide if such disputes should be submitted to binding arbitration, judicial or other. The governments have decided with good reason to avoid binding arbitration of disputes by a third party. When implementing social programs, an arbitration decision may have expensive consequences for the public purse. Especially in financially difficult times, governments must avoid as much as possible entrusting to third parties, who are not accountable to anyone, the responsibility for decisions that could carry high costs. In refusing binding arbitration, the first ministers have made a realistic choice.

The Framework Agreement contains various provisions that can facilitate the flexible and efficient resolution of disputes relating to mobility, intergovernmental transfers and the interpretation of the principles in the Canada Health Act. These provisions are based on a rule of parity according to which the parties involved in a dispute must be represented at each step of a resolution procedure and have responsibility for the decisions. This parity rule may prove to be cumbersome and increase costs in dispute resolution. However, it offers necessary guarantees of fairness in the resolution of disputes.

Conclusion

Claude Castonguay considers the Framework Agreement a breakthrough.[7] Among moderate Quebec federalists who follow these questions closely, he is the only one, to my knowledge, who has reacted favourably. André Burelle, former adviser to Pierre Trudeau, has severely condemned the Framework Agreement's centralizing nature.[8] Burelle's opinion is based on a rather narrow legal interpretation of the Constitution Act of 1867. He does not sufficiently take into account the major changes in the economic and social life of the country during the past century. In general, however, Burelle's reaction appears to be more representative than Castonguay's of opinion among moderate federalist Quebecers. The Framework Agreement will be remembered by Quebec federalists either as an important initiative, the objective of which was seriously compromised by the exclusion of Quebec, or as a long-winded and weak text opening the door to an increased preponderance of the federal government in social policy.

Seen from a distance, negotiating the Framework Agreement reproduced once again the inherent weaknesses of past attempts at changing the federation. On one side, the nation-builders of English Canada, some in Ottawa and others in provincial capitals, strive with unquestioned sincerity to develop Canada-wide initiatives aimed at harmonizing and integrating policies. Even when their projects seem to go beyond the letter of the Constitution, they have many good reasons to promote them. Conscious of the particular situation of Quebec, they generally attempt to associate the province with their initiatives. But because they fail to invest the effort needed to understand the true nature of the challenges deriving from Quebec's specific nature, they more often than not become tired of negotiating and in the end let down their embarrassing partner.

In the end, they come up with agreements that, because of Quebec's absence, are not really national agreements. Quebec, with its experience of Canada-wide initiatives, enters negotiations with caution, since any eventual agreement might go against its own values. Quebec gladly participates in information meetings and exchanges of correspondence. But when it comes to proposals to integrate the provinces and Ottawa and thereby dilute provincial jurisdictions, Quebec generally refuses to sign, whatever party may be in power in Quebec City. Before signing an agreement, Quebec often poses conditions that other provincial governments cannot accept. Each attempt at negotiations thus ends, more often than not, in failure which in turn aggravates frustration both in Quebec and the rest of the country.

How do we see the future in the wake of the failed negotiations on the social union? I exclude two extremes: that of Quebec's separation and that of a strategy that seeks to unite the country without reference to the distinct character of Quebec.

In September 1964, soon after my appointment as editor of *Le Devoir*, I expressed my clear preference for what I called the "Canadian hypothesis." Although I understood that agreement is more difficult when many cultures cohabit the same territory, I noted that, thanks to our diversity, we had the chance to build a political society in Canada respectful of individual liberty and also respectful of Quebec's own fundamental nature.[9] I added, however, that to be successful important changes to the Canadian Constitution, as well as to our political institutions, were needed. Thirty-five years later, even if the changes hoped for by Quebec are slow in coming, I still believe that the Canadian federal union is the best option for Quebec, and for the rest of Canada. That's why, with all due respect to those who are in favour of Quebec independence, I remain opposed to their option.

If the majority of the changes desired by moderate Quebec federalists have been refused to date, this is not because of a lack of sincere effort and understanding on behalf of those involved. In particular, I would like to emphasize the efforts of the many voices in the anglophone community who have shown an open spirit over the past years, whether it be in political circles, in universities, or in business. Where negotiations have failed, it is mostly because they have been thwarted by supporters of a rigid vision of Canadian unity. This vision contains an abstract and doctrinaire equality of individuals and provinces; it denies any form of asymmetry in our federal system. This vision was at the root of the failure of the Meech Lake Accord. It was also present in discussions leading to the Framework Agreement. Similar causes usually produce similar effects: no serious progress will ever be realized with Quebec as long as this vision prevails.

Once we escape the deeply rutted paths of separatism and rigid federalism, three avenues can be explored. One of them, put forward by the Reform Party, advocates extensive decentralization. It would provide Quebec with the same advantages as the other provinces. It goes without saying, however, that the degree of decentralization which would be justified in the case of Quebec might not be desirable for the Atlantic provinces. The Atlantic provinces, which have a greater dependence on the federal government, expect a substantial federal role.

The same applies to official-language minorities. The principal responsibility for language policy, under the Reform Party, would be given to the provinces. In light of past history, this is not reassuring to linguistic minorities, who have learned to count on the support of the federal government to defend their rights and to assure them appropriate public structures.

A second avenue has been suggested by André Burelle, who has repeatedly disassociated himself from the concept of Canadian unity dear to his former boss. According to Burelle, we should return to the spirit, and perhaps even to the letter, of the 1867 Constitution. Government action must be based on a clear, rigorous respect for the respective jurisdictions of each order of government, and on joint decision-making in areas of common interest.

In the absence of a more flexible approach, we may eventually seek refuge in this avenue. There are, however, three weaknesses to Burelle's approach. It is easier said than done to specify the areas of competence that belong to each order of government. This is even harder to do in the area of social policy, where memories of the Great Depression still linger, and where the country is changing at a rapid pace, both economically and socially. Also, since the 1982 Constitution, there is explicit joint responsibility of the two orders of government in the matter of equalizing individual opportunity. Those in favour of the Burelle approach attach great importance to interprovincial cooperation as a means to resolve problems common to the provinces. In light of the often divergent interests among provinces, and the rules of decision-making available under this type of cooperation, interprovincial cooperation would always be fragile. Furthermore, in order for interprovincial cooperation to be efficient, new structures would have to be set up, which would risk overlapping existing federal services. A third difficulty involves the rule of joint decision-making in matters involving the two orders of government. When there are convergent interests, joint decision-making produces excellent results. What happens when there is disagreement? For the parties to fall back upon their respective jurisdictions would not be a strategy adequate to resolve new problems that crop up more and more frequently in modern society.

A third avenue is that advocated by moderate Quebec federalists, with mixed results to date. Those in favour of this approach want a strong Quebec in a renewed Canadian federation, including a clear and operative recognition of the distinct character of Quebec. A first draft of this approach was proposed twenty years ago by the Pepin-Robarts Task Force on Canadian Unity, which recommended our federal system be more flexible and have room for asymmetrical measures. The conclusions of the Confederation 2000 Conference, held in Ottawa in the spring of 1996 under the auspices of the Business Council on National Issues, were also consistent with this approach.[10] Another version of asymmetrical federalism was proposed by the Quebec Liberal Party in a significant report published in 1996.[11] We would not need to bend over backwards in order to find solutions for Quebec, if only we could renounce the idea of treating it as "a province like the others."

This third avenue is much more promising than the bland consensus of the Framework Agreement. Along with it, we no longer need to seek uniform solutions applicable to everyone at the same time, but rather devise flexible arrangements which can allow for the pursuit of national objectives while taking into account the different situation in Quebec. Needless to say, these arrangements should not confer upon Quebec undue financial advantages, advantages which it is not seeking.

In the case of the spending power, this approach should take into consideration the fact that Quebec is considerably different and should be given the right to withdraw unconditionally from all Canada-wide programs within provincial jurisdiction. This withdrawal would be accompanied by financial compensation in the form of either cash or tax transfers.

Since the negotiations on the Canadian social union failed on the question of the spending power, we must sooner or later re-open conversation around this issue. I hope that in any future round of negotiation, the governments will find their inspiration along this third avenue. In my judgement, here lies the best if not the only way in which we may satisfy all Canadians, including Quebecers.

Originally published in *Inroads*, no. 8 (1999), pp. 25-41

1 Jean Charest, "L'Union sociale canadienne — L'occasion de progresser ensemble," *Le Devoir*, February 13, 1999.

2 Joseph Facal, "Facal sonne le réveil des souverainistes," *Le Devoir*, February 13, 1999.

3 Bernard Landry, "Les besoins sont à Québec, l'argent est à Ottawa," *La Presse*, February 25,1999.

4 Joseph Facal, "Pourquoi le Québec dit non à l'union sociale," *La Presse*, February 25, 1999.

5 Peter W. Hogg (ed.), *Meech Lake Constitutional Accord Annotated* (Toronto: Carswell, 1988), p. 76.

6 David Cameron, "The Social Union is not a Backward Step for Quebec," *Globe and Mail*, February 12, 1999.

7 Claude Castonguay, "Union sociale: un déblocage majeur," *La Presse*, February 10, 1999.

8 André Burelle, "Mise en tutelle des provinces," *Le Devoir*, February 15, 1999.

9 Claude Ryan, two articles published in Le Devoir, September 18 & 19, 1964. Reprinted in Who Speaks for Canada? (Toronto: McLelland & Stewart, 1998), p. 206.

10 Business Council on National Issues, *Confederation 2000 — Today and Tomorrow — An Agenda for Action — Ideas and Recommendations of the Confederation 2000 Conference Participants*. Report published under the sponsorship of the Business Council on National Issues, Ottawa, 1996.

11 Quebec Liberal Party, *Recognition and Interdependence: Quebec's Identity and Canadian Federalism* (December 1996).

Framework Agreement on Canada's Social Union (the Saskatoon consensus)

PREMIERS DISCUSSED THE STATUS OF NEGOTIATIONS ON A FRAMEWORK AGREEMENT for the social union. They noted that both orders of government are involved in Canada's social union and emphasized that a stronger partnership between the two orders of government is needed to secure Canada's social programs for the future.

Premiers strongly believe that a Framework Agreement for the Social Union will provide all Canadians with a better opportunity to participate fully in our economic and social life. It is about governments working together, within their constitutional responsibilities, to ensure strong and sustainable health, education and social services for Canadians. It is not about more power for one order of government or another.

Premiers expressed their unanimous support for the provincial/territorial consensus negotiating position developed by participating Ministers.

Premiers welcomed the Prime Minister's recent public commitment to concluding negotiations on an agreement. They recognized that the recent federal proposals on the Framework Agreement, although not a complete response to the provincial/territorial consensus negotiating position paper, permits the negotiations to proceed.

Premiers agreed that through negotiations they could accommodate many of the objectives of the federal proposals. The challenge now is for the federal government to work with the provinces/territories to resolve outstanding issues.

Premiers noted that the areas of common ground between the federal and provincial/territorial positions represent progress in the negotiations but stressed that collaborative arrangements on federal spending in areas of provincial/territorial jurisdiction, and a fair dispute resolution process are essential to a balanced and fair partnership. Premiers stressed that negotiations should now proceed with a view to concluding a draft agreement by the end of the year.

Premiers noted that the federal proposals contain provisions for opting out. Premiers emphasized that the flexibility afforded to provinces/territories through the ability to opt out of any new or modified Canada-wide social program in areas of provincial/territorial jurisdiction with full compensation, provided that the province/territory carries on a program or initiative that addresses the priority areas of the Canada-wide program, is an essential dimension of the provincial/territorial consensus negotiating position.

Premiers also agreed that new mechanisms to prevent and resolve disputes are an essential element of their negotiating position.

Premiers emphasized that disputes between governments undermine Canada's social union and that new cooperative mechanisms that both prevent disputes, and resolve them fairly when they arise, would strengthen Canadians' confidence in the ability of their governments to work together on their behalf.

Premiers emphasized that Canada's Social Union, and the programs that Canadians value most, particularly health care, must be supported by renewed fiscal arrangements that balance provincial/territorial program responsibilities with revenues.

Premiers concluded their discussions on the Framework Agreement negotiations by reiterating the negotiating ground rule that no element of the Framework Agreement is agreed to until everything is agreed to, and directed the Provincial Co-Chair of the negotiations, the Honourable Bernhard Wiens to set a date with the federal Co-Chair, the Honourable Anne McLellan, for a negotiating meeting of Ministers as soon as possible.

Securing Canada's Social Union into the 21st Century (the Victoria proposal)

1. Reflecting Canadian Values

GOVERNMENTS ARE COMMITTED TO WORKING BETTER TOGETHER TO ENSURE A strong social union that addresses the priorities of Canadians. This commitment is reflected in the following vision:

> The quality of our social union is one of the reasons that Canada is the envy of the world.
>
> The social union provides the foundation for the enhancement and preservation of social programs. It is the network of policies and programs that provides all Canadians with health care, education, training, employment insurance, and other social services. Canadians see these programs as essential to their well being and their sense of community.
>
> This Agreement is designed to improve social programs for Canadians by making them more efficient and effective. Canadians want and deserve governments working better together by clarifying responsibilities, eliminating overlap and duplication, and enhancing accountability.
>
> This Agreement offers Canadians financially sustainable health care and social programs, more accountable government, flexibility to meet different needs in different provinces and territories, and greater harmony among governments. Working together more effectively will strengthen the social union and benefit all Canadians.

2. Guiding Principles

THE FOLLOWING PRINCIPLES WILL GUIDE ALL GOVERNMENTS IN THE DESIGN AND delivery of social policies and programs:

Meeting the Needs of Canadians

- All Canadians are equal. Social programs should treat Canadians with fairness and equity.
- All Canadians should have reasonable access to essential public services of reasonable quality and appropriate assistance should be provided to support and protect those most in need.
- Governments are committed to the principles of medicare, which are comprehensiveness, universality, portability, public administration and accessibility. Governments agree there is a need for a joint mechanism for management and interpretation of these principles.[1]
- Social policy should assist all Canadians to participate actively in economic and social life by enhancing self-sufficiency and well-being, promoting prevention and early intervention and supporting the lifelong development of individuals.

Promoting Individual and Collective Responsibility

- Social policy should reflect Canadians' individual and collective responsibility for each other and their families, promote the dignity and independence of the individual, and support strong and healthy communities.
- Partnerships among governments, communities, the voluntary sector and social organizations, business, labour, families, and individuals are essential to modernizing and strengthening Canada's social union.

Ensuring Affordable, Effective and Accountable Programs

- All major federal/provincial/territorial funding arrangements should provide provinces and territories with adequate resources to meet their responsibilities to Canadians. To ensure that Canadians are treated equitably, the federal government will work with provinces and territories to ensure that they have the financial resources to allow them to provide reasonably comparable levels of public services at reasonably comparable levels of taxation.

Managing Canada's Social Union

- Under the Constitution, provinces and territories are primarily responsible for social policy and the delivery of social programs.
- Governments believe strongly in increasing accountability to the public and improving the effectiveness and efficiency of the social union. To this end, governments are committed to:
- reducing and avoiding overlap and duplication;
- clarifying roles and responsibilities by assigning, where appropriate, responsibility for areas of the social union to one order of government or the other; and,
- minimizing areas of joint responsibility where this would improve the effectiveness and efficiency of the social union.
- Governments are committed to working together in partnership where this would result in improved services to Canadians and explaining to Canadians their respective contributions to social programs.
- For the purpose of clarity, nothing in this agreement abrogates or derogates from Aboriginal, treaty or other rights of Aboriginal peoples, such as territorial self-government agreements.

3. Freedom of Movement

All governments support and promote the principle that Canadians are free to pursue social and economic opportunities anywhere in Canada. Mobility reflects our shared citizenship and is essential for equality of opportunity. Specifically:

> All governments are committed to freedom of movement of Canadians.
>
> All governments are therefore committed to eliminating unreasonable barriers to mobility while maintaining governments' ability to pursue legitimate public policy objectives.

All governments support the labour market provisions of the AIT under the current implementation process.

All governments are committed to promoting the mobility rights of Aboriginal Canadians by ensuring full access to, and portability of, federal social programs and benefits both on and off reserve.

4. Programs Canadians can Count on

A KEY PURPOSE OF THE SOCIAL UNION IS TO ESTABLISH A MORE EFFECTIVE PARTNERship among the governments which design, fund and deliver social programs. A renewed federal/provincial/territorial partnership is based, in large measure, on funding arrangements that ensure governments have the financial resources necessary to meet their social policy commitments to Canadians.

Adequacy, predictability and stability should characterize all major federal/provincial/territorial funding arrangements. Therefore, the following provisions apply to existing and new federal/provincial/territorial fiscal transfers and existing and new federal/provincial/territorial funding arrangements.

Adequacy

The federal government will work with provinces and territories to ensure that all major federal/provincial/territorial funding arrangements provide provinces and territories with adequate resources to meet their responsibilities to Canadians, including those described in this agreement. To ensure that Canadians are treated equitably, the federal government will work with provinces and territories to ensure that they have the financial resources to allow them to provide reasonably comparable levels of public services at reasonably comparable levels of taxation.

Adequacy and long-term balance will be addressed through:

- The federal government working with the provinces and territories to ensure that major federal/provincial/territorial funding arrangements adequately reflect provincial/territorial spending responsibilities. Full federal restoration of the funding cut from the Canada Health and Social Transfer is an important first step toward adequate funding for health care and other social programs. As a priority, provinces and territories agree that they will direct restored federal funds to core health services;

- The federal government working with the provinces to ensure that equalization payments adequately address the fiscal imbalances that exist between the provinces' revenue-raising capacities. The Equalization Program must provide provincial governments with sufficient revenues to provide reasonably comparable levels of public services at reasonably comparable levels of taxation; and,
- The federal government working with the provinces and territories to ensure sufficient federal resources through existing financial arrangements to address current and growing cost pressures in the areas of health, education and social services. An important step toward addressing cost pressures is the adequate escalation of current and future federal/provincial/territorial funding arrangements to ensure that the growing costs associated with funding health care and other social programs are reflected in the overlap level of funding.
- Under this Agreement, if the federal government withdraws from the funding of social programs, or if there is a realignment of responsibilities within the federation, commensurate federal resources must accompany these changes to provide provinces and territories with adequate funds to carry out their new or enhanced responsibilities.

Stability and Predictability

All major federal/provincial/territorial funding arrangements will be for a period of not less than five years and will be renewed automatically unless revised in accordance with this Agreement. CHST and Equalization, as well as any future major funding arrangements, will each be reviewed on a five-year schedule. Improvements to all major funding arrangements could still be made within the five-year time frame.

As required, and for the purposes of the five-year schedule referred to above, the federal government will provide provinces/territories three years' written notice before reducing major federal/provincial/territorial funding arrangements. The period for notification can be shortened upon agreement of all parties.

Non-Canada-wide federal and provincial/territorial funding arrangements must include provisions to ensure that they also are stable and predictable. These should include appropriate notice provisions for termination or adjustments and any mutually agreed-upon renewal provisions.

Federal constitutional, fiduciary, treaty and other historic responsibilities for assurance of Aboriginal, health, income support, social services, housing, training and educational opportunities must be fulfilled. The federal government must recognize its financial responsibilities for Aboriginal Canadians, both on and off reserve.

Dispute Resolution and Reporting

Provisions around adequacy, stability and predictability, as well as the provisions for the non-Canada-wide programs, could be subject to the dispute settlement mechanism — up to and including Step III.

Canadians should have access to appropriate information and reports regarding commitments made to them by governments under the Social Union Framework Agreement. Accordingly, the federal government agrees to report publicly, on an annual basis, regarding its commitments to adequate, predictable and stable funding arrangements.

5. Working Together in Partnership

Collaborative Initiatives

TO BETTER SERVE THE SOCIAL NEEDS OF CANADIANS, GOVERNMENTS NEED TO WORK collaboratively to strengthen Canada's social union. Provincial and territorial governments have primary responsibility for core social programs. The federal government also has an important role in the social union. Governments recognize that in areas of joint responsibility, or when one government acting within its own jurisdictional responsibility has a major impact upon another government, there must be a better means of managing these common interests. What follows is a continuum of collaborative initiatives to complement the collaborative approaches to federal spending on Canada-wide social programs:

Advance Notice and Information Sharing

Each order of government shall give the other written notice of any change proposed to a social policy or program in any area in which the actions of one government significantly affect another government. At the same time that notice of the proposed social policy or program change is given, written information about the change will be provided in sufficient detail to enable the receiving government to assess it adequately.

Mandatory Consultation

The government initiating the change shall be required to engage in meaningful consultation, including consideration of alternative initiatives, with the other government to ensure that the proposed change did not duplicate effort or operate in a counterproductive manner. Consultation could result in further collaborative action.

Joint Priority Setting

Governments agree to set joint overarching priorities. Where appropriate, governments also agree to broad goals, objectives and strategic directions for those priorities identified.

Outcome Measurement and Public Reporting

Governments agree to measure key social policy outcomes with a view to reporting on their actions to the public.

A Collaborative Approach to Federal Spending on Canada-Wide Social Programs

Building on precedents established by the National Child Benefit, provinces and territories are committed to working collaboratively to achieve consensus where federal spending on Canada-wide programs occurs in areas of provincial jurisdiction. Provincial/territorial flexibility in program design and delivery is a key component of social programs. The ability of a province/territory to address priority areas of Canada-wide programs within its jurisdiction is essential to an effectively functioning social union. Appropriate recourse to a consent rule is necessary to ensure that the collaborative approach in Step 1 is pursued.

Step 1 - Collaboration

- Joint priority-setting on federal cash and tax expenditures on new or modified Canada-wide programs in areas of provincial jurisdictions.
- Joint agreement on objectives and principles for new or modified Canada-wide programs, including:
    - program flexibility which respects provincial/territorial priorities,
    - clear roles and responsibilities for each order of government, and,
    - a commitment to reduce and avoid overlap and duplication.
- Agreement to develop, measure and publicly report on outcomes of new and modified Canada-wide programs, consistent with each government's roles and responsibilities.
- Agreements should incorporate measures to ensure the adequacy and certainty of funding.

Step 2 - Flexibility

Where the collaborative approach in Step 1 does not achieve agreement, the following provisions will be invoked:

- Any new or modified Canada-wide program in areas of provincial jurisdiction requires the consent of a majority of provinces. The consent of the territories will be sought.
- The federal government will provide full financial compensation to any provincial or territorial government that chooses not to participate in any new or modified Canada-wide program, providing it carries on a program or initiative that addresses the priority areas of the new or modified Canada-wide program.

Collaborative Approaches to Non-Canada-Wide Programs

Federal spending in an area of provincial jurisdiction which occurs in a province or territory must have the consent of the province or territory involved. Agreement should incorporate measures to ensure adequacy and certainty of funding.

The provisions of these sections should be subject to the dispute settlement mechanism.

6. Clear Roles for Government

Canadians need to know which order of government to hold responsible for specific decisions in areas of social policy. Clarifying roles and responsibilities in the management and delivery of social programs will enable Canadians to hold their governments accountable for decisions they make.

The considerations identified in the graphic attached will guide the development of federal and provincial/territorial roles and responsibilities in new social programs.

Within two years, sector Ministers will review current federal and provincial/territorial responsibilities, using the considerations below, and, where agreed, take measures to align responsibilities in accordance with them.

Sector Ministers will report annually to the Ministerial Council for Social Policy Reform and Renewal, on progress in realigning roles and responsibilities. The Ministerial Council will provide an annual public report to First Ministers, summarizing the progress made by sector Ministers.

7. Accountability for Canadians

Canadian's Social Union can be strengthened through enhancing each government's accountability to its constituents. Each government therefore agrees to:

Clarify the roles of [g]overnments and inform Canadians of the responsibilities of each government.

Ensure that social programs are delivered in a fair and transparent way.

Monitor and measure outcomes of their own social programs and report regularly to their constituents on how their social programs have performed.

Share best practices to enable jurisdictions to develop their own outcome measures.

Publicly report financial information to ensure Canadians understand the relative funding contributions of governments to programs.

Publicly report on their respective commitments of providing stable and adequate funding for social programs.

Involvement of Canadians

Governments agree that Canadians should have appropriate opportunities for public input in developing priorities and objectives for social programs.

Canadians should have access to fair and transparent administrative processes in social programs. Accordingly, governments agree to:

- Make publicly available eligibility criteria for their social programs.
- Have in place appropriate administrative mechanisms at the local level, that allow citizens to appeal when they believe they have been treated unfairly in the administration of a social program.

8. Working out Diffeences Between Governments

GOVERNMENTS ARE COMMITTED TO WORKING COLLABORATIVELY TO AVOID AND resolve intergovernmental disputes.

Mechanisms to avoid and resolve disputes should:

- be simple, timely, efficient, effective and transparent;
- allow maximum flexibility for governments to resolve disputes between them in a non-adversarial manner;

- provide for appropriate use of third parties while ensuring democratic accountability by elected officials; and
- respect existing legislative provisions.

A Three-step Mechanism for Promoting Adherence

The mechanism for promoting adherence to the framework agreement will consist of the following three steps:

Step 1: Avoiding Disputes

Governments are committed to preventing disputes through formal information-sharing and early consultation.

A number of elements in the framework agreement will help governments avoid disputes, including: collaborative approaches to federal spending on social programs, such as joint priority-setting; agreement on objectives and principles for new Canada-wide programs; policy and program flexibility which respects federal, provincial and territorial responsibilities and priorities; and, clear roles and responsibilities.

Step II: Resolving Disputes

In those cases in which disputes cannot be prevented in Step 1, governments will make every attempt to reach solutions through government-to-government negotiations.

These bilateral negotiations will normally involve the ministers from the governments involved in the dispute and from the appropriate social policy area affected by the dispute (e.g. health ministers, etc.). Alternatively, bilateral negotiations could involve the two representatives on the Federal/Provincial/Territorial Council on Social Policy Renewal from the governments involved in the dispute.

A further alternative will be to move the dispute up for the consideration by the First Ministers of the two governments involved in the dispute, should a negotiated solution to the dispute not be possible at the ministerial-level.

Step III: Involvement of a Third Party

In cases where a negotiated solution is not possible, governments will seek the assistance of a mediator to help them resolve their dispute. Governments are to agree on a mutually acceptable individual who will mediate the dispute.

If a solution is not reached, governments will call on an individual or a panel of three individuals to prepare a report on the dispute with recommendations for a solution. Governments will then hold new bilateral negotiations based on the report.

The individual that is to prepare the report will be jointly chosen by the two governments in the dispute. If a group of three individuals is to prepare the report, each government will appoint one member to the group, and these two appointees will together choose a third to chair the group.

If a negotiated solution is again not reached, the report will be made public and the governments are to be advised by the report and will have to publicly justify their respective positions.

Reporting to Canadians

Governments agree that the involvement of Canadians will help ensure the mechanism is effective. Canadians will be involved in a number of ways, including:

Outcomes reporting: Ensuring that all Canadians are informed on outcomes of the dispute settlement mechanism.

Annual public reporting: Annual reporting on the operation of the mechanism, its goals, performance and effectiveness in helping to avoid and resolve disputes.

Scope and Application of a Mechanism to Promote Adherence to the Framework Agreement on the Social Union[2]

The above dispute resolution and mechanism applies to federal spending power; stability, predictability and adequacy of funding; and the interpretation of the Canada Health Act principles.

1 With respect to CHA disputes, Newfoundland and Labrador believes that the final step, if necessary, should be mediation.

2 This is a preliminary outline of the scope and application of the mechanism to elements in the framework agreement. The scope and application of the mechanism will depend on the specific content and definitions in a final agreement. Quebec governments have never recognized the Canada Health Act and its principles even though, in practice, Quebec's health care services respect those principles.

A Framework to Improve the Social Union for Canadians (the Framework Agreement)

THE FOLLOWING AGREEMENT IS BASED UPON A MUTUAL RESPECT BETWEEN ORDERS OF GOVERNment and a willingness to work more closely together to meet the needs of Canadians.

1. Principles

CANADA'S SOCIAL UNION SHOULD REFLECT AND GIVE EXPRESSION TO THE FUNDAMENtal values of Canadians — equality, respect for diversity, fairness, individual dignity and responsibility, and mutual aid and our responsibilities for one another.

Within their respective constitutional jurisdictions and powers, governments commit to the following principles:

All Canadians are Equal

- Treat all Canadians with fairness and equity
- Promote equality of opportunity for all Canadians
- Respect the equality, rights and dignity of all Canadian women and men and their diverse needs

Meeting the Needs of Canadians

- Ensure access for all Canadians, wherever they live or move in Canada, to essential social programs and services of reasonably comparable quality
- Provide appropriate assistance to those in need
- Respect the principles of medicare: comprehensiveness, universality, portability, public administration and accessibility
- Promote the full and active participation of all Canadians in Canada's social and economic life
- Work in partnership with individuals, families, communities, voluntary organizations, business and labour, and ensure appropriate opportunities for Canadians to have meaningful input into social policies and programs

Sustaining Social Programs and Services

- Ensure adequate, affordable, stable and sustainable funding for social programs

Aboriginal Peoples of Canada

- For greater certainty, nothing in this agreement abrogates or derogates from any Aboriginal, treaty or other rights of Aboriginal peoples including self-government.

2. Mobility within Canada

All governments believe that the freedom of movement of Canadians to pursue opportunities anywhere in Canada is an essential element of Canadian citizenship.

Governments will ensure that no new barriers to mobility are created in new social policy initiatives.

Governments will eliminate, within three years, any residency-based policies or practices which constrain access to post-secondary education, training, health and social services and social assistance unless they can be demonstrated to be reasonable and consistent with the principles of the Social Union Framework.

Accordingly, sector Ministers will submit annual reports to the Ministerial Council identifying residency-based barriers to access and providing action plans to eliminate them.

Governments are also committed to ensure, by July 1, 2001, full compliance with the mobility provisions of the *Agreement on Internal Trade* by all entities subject to those provisions, including the requirements for mutual recognition of occupational qualifications and for eliminating residency requirements for access to employment opportunities

3. Informing Canadians — Public Accountability and Transparency

Canada's Social Union can be strengthened by enhancing each government's transparency and accountability to its constituents. Each government therefore agrees to:

Achieving and Measuring Results

- Monitor and measure outcomes of its social programs and report regularly to its constituents on the performance of these programs
- Share information and best practices to support the development of outcome measures, and work with other governments to develop, over time, comparable indicators to measure progress on agreed objectives.
- Publicly recognize and explain the respective roles and contributions of governments
- Use funds transferred from another order of government for the purposes agreed and pass on increases to its residents
- Use third parties, as appropriate, to assist in assessing progress on social priorities

Involvement of Canadians

- Ensure effective mechanisms for Canadians to participate in developing social priorities and reviewing outcomes

Ensuring Fair and Transparent Practices

- Make eligibility criteria and service commitments for social programs publicly available
- Have in place appropriate mechanisms for citizens to appeal unfair administrative practices and bring complaints about access and service
- Report publicly on citizen's appeals and complaints, ensuring that confidentiality requirements are met

4. Working in Partnership for Canadians

Joint Planning and Collaboration

The Ministerial Council has demonstrated the benefits of joint planning and mutual help through which governments share knowledge and learn from each other.

Governments therefore agree to

- Undertake joint planning to share information on social trends, problems and priorities and to work together to identify priorities for collaborative action
- Collaborate on implementation of joint priorities when this would result in more effective and efficient service to Canadians, including as appropriate joint development of objectives and principles, clarification of roles and responsibilities, and flexible implementation to respect diverse needs and circumstances, complement existing measures and avoid duplication

Reciprocal Notice and Consultation

The actions of one government or order of government often have significant effects on other governments. In a manner consistent with the principles of our system of parliamentary government and the budget-making process, governments therefore agree to:

- Give one another advance notice prior to implementation of a major change in a social policy or program which will likely substantially affect another government
- Offer to consult prior to implementing new social policies and programs that are likely to substantially affect other governments or the social union more generally. Governments participating in these consultations will have the opportunity to identify potential duplication and to propose alternative approaches to achieve flexible and effective implementation

Equitable Treatment

For any new Canada-wide social initiatives, arrangements made with one province/territory will be made available to all provinces/territories in a manner consistent with their diverse circumstances.

Aboriginal Peoples

Governments will work with the Aboriginal peoples of Canada to find practical solutions to address their pressing needs.

5. The federal Spending Power — Improving Social Programs for Canadians

Social Transfers to Provinces and Territories

THE USE OF THE FEDERAL SPENDING POWER UNDER THE CONSTITUTION HAS BEEN essential to the development of Canada's social union. An important use of the spending power by the Government of Canada has been to transfer money to the provincial and territorial governments. These transfers support the delivery of social programs and services by provinces and territories in order to promote equality of opportunity and mobility for all Canadians and to pursue Canada-wide objectives.

Conditional social transfers have enabled governments to introduce new and innovative social programs, such as Medicare, and to ensure that they are available to all Canadians. When the federal government uses such conditional transfers, whether cost-shared or block-funded, it should proceed in a cooperative manner that is respectful of the provincial and territorial governments and their priorities.

Funding Predictability

The Government of Canada will consult with provincial and territorial governments at least one year prior to renewal or significant funding changes in existing social transfers to provinces/territories, unless otherwise agreed, and will build due notice provisions into any new social transfers to provincial/territorial governments.

New Canada-Wide Initiatives Supported by Transfers to Provinces and Territories

With respect to any new Canada-wide initiatives in health care, post-secondary education, social assistance and social services that are funded through intergovernmental transfers, whether block-funded or cost-shared, the Government of Canada will:

- Work collaboratively with all provincial and territorial governments to identify Canada-wide priorities and objectives
- Not introduce such new initiatives without the agreement of a majority of provincial governments

Each provincial and territorial government will determine the detailed program design and mix best suited to its own needs and circumstances to meet the agreed objectives.

A provincial/territorial government which, because of its existing programming, does not require the total transfer to fulfill the agreed objectives would be able to reinvest any funds not required for those objectives in the same or a related priority area.

The Government of Canada and the provincial/territorial governments will agree on an accountability framework for such new social initiatives and investments.

All provincial and territorial governments that meet or commit to meet the agreed Canada-wide objectives and agree to respect the accountability framework will receive their share of available funding.

Direct Federal Spending

Another use of the federal spending power is making transfers to individuals and to organizations in order to promote equality of opportunity, mobility, and other Canada-wide objectives.

When the federal government introduces new Canada-wide initiatives funded through direct transfers to individuals or organizations for health care, post-secondary education, social assistance and social services, it will, prior to implementation, give at least three months' notice and offer to consult. Governments participating in these consultations will have the opportunity to identify potential duplication and to propose alternative approaches to achieve flexible and effective implementation.

6. Dispute Avoidance and Resolution

GOVERNMENTS ARE COMMITTED TO WORKING COLLABORATIVELY TO AVOID AND resolve intergovernmental disputes. Respecting existing legislative provisions, mechanisms to avoid and resolve disputes should:

- Be simple, timely, efficient, effective and transparent.
- Allow maximum flexibility for governments to resolve disputes in a non-adversarial way
- Ensure that sectors design processes appropriate to their needs
- Provide for appropriate use of third parties for expert assistance and advice while ensuring democratic accountability by elected officials

Dispute avoidance and resolution will apply to commitments on mobility, intergovernmental transfers, interpretation of the *Canada Health Act* principles, and, as appropriate, on any new joint initiative.

Sector Ministers should be guided by the following process, as appropriate:

Dispute Avoidance

- Governments are committed to working together and avoiding disputes through information-sharing, joint planning, collaboration, advance notice and early consultation, and flexibility in implementation

Sector Negotiations

- Sector negotiations to resolve disputes will be based on joint fact-finding
- A written joint fact-finding report will be submitted to governments involved, who will have the opportunity to comment on the report before its completion
- Governments involved may seek assistance of a third party for fact-finding, advice, or mediation
- At the request of either party in a dispute, fact-finding or mediation reports will be made public

Review Provisions

- Any government can require a review of a decision or action one year after it enters into effect or when changing circumstances justify

Each government involved in a dispute may consult and seek advice from third parties, including interested or knowledgeable persons or groups, at all stages of the process.

Governments will report publicly on an annual basis on the nature of intergovernmental disputes and their resolution.

Role of the Ministerial Council

The Ministerial Council will support sector Ministers by collecting information on effective ways of implementing the agreement and avoiding disputes and receiving reports from jurisdictions on progress on commitments under the Social Union Framework Agreement.

7. Review of the Social Union Framework Agreement

BY THE END OF THE THIRD YEAR OF THE FRAMEWORK AGREEMENT, GOVERNMENTS will jointly undertake a full review of the Agreement and its implementation and make appropriate adjustments to the Framework as required. This review will ensure significant opportunities for input and feed-back from Canadians and all interested parties, including social policy experts, private sector and voluntary organizations.

Assessing ACCESS: Towards a New Social Union. Proceedings of the Symposium on the Courchene Proposal (Kingston: Institute for Intergovernmental Relations, Queen's University, 1997).

Bakan, Joel and David Schneiderman (eds.). *Social Justice and the Constitution: Perspectives on a Social Union for Canada* (Ottawa: Carleton University Press, 1992).

Banting, Keith G. "The Past Speaks to the Future: Lessons from the Postwar Social Union," in Harvey Lazar (ed.), *Canada: The State of the Federation 1997* (Kingston: Institute of Intergovernmental Relations, 1998), pp. 3-32.

Biggs, Margaret. *Building Blocks for Canada's New Social Union*, Working Paper no. F02 (Ottawa: Canadian Policy Research Networks, 1996).

Browne, Paul Leduc (ed.). *Finding Our Collective Voice: Options For a New Social Union* (Ottawa: Canadian Centre for Policy Alternatives, December 1998).

Burelle, André. "Mise en tutelle des provinces," *Le Devoir*, February 15, 1999, p. A7.

Cameron, Barbara. *Rethinking the Social Union: National Identities and Social Citizenship* (Ottawa: Canadian Centre for Policy Alternatives, December 1997).

Cameron, David. "The Social-Union Pact is not a Backward Step for Quebec," *The Globe and Mail*, February 12, 1999, p. A17.

Castonguay, Claude. "Union sociale: un déblocage majeur," *La Presse*, February 10, 1999, p. B3.

Charest, Jean J. "L'union sociale canadienne: l'occasion de progresser tous ensemble," *Le Devoir,* February 13, 1999, p. A13.

Courchene, Thomas. "ACCESS: A Convention on the Canadian Economics and Social Systems," Working Paper prepared for the Ministry of Intergovernmental Affairs, Toronto, Government Printers, 1996. Also published in *Canadian Business Economics*, Vol. 4, no. 4 (July/September 1996), pp. 3-36.

Dion, Stéphane and Anne McLellan. "Collaborative Use of the Spending Power for Intergovernmental Transfers: The Race to the Top Model," Ottawa, February 5, 1999.

Dufour, Christian. *Rapport sur le projet d'union sociale en regard de la vision québécoise du fédéralisme canadien* (Quebec: Secrétariat aux Affaires intergouvernementales canadiennes, 1998).

"Forum on the Social Union: Staking Out the Future of Federalism." *Policy Options*, Vol. 19, no. 9 (November 1998).

Kennett, Steven A. *Securing the Social Union: A Commentary on the Decentralized Approach* (Kingston: Institute of Intergovernmental Relations, 1998).

Johnston, Larry. "Behind The 'Social Union'." *Issue Gateway* 3 (Toronto: Ontario Legislative Library Legislative Research Service, February 9, 1999).

Lazar, Harvey. "The Federal Role in a New Social Union: Ottawa at the Crossroads," in Harvey Lazar (ed.), *Canada: The State of the Federation 1997* (Kingston: Institute of Intergovernmental Relation, Queen's University, 1998).

Maxwell, Judith. "Governing Canada's Social Union," *Canadian Business Economics*, Vol. 5, no. 1, pp. 15-19.

Poirier, Johanne. *The Social Union: Solution or Challenge for Canadian Federalism* (Larcier, Verschenen in Sociaal Beleid en Federalisme, 1999).

O'Hara, Kathy (with the assistance of Sarah Cox). *Securing the Social Union*, CPRN Study no. CPRN|02 (Ottawa: Canadian Policy Research Networks, July 1998).

Robson, William B.P and Daniel Schwanen. *The Social Union: To Flawed to Last* (Toronto: C.D. Howe Institute, February 1999).

Schwanen, Daniel. *More Than the Sum of Our Parts: Improving the Mechanisms of Canada's Social Union* (Toronto: C.D. Howe Institute, January 1999).

Secrétariat aux affaires intergouvernementales canadiennes. *Québec's Historical Position on the Federal Spending Power, 1944-1998* (Québec: ministère du Conseil exécutif, 1998).

Secrétariat aux affaires intergouvernementales canadiennes. *Québec's Traditional Constitutional Positions, 1936-1990* (Québec: ministère du Conseil exécutif, 1991).

Smith, Jennifer. "The Québec Election and the Social Union," *The Dalhousie Review*, Vol. 78, no. 1, pp. 59-70.

Youing, Robert (ed.). *Stretching the Federation: the Art of the State in Canada* (Kingston: Institute of Intergovernmental Relations, 1999).

André Binette is an attorney with the law firm of Joli-Coeur, Lacasse, Lemieux, Simard & St-Pierre, s.e.n.c. in Sillery, Quebec. In 1997-1998, he worked as a constitutional and international law adviser to André Joli-Coeur, the *amicus curiae* in the Reference on Quebec Secession before the Supreme Court of Canada and, from 1988 to 1990 and 1995 to 1996, to the Executive Committee of the Government of Quebec (Secrétariat aux Affaires intergouvernementales canadiennes). In 1991-1992 he served as the constitutional and international law research coordinator for the Secretariat of the Committee to Examine Matters Relating to the Accession of Quebec to Sovereignty. Together with Ivan Bernier he published *Les provinces canadiennes et le commerce international* (Sainte-Foy: Les Presses de l'Université Laval, 1988).

Jacques Frémont is a professor at the Faculty of Law at the University of Montreal. He is a researcher at the Centre de recherche en droit public and was the director of the Centre from 1994 to 1999. His major fields of research include constitutional and administrative law. Jacques Frémont was a guest professor in various universities including Geneva University and Osgoode Hall Law School, where he held the Bora Laskin Chair in Public Law. He recently published "Supranationalité canadienne et sécession du Québec," *National Journal of Constitutional Law* (Vol. 8, 1997, pp. 161-204) and co-edited *Le temps et le droit* (Cowansville: Éditions Yvon Blais, 1996) as well as *Les autoroutes de l'information: enjeux et défis* (Lyons, France: Éditions Les Chemins de la recherche, 1996).

Alain-G. Gagnon is a professor in the Political Science Department of McGill University and director of the Quebec Studies Program. He has been the editor of *Politique et Sociétés* since 1995 and is the vice-president of the International Association of Quebec Studies. He has edited and published more than twenty-five works in the fields of multinational federations, collective and individual rights, social movements and the sociology of intellectuals. Among his most recent books are: *Ties that Bind: Parties and Voters in Canada* (Toronto: Oxford University Press, 1999), with James Bickerton and Patrick Smith; *Canadian Politics* (Peterborough: Broadview Press, 1999, 3rd ed.), with James Bickerton; *Quebec* (Oxford: ABC Clio, 1998) and *Quebec: State and Society* (Montreal: Québec Amérique, 1994 — Prix Richard Arès 1995). He is currently editing a book with James Tully entitled *Struggles for Recognition* (Cambridge: Cambridge University Press, forthcoming).

Alain Noël is an associate professor in the Political Science Department of the University of Montreal. His fields of specialization include comparative politics (North America and Western Europe), political economy, Canada-Quebec politics and social policy. During the 1997-1998 academic year, Alain Noël was Visiting Scholar at the School of Social Welfare and John A. Sprout Postdoctoral Fellow in Canadian Studies at the University of California, Berkeley. He has published many works on Canadian politics, the welfare state in OECD countries and social welfare policies. Together with Alain-G. Gagnon he edited *L'espace québécois* (Montreal: Québec Amérique, 1995) and recently wrote "The Federal Principle, Solidarity and Partnership," in *Beyond the Impasse: Toward Reconciliation* (Montreal: Institute for Research on Public Policy, 1998), edited by Roger Gibbins and Guy Laforest.

Ghislain Otis is a professor at the Law Faculty of Laval University and associate dean for graduate studies and research. Among his fields of expertise are constitutional law, human rights and Aboriginal law. His publications include *Peuples autochtones et normes internationales: analyse et textes relatifs au régime de protection identitaire des peuples autochtones* (Cowansville: Éditions Yvon Blais, 1996), with Bjarne Melkevik; "Opposing Aboriginality to Modernity: The Doctrine of Aboriginal Rights in Canada," *British Journal of Canadian Studies* (Vol. 12, no. 2, 1997); and "L'identité autochtone dans les traités contemporains: de l'extinction à l'affirmation du titre ancestral," *McGill Law Journal* (Vol. 41, 1996), with André Émond.

Claude Ryan was the editor of *Le Devoir* newspaper from 1963 to 1978 and served as leader of the Quebec Liberal Party from 1978 to 1982. Elected to the National Assembly for the riding of Argenteuil, which he represented from 1979 to 1994, he served in various Cabinet portfolios over a period of nine years. In 1995, he published *Regards sur le fédéralisme canadien* (Montreal: Boréal) and more recently he has written about the Supreme Court Reference on Quebec Secession and the Canadian Social Union agreement.

Hugh Segal is President of the Institute for Research on Public Policy (IRPP). A graduate of the University of Ottawa, Mr. Segal is a Senior Fellow at the School of Policy Studies and Professor of Public Policy at the School of Business at Queen's University. He is a Director of the Atlantic Council, the Canadian

Institute for Advanced Research, and various corporations. Hugh Segal has also held a series of senior positions in the public sector including Associate Secretary of Cabinet for federal provincial relations in Ontario and Chief of Staff to the Prime Minister of Canada.

André G. Tremblay is a lawyer and a full professor at the Law Faculty of the University of Montreal. Specializing in constitutional law and human rights, as well as federalism, Professor Tremblay was a senior adviser to the Quebec government in constitutional matters from 1986 to 1993, and has appeared before the Supreme Court of Canada on several occasions. Included among his publications are *Droit constitutionnel — Principes* (Montreal: Éditions Thémis, 1993) and *Droit constitutionnel canadien et québécois — Documents* (Montreal: Éditions Thémis, 1999).

Guy Tremblay has been a professor in the Law Faculty of Laval University since 1984. Concentrating his research mainly on constitutional law and legal methodology, Professor Tremblay published *Droit constitutionnel* (Cowansville: Les Éditions Yvon Blais, 1990, 2nd ed.), with Henri Brun. He also wrote *Une grille d'analyse pour le droit du Québec* (Montreal: Wilson & Lafleur ltée, 1993, 3rd edition) as well as "La constitutionnalité des infractions provinciales pures et simples," *Thémis* (Vol. 27, 1993).

Education:

Derek Hum and Wayne Simpson (1996), *Maintaining a Competitive Workforce: Employee-Based Training in The Canadian Economy*

Thomas T. Schweitzer (1995), *The State of Education in Canada*

Stephen B. Lawton (1995), *Busting Bureaucracy to Reclaim our Schools*

Bruce Wilkinson (1994), *Educational Choice: Necessary But Not Sufficient*

Peter Coleman (1994), *Learning About Schools: What Parents Need to Know and How They Can Find Out*

Governance:

John Meisel, Guy Rocher and Arthur Silver *et al.* (1999), *As I Recall Si je me souviens bien: Historical Perspectives*

John Meisel, Guy Rocher et Arthur Silver *et al.* (1999), *Si je me souviens bien As I Recall : Regards sur l'histoire*

Guy Laforest and Roger Gibbins (eds.) (1998), *Beyond the Impasse: Toward Reconciliation*

Guy Laforest et Roger Gibbins (dir.) (1998), *Sortir de l'impasse : les voies de la réconciliation*

Peter Aucoin (1995), *The New Public Management: Canada in Comparative Perspective*

Kirk Cameron and Graham White (1995), *Northern Governments in Transition: Political and Constitutional Development in the Yukon, Nunavut and the Western Northwest Territories*

G. Bruce Doern (1994), *The Road to Better Public Services: Progress and Constraints in Five Canadian Federal Agencies*

Donald G. Lenihan, Gordon Robertson and Roger Tassé (1994), *Canada: Reclaiming the Middle Ground*

F. Leslie Seidle (ed.) (1994), *Seeking a New Canadian Partnership: Asymmetrical and Confederal Options*

Family and Social Policy:

Adil Sayeed (ed.) (1995), *Workfare:Does it Work ? Is it Fair ?*

Ross Finnie (1994), *Child Support: The Guideline Options*

Telecommunications:

W.T. Stanbury (ed.) (1996), *Perspectives on the New Economics and Regulation of Telecommunications*

Yves Rabeau (1995), *Les télécommunications : problématique d'une industrie en évolution rapide*

Charles Sirois and Claude E. Forget (1995), *The Medium and the Muse: Culture, Telecommunications and the Information Highway*

Charles Sirois et Claude E. Forget (1995), *Le médium et les muses : la culture, les télécommunications et l'autoroute de l'information*

City-Regions:

Tom Hutton (1998), *The Transformation of Canada's Pacific Metropolis: A Study of Vancouver*

Paul A.R. Hobson and France St-Hilaire (eds.) (1997), *Urban Governance and Finance: A Question of Who Does What*

Andrew Sancton (1994), *Governing Canada's City-Regions: Adapting Form to Function*

William Coffey (1994), *The Evolution of Canada's Metropolitan Economies*

Health:

Monique Jérôme-Forget and Claude E. Forget (1998), *Who is the Master? A Blueprint for Canadian Health Care Reform*

Monique Jérôme Forget et Claude E. Forget (1998), *Qui est maître à bord ? projet de réforme du système de santé canadien*

Monique Jérôme-Forget, Joseph White and Joshua M. Wiener (eds.) (1994), *Health Care Reform Through Internal Markets: Experience and Proposals*

Choices\Choix

Public Finance:

Donald J.S. Brean and Jeremy A. Leonard (1998), *Technology, Taxation and Canada's Competitiveness: Policies for the New Global Economy*

Jacques Henripin, *Les pensions de retraite dans une société vieillissante*

Philip Oreopoulos (1996), *Bad Tasting Medicine: Removing Intergenerational Inequity from the CPP*

Jack Mintz and Thomas Wilson (1996), *The Taxing Question of Savings: Should Retirement Savings be Taxed ?*

France St-Hilaire (1996), *A qui profitent les avantages fiscaux ? / For Whom the Tax Breaks*

Philip Oreopoulos and Laurence J. Kotlikoff (1996), *Restoring Generational Balance in Canada*

Michel Leblanc and François Vaillancourt (1995), *Répartition régionale des dépenses fiscales touchant les corporations / Regional Distribution of Federal Corporate Tax Expenditures*

Governance:

Jean-Claude Deschênes (1996), *Les agences britanniques, source d'inspiration des modernisations administratives*

Peter Aucoin and Jean-Claude Deschênes (1996), *Operational Agencies: From Half-Hearted Efforts to Full-Fledged Government Reform*

Family Policy:

Robert Baril, Pierre Lefebvre, Philip Merrigan (2000), *Quebec Family Policy: Impact and Options*

Gordon Cleveland and Douglas Hyatt (1998), *Subsidizing Child Care for Low-Income Families: A Good Bargain for Canadian Governments?*

Robert Baril, Pierre Lefebvre, Philip Merrigan (1997), *La politique familiale: ses impacts et les options*

Michel Leblanc, Pierre Lefebvre and Philip Merrigan (1996), *Comment accroître le soutien public en faveur des enfants*

Social Policy:

Guy Lacroix, Jean-Michel Cousineau and Pierre Lefebvre (1995), *La sécurité du revenu au Québec: une critique de la réforme proposée*

Commentaries on the Axworthy Green Paper (1995), *IRPP prend position / The IRPP Position*

Health:

Monique Jérôme-Forget and Claude E. Forget (1995), *Les marchés internes dans le contexte canadien*

Série Québec-Canada:

Armand de Mestral and François Rocher (1995), *Un Québec souverain et l'union économique Québec-Canada*

Stéphane Dion and Christian Dufour (1995), *L'évolution du fédéralisme canadien*

Reuven Brenner, Fred Lazar and David W. Slater (1995), *La monnaie d'un Québec souverain*

Josée Legault and Jeremy Webber (1995), *L'avenir de la communauté anglophone au Québec / The Future of the Anglophone Community in Québec*

Gerald R. Alfred and Renée Dupuis (1995), *Les peuples autochtones et l'avenir du Québec*

Marcel Côté and Pierre-Paul Proulx (1995), *Les implications économiques d'un Québec souverain*

Patrick J. Monahan and José Woehrling (1995), *L'accession du Québec à la souveraineté: aspects juridiques*

Courts and Legislatures:

Frederick Vaughan and Kate Malleson (1999), *Judicial Power in Canada and Britain*

Jacob S. Ziegel (1999), *Merit Selection and Democratization of Appointments to the Supreme Court of Canada*

Jacob S. Ziegel (1999), *Sélection au mérite et démocratisation des nominations à la Cour suprême du*

Janet L. Hiebert (1999), *Wrestling with Rights: Judges, Parliament and the Making of Social Policy*

Janet L. Hiebert (1999), *Des droits à interpréter : les juges, le Parlement et l'élaboration des politiques sociales*

These and other publications are available from:

IRPP
1470, rue Peel, bureau 200
Montréal, Québec
H3A 1T1
Téléphone : (514) 985-2461
Télécopieur : (514) 985-2559
Courriel/e-mail: irpp@irpp.org
Site web/Web site: www.irpp.org

and many bookstores.